Understanding Employee Ownership

Corey Rosen

Karen M. Young

EDITORS

ILR Press
Ithaca, New York

Copyright © 1991 by Cornell University
All rights reserved

Cover design by Kat Dalton

Library of Congress Cataloging-in-Publication Data

Understanding employee ownership / Corey Rosen and Karen M. Young,
  editors
      p.   cm.
   Includes bibliographical references (p.   ) and index.
   ISBN 0-87546-171-9 (cloth : alk. paper). — ISBN 0-87546-172-7
(pbk. : alk, paper)
   1. Employee ownership—United States. 2. Employee ownership.
I. Rosen, Corey M. II. Young, Karen M., 1942–
HD5660.U5U64 1991
338.6—dc20   90-24359

Copies may be ordered through bookstores or directly from
ILR Press
New York State School of Industrial and Labor Relations
Cornell University
Ithaca, NY 14851–0952

Printed on acid-free paper in the United States of America
5 4 3 2 1

Contents

Preface

This book is being published on the tenth anniversary of the National Center for Employee Ownership (NCEO). When we founded the center in 1981, it seemed unlikely that ten years later employees would be principal owners of such major companies as Avis, HealthTrust (a thirty thousand–employee hospital chain), Weirton Steel (the seventh largest steelmaker), and the Parsons Corporation (a ten thousand–employee construction company). Given that employee-owners, to that point, owned under $2 billion in assets and the largest employee ownership transaction had been just $25 million, it seemed even less likely that by 1990 employee ownership plans would control $60 billion in assets and that billion dollar–plus transactions would no longer be unusual. Hard as these eventualities were to imagine, it would have seemed even more farfetched in 1981 that by 1990 employee ownership would be being seriously considered as a means to privatize state-owned businesses in Eastern Europe and the Soviet Union.

Nonetheless, thanks to the hard work of hundreds of people, all of these hard-to-imagine scenarios have come true. We hope the National Center for Employee Ownership has played a constructive role in this process. The role of the NCEO, with which we all are or have been closely associated, has been to serve as the main source of information on this concept. We conduct research, hold workshops, publish a newsletter and other publications, provide information to the media, and otherwise attempt to help people understand what employee ownership is, its advantages and disadvantages, and the conditions under which it works best for companies and their employee-owners.

It seems appropriate that after ten years we are stepping back and assessing where we are. Employee ownership has gone from a seemingly fringe notion to the topic of cover stories in one business magazine after another. While the general understanding of employee ownership is much greater today than in 1981, many assessments of the idea are still based on limited information and experience. Some people still see it as an economic cure-all; others see it as little more than a management-controlled "rip-off" of the taxpayer and employees. Our goal in this book is to provide an overview based on the best information and research currently available.

We make no apology for being advocates of employee ownership. We think it offers the best hope for combining the goals of social justice with the need for economic efficiency. Our guiding principle all along, however, has been that if employee ownership is as good an idea as we think it is, it can stand on its own merits. Advocates who artificially pump up its merits and obscure its problems will only lose credibility for themselves and the idea. Employee ownership can only realize its often lofty ambitions if those involved with it understand when it is not an appropriate option and how to make it work best when it is. Objective, reliable information is essential. We have tried to provide such information in this book.

Acknowledgments

In compiling the material for this book, we have relied on the research efforts of many people outside the National Center for Employee Ownership: Michael Conte of the University of Baltimore; Katherine Klein of the University of Maryland; Joseph Blasi and Douglas Kruse of Rutgers University; Patrick Rooney of Indiana-Purdue University at Indianapolis; William Foote Whyte, Tove Hammer, and Robert Stern of Cornell University; Richard Long of the University of Saskatchewan; Raymond Russell of the University of California at Riverside; and researchers at the U.S. General Accounting Office. All have done important and pioneering work in this field. Michael Conte also provided detailed comments on an earlier draft of this book. Special recognition must go to our first employee, Lisa Gilman. In addition, former NCEO employees and research associates, including Michael Quarrey, Michael Yoffee, Ira Wagner, Cathy Ivancic, and Andy Lisak have made critical contributions. Through the years, our interns and our board have also been of invaluable assistance.

This book is a reflection of the work we have done over the last ten years. Many people have helped make that effort possible. Joseph Blasi, Jack Curtis, and Robert Smiley, for instance, were actively involved from the start in helping the center develop as an organization. William Foote Whyte provided the initial inspiration for the founders of the center to get involved in employee ownership and offered a model for how research can be used to help encourage social change. Former senator Russell Long and Louis and Patricia Kelso made employee ownership possible and have provided valuable advice for the center. Dozens of business leaders have been a source of both inspiration and leadership. Karl Reuther, Rich Biernacki, Robert Fien, Michael Quarrey (who moved from the NCEO to business), and Gil Phillips are but a few of the many who have made employee ownership more than an idea.

The efforts of many colleagues in other employee ownership organizations have also been invaluable. David Binns and Martin

Staubus of the ESOP Association, Jim Megson of the Industrial Co-operative Association, John Logue and Cathy Ivancic of the Northeast Ohio Employee Ownership Center, Jan Stackhouse of the New York Center for Employee Ownership and Participation, June Sekera of the Massachusetts Program for Employee Ownership and Involvement, Jim Houck and Mike Polzin of the Michigan Center for Employee Ownership, Richard Callicrate of the Community Economic Stabilization Corporation, Jim Keogh of the Washington Employee Ownership Program, and Seth Borgos and Deborah Groban Olson of the Midwest Employee Ownership Center have all made vital contributions.

Finally, we want to thank the people at ILR Press, especially Erica Fox and Andrea Fleck Clardy, for their excellent work in producing this manuscript in a timely and readable form. It was a pleasure working with them.

In any acknowledgment, many people inevitably are left out. We apologize to those who deserve to be included but were not because space precluded their being mentioned. One of the great pleasures of working in this field has been the opportunity to associate with so many dedicated, talented people. Many of these people are now friends as well as colleagues. Our modest efforts in this book are a tribute to the extraordinary efforts so many of them have made.

Understanding Employee Ownership

1 Employee Ownership: Performance, Prospects, and Promise

Corey Rosen

In Weirton, West Virginia, 8,200 capitalists go to work every day in the steel mill they own. At just about the time they are entering the plant gate, 650 more capitalists are leaving work at the company they own, the Khljupin Building Materials Plant in Moscow.

In the U.S. Congress, Senator Jesse Helms has sponsored legislation to encourage employee ownership in Poland. The beneficiaries of the bill will be receptive; Poland has already made employee ownership a major element in its economic reform program.

In a national advertising campaign, Avis is telling people to rent from the owners, the 12,500 employees who own 100 percent of the company's common stock. Perhaps Avis cars will someday use tires made by employee-owners of Alexandria Tire Company in Egypt.

In the last few years, Carl Icahn, T. Boone Pickens, and Saul Steinberg, among others, have borrowed billions of dollars to buy American companies. So have Penny Minton, Jim Olson, and Nellie Feggett. The first three names may be familiar, but the others probably are not. That is because Penny Minton is a nurse at HealthTrust, Jim Olson is a steelworker at Northwestern Steel and Wire, and Nellie Feggett is a waitress at Wyatt Cafeterias. Like their better-known capitalist counterparts, they, along with forty-two thousand of their co-workers, borrowed money to buy their companies. Each of them could end up owning over $100,000 in stock.

Just a decade ago, the concept of widespread employee ownership would have seemed like fanciful musing. Today, at least eleven thousand U.S. companies, including some of America's largest and most successful firms, are wholly or partly owned by

12 million of their employees. Employees own a majority of the stock in three of the country's ten largest integrated steel manufacturers, two of the ten largest private hospital management companies, two of the three largest shipbuilders, two of the ten largest construction companies, and many others. Overall, employees own an estimated $60 billion worth of stock through the principal vehicle for employee ownership in the United States, employee stock ownership plans, or ESOPs, and may own this much or more through a variety of other plans.

The success of employee ownership here has spurred imitation abroad. England, Egypt, Argentina, and Poland have enacted laws to encourage employee ownership, and Costa Rica, Australia, Hungary, and the Soviet Union are considering such legislation. The idea is being touted by several leading Soviet thinkers and seriously discussed in most of the emerging social democracies in Eastern Europe.

These trends are being fueled by a convergence of economic concerns. The economic inefficiency of communism has become increasingly apparent, yet traditional capitalist countries continue to struggle with the question of how to ensure economic equity. Competition spurs production, but it also leaves too many people behind. Increasingly, both East and West are seeking to stimulate economic growth in ways that are socially just. Employee ownership is purported to be an alternative that can create a system of mutual self-interest in which rewards are shared while preserving incentives.

In the context of the extraordinary changes toward increased democracy taking place worldwide, expanding democratic ownership to the workplace seems both fitting and possible. But beneath the high plane of theoretical vision lies the much more difficult and complex terrain of practical problems. How exactly is the transition made from existing ownership patterns to much broader ones? What will be the role of employee-owners in their companies? Can employee ownership be a systemic change, or will it always occur only in certain special cases?

To address these broad issues of policy, we must ask what has actually happened. How well has employee ownership worked? Has it increased employees' wealth? Does it lead to an improvement in corporate performance? Does it give employees any greater role in decisions affecting their jobs or their company? Does it require either massive government incentives or mandatory economic decree to gain companies' acceptance? If so, are the benefits worth the costs?

This book aims to answer these questions while providing a general overview of the growth of employee ownership here and abroad. Because employee ownership is so much more developed in the United States than elsewhere, however, most of our attention will focus on this country.

The research and analysis we present in this book provide a generally encouraging account of employee ownership, although there are always caveats. When employee ownership is combined with participative management practices, for instance, substantial performance gains result. Ownership alone, however, has no clear effect; neither does participative management. Employee-owners are accumulating substantial amounts of capital in their companies, and they rarely have to make sacrifices to get it. But ownership is not always an economic boon, and in some cases, employees have ended up much worse off than they were before. And although U.S. government tax incentives have resulted in ESOPs alone putting $60 billion worth of productive capital in the hands of employees, this still represents only 3 percent of the value of all stock in the United States.[1] By contrast, just one non-ESOP transaction, the leveraged buyout of RJR Nabisco by Kohlberg, Kravits, Roberts in 1989, put $24 billion in the hands of just a few investors.

The cost of these ESOP tax incentives is substantial—about $500 million to $1.5 billion a year.[2] This is but a trickle, however, compared to the billions spent subsidizing the ownership of capital by the very rich through existing tax code benefits. Still, $60 billion is a substantial sum, and it has been accumulated largely in the last three years.

In short, though the record of employee ownership in the United States is imperfect, it is impressive enough that many other countries are pursuing the idea. These efforts are in their very early stages, but there is every reason to believe that several other countries will have well-developed programs within the next decade. It may well be that just as feudal ownership in agrarian society gave way to individual ownership under industrial capitalism, so individual ownership will give way to employee ownership in the postindustrial information economy. It will be an economy that relies increasingly on knowledge and ideas rather than the rote execution of preset tasks. This would be an ideal environment for employees to share these crucial resources as owners. In a comparison of employee ownership versus less equitable forms of ownership in which the few, or governments, own and the rest work for them, employee ownership seems to stand up well.

Origins of Employee Ownership in the United States

Employee ownership has always existed in the United States. Albert Gallatin, a founding father and early secretary of the treasury, argued that democracy should not be limited to politics but "should extend to the economic sphere" as well. Later, William Meredith, secretary of the treasury under President Zachary Taylor, wrote in his 1849 annual report that "in many of the New England factories, the laborers are encouraged to invest their surplus earnings in the stock of the company by which they are employed, and are thus stimulated, by direct personal interest, to the greatest extent." Meredith expected this idea would expand, instructing "all men in the great truth of the essential harmony of capital and labor."[3]

Meredith was describing management-initiated plans, but laborers showed an interest in starting their own companies as well. Periodic experiments with employee ownership can be traced back to the 1790s,[4] and in the nineteenth century both the Knights of Labor and the National Labor Union started worker cooperatives.[5] Although many of these cooperatives were successful, union strategy ultimately shifted to collective bargaining and neglected employee ownership.

In the 1920s, employee ownership became a full-fledged movement, called the New Capitalism, replete with theorists, publicists, a national organization, and considerable success. Management, reflecting the economic optimism of the time, thought employee-owned stock investments would pay handsomely. At a time when socialism and communism were gaining abroad, employee ownership seemed a logical American response. The shares purchased by employees provided a new source of capital, and their stake in the business was expected to motivate employees to perform better. Robert Brookings, founder of the Brookings Institution, wrote in his book *Economic Democracy: America's Answer to Socialism and Communism*: "Many of the large corporations are encouraging the thrift of their employees by assisting them to invest their savings in the stock of the corporation . . . thus creating a real 'economic democracy,' which is America's answer to socialism and communism with their inherent weaknesses."[6]

Even an editor of the *Wall Street Journal* was enthusiastic. According to Arundell Cotter of the paper, "Anything that helps reduce that friction [between capital and labor] makes for the good of the entire social body. And, I believe, employee ownership more nearly achieves this than any other means yet devised."[7]

Employees were encouraged to buy shares out of their savings or through bonuses paid by the companies. By 1930, about 2.5 percent of the work force had bought shares valued at over $1 billion, which was equivalent to the value of ESOP holdings in the early 1980s. Employees gained majority ownership of such companies as the Bank of Italy (a Transamerica company) and Dennison Manufacturing.[8] The stock market crash put an abrupt end to this movement. Workers were left with largely worthless paper, and the idea, once the subject of hundreds of scholarly and popular articles, disappeared.

Louis Kelso and His Two Factors

In the 1950s, an eccentric, persistent, and visionary San Francisco attorney and investment banker named Louis Kelso developed what he called the "two-factor theory." In *The Capitalist Manifesto*, which Kelso co-authored with the well-known philosopher Mortimer Adler, they wrote, "The ownership of productive property by an individual or a household must not be allowed to increase beyond the point where it injures others by excluding them from the opportunity to earn a viable income."[9] When Kelso looked at the United States, he found this principle was being violated in a most egregious way. Just 1 percent of the population owned 50 percent of the privately held corporate securities, and 10 percent owned 90 percent.[10] Some people earned from ownership far more than they could ever spend, while most people were dependent on making what they could from their own labor. Although the result was a fairly high standard of living, Kelso argued that a different system of ownership could produce far better results.

Kelso believed there were only two factors of production: capital and labor. As society became more industrialized, capital contributed more to production than labor. The problem was that although all workers owned their labor, only a few owned and thus could get more capital. Kelso was not at all surprised when in the 1980s a handful of investment bankers could gain control of tens of billions of dollars worth of capital and wealth became increasingly concentrated. The outrageously rich could not spend all this money on themselves, so they spent it speculating, buying and selling companies, producing nothing.

To this point, it might seem that Kelso was rehashing Marx. But Kelso had no patience with communism either. By expropriating the rights of ownership, Kelso contended, the state violated the basic right of individuals to acquire the means to a decent livelihood. Communism thus resulted in a dispirited economy, lacking both the incentive to excel and the dynamism to adapt.

The solution, Kelso argued, was simple. Capitalism is marvelous for creating economic growth but poor for creating economic justice. The problem was that to acquire the most important factor of production, capital, it was necessary to have capital. So the rich get richer, unless the government steps in to redistribute wealth, which would deter economic growth. What was needed was a mechanism by which the economically disfranchised could acquire capital in the form of buildings, machinery, computers, and the like.

The answer was the ESOP, a kind of company-funded benefit plan for employees that invested its assets in the employer's stock. The ESOP, Kelso contended, could be a means whereby rank-and-file employees could gain access to capital credit. After all, most new capital is funded by debt, even for the very rich. They borrow money to buy productive capital, which then earns enough money to repay the loan. If the lenders and the borrowers did not think the capital could do this, they would be foolish to fund or to make the acquisition. Employees acting alone could not acquire capital this way because lenders were not persuaded they had either the skills to manage it or the resources to repay the loans if the project did not succeed. If the employees had the backing of their company, however, they would have both management and collateral. Now the lender could loan them the money with which to buy stock in their company. The company would use the money to acquire capital, repaying the loan out of the earnings from that acquisition. Everyone would be better off.

Kelso believed the ESOP could be implemented under existing law, although several major changes would help make the system work. He argued that companies could borrow the money through the ESOP and deduct both the principal and the interest on the loans, rather than just the interest as in a conventional loan. Here was the hook, Kelso thought, that would get companies interested. The availability of low-cost capital would start the ESOP movement.

Theory into Practice

Kelso's ESOP was met with some interest by the public, scorn by economists, doubt by managers, and serious reservations by attorneys. But Kelso was not discouraged; he knew he was right. In 1957, he persuaded his first company—Peninsula Newspaper Group—to set up an ESOP. Over the next sixteen years, he found another three hundred or so converts, mostly "middle-market" companies of a few hundred employees or less.

The difficulties were manifold. Lawyers worried that the Internal Revenue Service (IRS) would not allow the tax benefits Kelso claimed for his ESOP. Under existing law, companies could set up "stock bonus plans" to put stock in the hands of employees. Normally, a company either contributed its own shares to the plan or contributed cash to buy the shares. A few well-known firms, most notably Sears, had such plans. Kelso said these plans could borrow money to buy the stock, though the law did not clearly say they could, or that the company could repay the loan with tax-deductible dollars. Economists either ignored Kelso or said he knew nothing about economics (after all, he did not have a Ph.D. in the field). Companies were not comfortable with employees as owners regardless of the tax incentives, and lenders were not comfortable with change.

Kelso realized that to make any progress, legislation was needed. He made a few early converts, but none was in a position of power. Then in 1973 he managed to get an audience with Louisiana's Democratic senator Russell Long. Long was chair of the Senate Finance Committee, which writes tax law, and was probably the most powerful member of the Senate.

He was also Huey Long's son. Huey, the fabled "kingfish," the governor of Louisiana in the Depression and later a senator and candidate for the presidency, wanted to give every family a guaranteed annual income, taking from the rich to assure a decent life for the poor. Some think he would have won on his platform of "every man a king" had he not been assassinated in 1935.

Russell Long was not persuaded of the wisdom of his father's radical proposal. He was a much more cautious and conservative politician than his father and as chair of the Finance Committee had gained a reputation for favoring business. But he did believe that capitalism was not working as well as it should. There were too few capitalists, and the result was an inequitable distribution of wealth. Thus his meeting with Louis Kelso was serendipitous. Kelso's idea could use the economic system itself, with just a push from government, to create more owners. It was, he would later say, "Huey without the Robin Hood."

Soon after the meeting, Long set to work persuading his colleagues. Some were convinced by his arguments, some by his power. By 1974, Long had enough votes to pass a law providing a specific legal structure for ESOPs, making it clear that they could borrow money and that companies could deduct payments made to the plan. In the next twelve years, not a Congress went by that Long did not create yet another ESOP tax incentive. By the mid-1980s, employee ownership was endorsed by Jesse Helms and Jesse Jackson, Ted Kennedy and Ronald Reagan, the United Steelworkers and the Chamber of Commerce, and the Catholic church and the Republican party. What could be more conservative than making everyone a capitalist? And what could be more liberal than giving everyone a piece of the pie?

There were skeptics, of course. Some unions saw ESOPs as a ploy to co-opt workers or force them to buy failing companies (even though only 2 to 4 percent of all ESOPs were set up in distressed companies).[11] Some members of Congress thought the tax incentives were excessive. Some conservatives argued that employees could buy stock if they wanted to be owners; some liberals said that ESOPs provided unreliable financial benefits and too little employee control.

These critical voices would have more effect by the end of the 1980s, but for most of their early history, the growth of ESOPs was hindered more by inertia and lack of awareness. Employee ownership was unknown to most people who were in a position to implement it and too great a departure from comfortable norms for those who understood it.

The Growth and Use of ESOPs

Nonetheless, employee ownership began to grow, although not in the way Kelso envisioned. Few companies used their plans to borrow money to acquire new capital. Instead, the plans were typically used to buy existing shares, often from owners of successful, privately held companies who wanted to sell their stock. Other companies found ESOPs were an inexpensive way to create an employee benefit plan or to augment other existing plans. A few companies were simply attracted to the idea of employees being owners. Until ESOPs, there were few ways to share ownership that did not have major tax drawbacks. Large companies were lured by a special ESOP called a tax credit ESOP that saved them a dollar in taxes for every dollar they

Figure 1.1.   Cumulative Growth of Employee Ownership Plans, 1975–1989

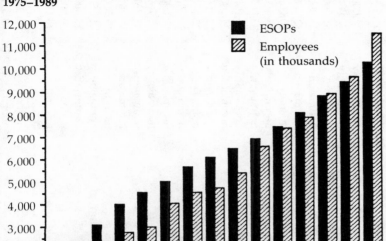

Source: NCEO.

put into stock for employees. These plans were responsible for most of the government expenditures on ESOPs between 1978 and 1986, when tax credit ESOPs were eliminated, but they limited corporate contributions to a very small amount per employee and so never amounted to much in any one company. The growth of ESOPs after 1975, excluding tax credit plans, is shown in figure 1.1; table 1.1 lists the fifty largest companies that are at least 25 percent owned by employees.

How ESOPs Work

The financial and legal structure of ESOPs will be explored in detail in chapter 2, but a basic understanding can be gained by studying the examples that follow. For readers who are not familiar with basic business concepts and terminology, the appendix, "A Primer on Business," provides an introduction.

Table 1.1. Fifty Largest Employee Ownership Companies

Company	Location	Business	Ownership	Employees
Kroger Co.	Cincinnati, Ohio	Supermarkets	nonmajority	178,000
J. C. Penney Co.	Dallas, Tex.	Retail	nonmajority	177,000
Publix Supermarkets	Lakeland, Fla.	Supermarkets	majority	65,000
Carter Hawley Hale	Los Angeles, Calif.	Retail	nonmajority	35,000
Merrill Lynch	New York, N.Y.	Financial	nonmajority	32,000
HealthTrust	Nashville, Tenn.	Hospital management	majority	30,000
Phillips Petroleum	Bartlesville, Okla.	Petroleum	nonmajority	28,400
FMC Corp.	Chicago, Ill.	Industrial manufacturing	nonmajority	28,000
Tyson Foods	Springdale, Ariz.	Chicken processing	nonmajority	25,000
Coldwell Banker	Chicago, Ill.	Real estate	nonmajority	24,000
Ashland Oil	Russell, Ky.	Oil refinery	nonmajority	22,800
USG	Chicago, Ill.	Construction material	nonmajority	22,000
Colt Industries	New York, N.Y.	Industrial products	nonmajority	19,700
Olin Corp.	Stamford, Conn.	Chemicals/defense	nonmajority	17,000
Dyncorp	Reston, Va.	Technical services	nonmajority	15,700
Hallmark Cards, Inc.	Kansas City, Mo.	Greeting cards	nonmajority	15,521
Lowe's Companies, Inc.	N. Wilkesboro, N.C.	Lumber and hardware	nonmajority	14,700
Avis, Inc.	Westbury, N.Y.	Car rental	majority	13,500
CBI Industries	Oak Brook, Ill.	Energy and manufacturing	nonmajority	11,400
Stone and Webster	New York, N.Y.	Engineering	nonmajority	10,000
EPIC Healthcare	Irving, Tex.	Hospitals	majority	10,000
Science Applications, International	San Diego, Calif.	Research and development and computers	majority	10,000
Parsons Corp.	Pasadena, Calif.	Engineering, mining, construction	majority	10,000
Ruddick Corp.	Charlotte, N.C.	Holding company	nonmajority	9,390

Company	Location	Industry		Employees
Price Chopper	Schenectady, N.Y.	Supermarkets	nonmajority	9,000
Charter Medical	Macon, Ga.	Hospitals	majority	9,000
Amsted Industries	Chicago, Ill.	Manufacturing	majority	8,300
Weirton Steel Corp.	Weirton, W.Va.	Steel manufacturing	majority	8,100
Harcourt Brace Jovanovich	Orlando, Fla.	Publishing	nonmajority	8,000
America West Airlines	Phoenix, Ariz.	Airline	nonmajority	8,000
Avondale Shipyards	New Orleans, La.	Shipbuilding	majority	7,500
AST General Corp.	Houston, Tex.	Supermarkets	nonmajority	7,000
Wyatt Cafeterias, Inc.	Garland, Tex.	Cafeterias	majority	6,500
Austin Industries	Dallas, Tex.	Construction	majority	6,500
The Journal Company	Milwaukee, Wisc.	Newspapers and communications	majority	6,200
Pamida	Omaha, Nebr.	Discount retail	nonmajority	5,000
Herman Miller, Inc.	Zeeland, Mich.	Furniture manufacturer	nonmajority	5,000
W. L. Gore Associates	Newark, Del.	High-tech manufacturer	majority	5,000
Republic Engineered Steel	Canton, Ohio	Steel manufacturer	majority	4,900
Simmons Co.	Atlanta, Ga.	Furniture manufacturer	majority	4,900
Graybar Electric	St. Louis, Mo.	Electrical equipment	majority	4,700
King Kullen	Westbury, N.Y.	Grocery retail	nonmajority	4,200
Treasure Chest Advertising	Glendora, Calif.	Printing	majority	4,000
National Steel Shipbuilding	San Diego, Calif.	Shipbuilding	majority	4,000
Stebbins Engineering	Watertown, N.Y.	Engineering	majority	4,000
Davey Tree Expert Co.	Kent, Ohio	Tree service	majority	3,800
Dentsply International	York, Pa.	Dental supplies	nonmajority	3,500
Applied Power, Inc.	Butler, Wisc.	Automotive equipment	nonmajority	3,400
Swank, Inc.	Attleboro, Mass.	Leather goods	nonmajority	3,100
Lifetouch	Minneapolis, Minn.	Photography studios	majority	3,000

Source: NCEO.

Imagine you are an owner of a company and you want your employees to become owners too. What can you do? You could give them stock, but they would have to pay tax on this benefit, even though the shares would provide them with only the possibility of money when they were sold later. You could sell them the stock, but the employees would have to buy the shares with their after-tax earnings. Most employees have never owned stock, however, and probably do not have the disposable income to invest.

Now imagine you are leading a group of employees who want to buy stock or even the whole company. Even if you could get people to buy shares individually, it is unlikely they could put up enough money to buy a significant part of their business. After all, a typical business could well be capitalized at $10,000 to $100,000 per employee. You have seen the truly rich buy companies, and they just borrow the money. But who would lend it to you, and how would you repay it? Would you have to pledge your car, your house, and your first born as collateral?

A solution for both situations is the ESOP. An ESOP is an employee benefit plan similar in some ways to a profit-sharing plan. In an ESOP, a company sets up a trust fund to which it contributes new shares of its own stock or the cash to buy existing shares. Alternatively, the ESOP can borrow money to buy new or existing shares, with the company making cash contributions to the plan to enable it to repay the loan. Regardless of how the plan acquires stock, the company's contributions to the trust are tax-deductible, within certain limits. The ESOP has solved everyone's problems. An employee's stock remains in the plan, and no taxes are due until the employee leaves. The company can deduct any money it puts into the plan from its taxable income. For a company in a 34 percent tax bracket, that means saving 34 cents on every dollar spent. The employees do not need to put up any money directly. If they need to buy a lot of stock, the plan can borrow the money, then repay the loan gradually (usually over five to ten years) out of company earnings contributed to the plan. Should the company default on the loan, the employees are not personally liable for repaying it.

The idea gets complicated in practice but is simple in theory. Employees cannot or will not buy stock with their own money so the company buys it for them, either with money it already has or with money it borrows through the plan and repays. The company gets a tax benefit to cover part of the cost and hopes the employees can do well enough as owners to pay for the rest. Shares are allocated to employees, who actually get the shares when they leave the company or retire. If employers do not trade the stock on a stock market, the company buys the shares back at a value set by an outside stock appraiser.

ESOPs are used in a number of ways. The tax advantages of these approaches are discussed in chapter 2.

To buy the shares of a departing owner. Fred Wright's insurance company had been family-owned for decades, but Wright was in his seventies, ready to retire, and had no family members to take over the business. He could have sold the company to someone else, but he was concerned that a new owner would not treat his employees well. Wright was lucky to have potential buyers; many profitable companies can find only people who want to buy their assets, leaving their employees on the street. Buying a business is a high-risk investment. Purchasers are less likely to buy a company that makes a 10 or 12 percent return on investment a year than to buy stocks or bonds that have as good a return with less work and worry. An ESOP was the solution. Over a period of about ten years, Wright gradually sold all his stock to the plan.

Wright's insurance company had only thirty-five employees, but very large companies have also used an ESOP to buy out owners. When the family that owned Wyatt Cafeterias, employing sixty-five hundred people, wanted to sell, for instance, they looked first to competitors such as Furr's, which offered close to $200 million. Then Mark Shackleford, Wyatt's controller, read an article about ESOPs. The family agreed to sell to an ESOP for less than Furr's would pay because the tax concessions made the ESOP a better deal. They also liked the idea of employees becoming owners, especially since Furr's would probably close some of the cafeterias. The employees, mostly low-income minority group members and women, ended up owning the company, even though they put up none of their own money. A typical employee can now expect to own $70,000 or more in stock after fifteen years of employment.

About half of all ESOPs are formed to promote business continuity. Sometimes the plan buys a majority of the stock, sometimes less. In either case, members of the family of the retiring owner or other investors get the rest.

To borrow money at a lower after-tax cost. When the employees of Weirton Steel Company needed $322 million to buy their business from its parent, National Intergroup, they used an ESOP. The profits their company now earns go to the plan to repay the loan. When Chevron wanted to put stock in the hands of employees quickly to help fend off a hostile takeover attempt, it used an ESOP to borrow

$1 billion to buy 4 percent of its stock. When Marshall and Sterling, a growing private insurance company, wanted to expand, it used its ESOP to borrow money to buy acquisitions.

Surprisingly, ESOPs are almost never used to borrow money to buy productive capital, as Kelso envisioned. To use the ESOP this way, the company issues new shares, which the ESOP buys with borrowed money. The company then uses the money to buy equipment or other goods to improve its operation. Stockholders end up owning a smaller percentage of the company, and even though they will come out ahead if the new equipment pays for itself (because now they will own a smaller piece of a bigger pie), so far little enthusiasm has been shown for this idea, primarily because it dilutes the ownership interests of non-ESOP shareholders.

Nor are ESOPs always leveraged. Of the ten thousand plans calling themselves ESOPs (about 40 percent of which technically are not, although they operate much like ESOPs), only about one-third borrow money. The tax benefits of borrowing are attractive, but many companies simply do not want to take on the debt.

To create an additional employee benefit. When John Stack and a group of managers bought Springfield Remanufacturing Company from International Harvester, they wanted to make sure employees had the same interest in the company's bottom line they did, so they set up an ESOP. Each year, the company contributes up to 15 percent of each employee's pay to the plan out of its profits. The result seems to be a success. Stock in the company increased in value from 10 cents to $15 a share in just four years. Approximately 40 percent of all ESOPs are set up primarily as benefit plans, rather than as means to buy shares from existing owners.

Other uses. When companies ask for wage concessions, they sometimes offer stock in return. ESOPs resulting from employees buying out troubled companies account for about 3 to 4 percent of all ESOPs, according to the U.S. General Accounting Office (GAO). Public companies have found that ESOPs can be combined with existing benefit plans to produce the same or greater benefits at lower cost, and these account for another 4 percent of ESOPs. About the same percentage of plans is accounted for by ESOPs formed to avoid hostile takeovers.[12]

Alternatives to ESOPs. ESOPs are not the only way for employees to own stock. Joseph Blasi and Douglas Kruse of Rutgers University estimate that employees may own as much stock in their employers through profit-sharing and other employee benefit plans as they own in ESOPs. Typically, only a minority of the assets of these plans are in company stock, however, and employees usually do not think of themselves as owners. Instead, they focus on how much their total investment is worth. Still, a few companies do invest most of the assets from their profit-sharing plans in company stock. There are fewer tax incentives than for ESOPs, but there are also fewer rules with which to comply. Employees of Hallmark Cards, for instance, own 33 percent of their company through a profit-sharing plan.

Most public companies and some private ones offer employees a chance to buy shares, either directly or through an employer-sponsored savings plan. The most common savings plan is a 401(k) (named for its tax code section), which allows employees to divert part of their earnings into a savings account set up by the company, offering different investment options. Employees pay no tax on the money saved. Companies often match part or all of the employees' contributions. According to the General Accounting Office, 7 percent of the companies sponsoring 401(k) plans offer their own stock as an investment choice. Because the companies that match with their own stock tend to be larger companies, 29 percent of all 401(k) assets are invested in the stock of the employer, which amounted to about $21 billion at the end of 1986.[13]

A few companies, most notably PepsiCo, offer stock options to all their employees. In most companies, options are available only to executives. For instance, an executive might be given an option to buy shares in the company for which he works for $100 any time between 1991 and 1995. If the stock goes above $100, the executive will buy at the lower price, sell, and make a profit. Options are commonly part of executive compensation, and some corporate leaders have become enriched by tens of millions of dollars as a result. In 1989, PepsiCo gave all of its employees a chance to buy options worth up to 10 percent of their pay each year.

Employee cooperatives are another approach. More than two hundred thousand employees in France, Italy, and Spain own their companies through cooperatives, and some of these companies have grown to be very large and successful. In a cooperative each owner has one vote and shares in the cooperative are usually allocated equally. This structure has some important tax advantages, but it is too democratic for most companies. In the United States, there may be more than a thousand cooperatives, although no one knows for sure. Very few have more than a handful of employees.

The Evolution of Employee Ownership since ERISA

When the Employee Retirement Income Security Act (ERISA) was passed in 1974 and ESOPs were incorporated into the tax law, it seemed that they would appeal primarily to small companies. Large firms were too inertial or too committed to existing benefit plans to change. Senator Long created the tax credit ESOP to encourage public firms. For every dollar they put into a plan, the government paid them a dollar back at tax time. The amounts were limited, however, and most employees ended up with only a few thousand dollars worth of shares. (Tax credit plans were eliminated in 1984.)

Although the tax credit plans created many small ESOPs in public companies, the real growth of employee ownership remained concentrated in the hands of companies with twenty to a thousand employees, almost all of which were closely held (that is, their stock was not traded on a stock exchange). According to data collected by the National Center for Employee Ownership (NCEO), ESOPs typically borrowed around $500 million a year.

In 1984, Congress passed legislation allowing lenders to exclude 50 percent of the interest income they received from loans to ESOPs from their taxable income. Not only did this help lower ESOP loan rates because lenders passed on part of the savings to borrowers, but it also aroused lenders' interest in ESOPs. Until then, most lenders had looked at ESOPs skeptically; now they had a financial interest in reevaluating that position.

The new law created a great deal more interest in using ESOPs for large leveraged transactions in which the ESOP might borrow tens or even hundreds of millions of dollars to buy all or part of a major company. In 1985, for instance, the Parsons Corporation used its ESOP to borrow over $500 million to buy back from the public market the 71 percent of the shares it did not already own. In 1987, Avis and HealthTrust were bought by employees in $1.7 billion transactions.

ESOP borrowing reached $1.2 billion in 1986 and $5.5 billion in 1987, mostly on the strength of twenty to thirty very large transactions each year. Private companies were still the major borrowers, and the largest deals were those in which the ESOP bought controlling interest in a company. But the ESOP market in smaller firms continued at much the same pace as before.

In 1986, Congress allowed companies to deduct dividends paid on shares in an ESOP, provided the dividends were paid directly to employees or used to repay an ESOP loan. Dividends are otherwise not deductible so the company pays taxes on them as profits, then the shareholders pay taxes on them too. By late 1988, ESOP advisers (the majority were lawyers) had created ways under the new law to restructure benefit plans that were very appealing to public companies.

The details of this development are complex. A company such as J. C. Penney would borrow money through its ESOP to buy its own common stock, on which it had been paying shareholders a dividend. This stock would now be retired. The company would no longer be paying a nondeductible dividend on those shares. Penney would then create an equivalent amount of convertible preferred shares to contribute to the ESOP. These shares differ from common stock in that they pay a higher dividend, put their owners ahead of common shareholders in getting any money if the company goes bankrupt, and fluctuate in price less.

The employees now get an allocation of preferred shares every year. In most cases, the company uses that allocation to replace some other benefit it was providing, typically its matching contribution to an employee savings plan. It repays the loan to buy the shares out of tax-deductible dollars and can use the deductible earnings of the stock (the dividends) to help repay the loan. If the stock does reasonably well, its earnings can contribute to the repayment. As a result of the 1986 law, a company could fund its employee benefit plans in a way that allowed it to deduct more dollars than it could before and to borrow money at a lower cost than it could otherwise (because of the interest income exclusion for lenders).

In early 1989, Polaroid used an ESOP against a hostile takeover attempt and won a court case challenging its legality. Until the Polaroid ruling, it was not clear whether an ESOP could be used for that purpose. The concern was that state law might prohibit companies from setting up ESOPs in response to a takeover because they could prevent other shareholders from realizing the share price premium that takeovers often generate. Federal law might force the trustee of an ESOP to sell the shares to a raider because that would generate a higher price for the employee-owners. By winning a ruling on the state law issue, Polaroid avoided adverse action on the federal issue (although the federal law remains undecided).

After this ruling public companies scrambled to set up ESOPs to block real and imagined raiders. In the efforts to avoid takeovers and to restructure benefit plans, ESOPs borrowed $24 billion in 1989. In a reversal of previous trends, 85 percent of the money was borrowed by public companies.

Congress responded, worried about deficits and thinking this growth had gotten out of hand. The interest income exclusion was limited to companies in which the ESOP owned over 50 percent of the stock and that gave employees full voting rights on shares acquired by the loan. This saved the taxpayers something over $1 billion annually, but it was only a minor blow to ESOPs in public companies. In 1990, two more effective forces came into play. First, the "junk bond market" collapsed. Junk bonds are essentially loans by investors to companies that pay high interest rates and that can be sold on securities markets. Investors became worried that the borrowers could not pay off the loans, and some of the key junk bond players, such as Drexel Burnham Lambert went bankrupt. Corporate raiders had relied on junk bonds, so the demise of one was the demise of the other—and of ESOPs as a defense against takeovers. Then the accounting profession decided to change the way ESOPs are reported on a company's balance sheet. The seemingly arcane changes made ESOPs less attractive to public companies, most of which are very sensitive to how their financial picture appears to shareholders.

As a result, ESOPs will probably borrow only about $6 to $7 billion in 1990. Public companies are still setting up plans, but they are smaller and there are fewer of them. Private companies continue to set up ESOPs much as they did throughout the 1980s. After the dust settled, the NCEO estimated that about 15 percent of all ESOPs are in public companies, but about 40 percent of the participants in ESOPs work for these firms.

Ownership Abroad

Except for the cooperative sectors in Europe, employee ownership is not a significant force outside the United States, but interest in the idea is growing quickly. In England, for instance, 1988 and 1989 tax laws encouraged the creation of something similar to U.S. ESOPs (they are even called that there), although with fewer tax incentives. A few dozen English firms have set up plans, including several bus companies that employees bought when the government privatized them. Some Canadian provinces have laws encouraging employees to buy stock in their companies, but so far not much has come of the effort. Australia recently allowed companies to deduct contributions of their own shares to employee benefit funds, a change that could stimulate some interest. Several other countries are considering legislation to encourage employee ownership.

In some countries, employee ownership is being considered as a means of privatizing government-owned businesses. Costa Rica, Argentina, Mexico, and Korea are looking seriously at this alternative. In the Philippines and Guatemala, major agricultural estates have given employees stock in the plantation business rather than break up the land through land reform.

Interest is perhaps strongest in Eastern Europe and the Soviet Union. Poland has passed legislation to encourage employee ownership, and the Communist party in the Soviet Union stated in its 1990 platform that turning companies over to employees would be an acceptable way to move toward a market economy. Czechoslovakia, Yugoslavia, and Bulgaria are also considering legislation to allow employee ownership.

The appeal of the idea in these countries is obvious. Employee ownership offers a way to move toward the efficiency of the market without sacrificing the goals of social equity that are central to leaders and workers alike. The difficulties are great, however. These countries lack recent experience with private markets, do not have accountants and financial experts to help plan the transition to an employee-owned company, have traditions of worker indifference and broad skepticism toward capitalism, lack legal structures that can easily accommodate the ESOP-like vehicles that would be the most practical forms of ownership, and have underlying economic weaknesses that could imperil any move toward employee ownership. If employee ownership were used as a transition mechanism, for instance, and failed because of basic economic problems, the idea would probably be permanently discredited. Despite all these drawbacks, advocates of employee ownership are excited by the possibility that moves toward democracy could lead to systemic implementation of their idea.

Employee Ownership in the United States

The growth of ESOPs and ESOP-like plans in the United States is shown in table 1.2. It is impossible to estimate how many other companies and employees are involved in other forms of employee ownership. About 12 percent of the civilian work force now participates in one such plan. Combining the $60 billion in ESOP assets with the more than $60 billion Blasi and Kruse believe is held by employees in major companies outside ESOPs results in a total of over $120 billion, or about 4 percent of the total corporate stock in the United States.[14]

The General Accounting Office took a survey in which it asked companies why they set up ESOPs. Respondents could list more than one reason. This format, however, makes it difficult to say that any particular percentage of plans is used primarily for one purpose (see table 1.3). A failing company, for instance, may also give wage concessions as an answer; for a company buying out a shareholder, tax

Table 1.2.   Cumulative Growth of Employee Ownership Plans, 1974–1989

Year	Cumulative No. of Plans	Cumulative No. of Employees
1975	1,601	248,000
1976	2,331	503,000
1977	3,137	1,658,000
1978	4,028	2,800,000
1979	4,551	3,039,000
1980	5,009	4,048,000
1981	5,680	4,537,000
1982	6,082	4,745,000
1983	6,456	5,397,000
1984	6,904	6,576,000
1985	7,402	7,353,000
1986	8,046	7,860,000
1987	8,777	8,860,000
1988	9,407	9,630,000
1989	10,237	11,530,000

SOURCE: NCEO.

advantages and possibly turning over majority ownership could be important reasons. The table does, however, clarify a few questions. Tax incentives, although important, are only one reason for setting up plans. There was little employee ownership in the United States before ESOP tax incentives were created, but rather than being the primary motivation, the incentives seem to push people with other needs over the decision-making edge.

ESOPs are seldom used to save failing companies or to prevent takeovers, although these are the reasons most frequently reported in the press. Because the GAO excluded ESOP-like plans from its survey, even the percentages for those categories may be exaggerated. ESOP-like plans are "like" in most ways except they cannot borrow money, yet employee buyouts of troubled firms and defenses against hostile takeovers almost always require borrowing money to buy large amounts of stock quickly. ESOPs are usually more mundane affairs, set up for business continuity or as an employee benefit plan, with the attendant hope that improvements in productivity and morale will result.

Employee ownership companies are a diverse lot. They occur in all types and sizes of companies except those with fewer than fifteen to twenty employees because for them the legal costs are too high. About one-fifth of ESOPs employ fewer than one hundred people; two-thirds

Table 1.3.   Reasons Companies Formed ESOPs

Reason	Percentage
Provide an employee benefit	91
Tax advantages	74
Improve productivity	70
Buy stock of major owner	38
Reduce turnover	36
Transfer majority ownership	32
Raise capital	24
Decrease absenteeism	14
Avoid unionization	8
Avoid hostile takeover	5
Save failing company	4
Exchange for wage concessions	3
Take company private	1

SOURCE: U.S. General Accounting Office, *Benefits and Costs of Employee Stock Ownership Plans*, PEMD–87–8 (Washington, D.C.: U.S. General Accounting Office, 1986), p. 20.

employ between one hundred and one thousand, and one-eighth employ over a thousand. These largest companies account for about 40 percent of the plan participants.[15] About 10 percent of ESOPs are in public firms.

ESOPs tend to be concentrated in manufacturing and finance. About 30 percent of all plans are in manufacturing, compared to 18 percent of all corporations large enough to consider a plan; 13 percent of ESOPs are in finance, real estate, and insurance, compared to 7 percent of all corporations of sufficient size. By contrast, wholesale and retail trade account for only 24 percent of ESOPs but make up almost half of all companies large enough to set up plans.[16] Other business sectors have about the expected representation. These numbers are largely a consequence of the different work forces in these industries. Wholesale and retail firms have a high concentration of transient and low-paid employees. Ownership plans are designed to encourage and reward longevity by providing a substantial economic benefit. Many firms in these sectors either do not want to or cannot obtain a more permanent work force, and often they do not need to provide good benefits to attract employees. These businesses also have relatively few profit-sharing and pension plans. Manufacturing companies, by contrast, tend to pay higher wages and have more stable work forces. Banks like to sponsor their ESOPs for idiosyncratic reasons having to do with the legal and financial requirements of banks.

The percentage of ownership held by ESOPs varies considerably as well. Different surveys produce very different numbers, but a conservative estimate would be that one-third of all ESOPs own or will own a majority of their companies' stock. Estimates of the distribution of nonmajority ownership diverge dramatically, but it seems likely that half or more of all ESOPs currently own less than 20 percent of their companies' stock. This number is somewhat deceptive, however. ESOPs often start out owning much less of their companies than they will a few years later. Because a significant percentage of ESOPs have been created relatively recently, information on a cross section of plans at any time is misleading as an indicator of what ESOPs will own later on.

From the employee's perspective, this is mostly an academic issue. Individual participants in the plan primarily want to know how much is contributed for them each year. It is better, after all, to participate in an ESOP that contributes 25 percent of one's pay per year and own 30 percent of the stock than one that contributes 5 percent of one's pay and own all the stock (either scenario is possible depending on how fast the company is growing and how mature the plan is). Various surveys indicate that about one-third of all ESOPs contribute less than 5 percent of employees' pay per year, one-third contribute 6 to 14 percent per year, and another one-third contribute over 14 percent. The median contribution is about 8 to 9 percent of pay.[17]

How Are ESOPs Working?

"All this is very interesting," the skeptic would say. "Congress created a package of tax incentives to get companies to share ownership with employees, and they did. But has it been worthwhile? After all, only 12 percent of civilian employees participate in the plans, and many of the plans do not contribute very much. From what I have heard, most of these plans give most of their benefits to those who are already pretty well off and do not give any control to employees. And though there is a lot of talk about employee ownership improving corporate performance, there is not much evidence, is there?"

This hypothetical skeptic is a composite of real people. A 1987 *Newsweek* story, for instance, began as follows:

How's this for a hot investment? A new company owns 104 hospitals, most of them fairly small and rural—one of the weakest segments of the industry. Some of the firm's biggest customers, the federal and state governments, have sharply restricted payments for Medicare and Medicaid. To top it all off, a lot of the company's debt is in junk bonds. . . . Now that you've heard all about the firm, here's an offer you can't refuse: how'd you like to invest *your entire company pension* in it?[18]

In 1989 a *Fortune* article commented: "ESOPs don't always work as advertised. ESOPs can do long-term damage to shareholders because the plans can entrench management while offering little motivation for employees to become more productive."[19] A House of Representatives aide on the tax-writing Ways and Means Committee opined, "If the only reason management puts these in place is to get cash to save their own skins, why have tax breaks that encourage that?"[20]

One response to these critics is that employees want to be owners, despite the risks. According to a 1987 poll commissioned by the National Center for Employee Ownership and the Bureau of National Affairs, 57 percent of the people surveyed would give up their next paycheck in return for stock in their company. In a 1990 survey by the Gallup Organization, 44 percent of the respondents said they would trade their next pay increase for stock even if they were not assured of getting any money back when they left the company. Forty-four percent said they would not, and 12 percent said they did not know.[21]

Another response is to say these criticisms are in error in characterizing ESOPs. ESOPs are not commonly used to prevent takeovers or save failing companies, even if that is the common perception. And *Newsweek* was completely wrong about HealthTrust, the "hot deal" it was critiquing. HealthTrust, one of the largest majority employee-owned companies in the country with thirty thousand employees, was bought by an ESOP, but employees did not give up anything to get it. In fact, their benefit plan increased from 6 percent of pay to 25 percent, and their company is now doing better than the parent firm, Hospital Corporation of America, which sold it to focus on its profitable enterprises.

But though many critics of ESOPs are simply shooting at the wrong targets, others, such as sociologist Joseph Blasi, have asked more pertinent questions. Our hypothetical skeptic outlined most of them.

Sometimes there is a very good answer; sometimes the experience is more mixed.

ESOPs and the Distribution of Wealth

Proponents of ESOPs rightly complain that the distribution of wealth in the United States is a disgrace that would not be tolerated in virtually any other developed country in the world. Japanese executives regularly tell us we should be ashamed of what our corporate chief executive officers (CEO) make and own. Critics of ESOPs just as rightly complain that ESOP financing, even in its heyday year of 1989, accounted for just 8 percent of the total capital financing that year and, altogether, ESOPs own only 3 percent of the estimated total productive capital in the United States.

Blasi has appropriately raised the issue of whether ESOPs can ever make much of a dent in the overall distribution of wealth. Even if they do acquire more stock, stock is only one form of wealth; real estate, collectibles, bonds, savings accounts, and other vehicles exist as well and similarly are held in intense concentrations. According to the Federal Reserve Board, in 1983, American households had $10 trillion in net worth, of which only 10 percent was stock (stock is also owned by corporations, pension funds, and other nonhousehold owners). Sixty percent of these nonstock assets are held by 10 percent of the population and 30 percent by the top 1 percent.[22] Judged by these standards, even sustained rapid growth in ESOPs would still leave most wealth in the hands of relatively few.

Another way to look at the problem, however, is to recall Penny Minton, Jim Olson, and Nellie Feggett, who were mentioned at the beginning of the chapter. Each of them could own $100,000 in stock if they stay with their companies for fifteen to twenty years and the companies do even modestly well. Another example is the employees of SeaRay Boats. That company had an ESOP for a few years, then was bought by Brunswick. The typical employee got $200,000 in stock and became a participant in Brunswick's ESOP. Charles Valentine, an employee of the Lowe's Companies in North Carolina, never made more than $125 a week, but he left Lowe's owning over $500,000 in stock. The only other way these people and many others could acquire so much money would have been to win a lottery. After all, in 1983, the median net financial assets of a family at retirement, excluding home equity, came to just $11,000.[23]

Of course, critics can point to other examples. Remember Drexel Burnham Lambert? Although the company did not have an ESOP, it encouraged employees to buy shares, and more than a thousand of them did, buying 54 percent of the company. On February 14, 1990, they got an unlucky valentine: Drexel declared bankruptcy and the stock became virtually worthless. Fortunes disappeared overnight.

Unfortunately, argument by example may be emotively persuasive, but it is not empirically convincing. The best way to analyze the issue is to determine just how much employees get from an ESOP and how much they give up, if anything, for the privilege.

According to a 1986 U.S. General Accounting Office report, in 1984, the average ESOP participant had accumulated about $7,000 in assets. This figure is somewhat misleading, however, because most of the plans in the sample had existed for only a few years.

To look at the data another way, the NCEO conducted a random sample of current private company plan contributions and growth rates for the period 1985–89. Based on the actual growth in account balances over that time, the NCEO projected how much an employee making $20,000 per year would get over ten years and twenty years. In current dollars, the employee would accumulate $31,000 over ten years and $83,000 over twenty. The present value of these amounts is $16,713 for the ten-year period and $22,859 for the twenty-year period (present value indicates how much these amounts would be worth, assuming a 7 percent discount rate, if an employee had the option of receiving the cash today, not in the future).[24]

The NCEO also surveyed forty-five private employee ownership companies in California to determine what and how much employees gave up to participate in an ESOP. Thirty-seven companies provided usable responses. Of these, the ESOP was the first benefit plan in nine. Ten had added the ESOP onto existing plans; seven used the ESOP to replace a pension plan; and fifteen replaced a defined contribution plan such as profit sharing (four companies had two employee benefit plans; eighteen companies replaced some kind of overall employee benefit plan). Of the eighteen firms that replaced plans, seven were not sure if they contributed more or less to the ESOP than to previous plans, one contributed less, and six contributed more.[25]

These data are similar to broader survey data with a less explicit focus. A survey of members of the ESOP Association, a trade group, for instance, suggests that ESOP companies are about as likely as other companies of similar size to have other deferred income benefit plans, and the GAO report mentioned above indicated that only about 8 percent of ESOPs replace pension plans.[26] A survey of Ohio firms indicated that in only three of sixty-one companies did employees give up any benefits to get their ESOPs.[27] It is unknown, however, whether the other plans in these private firms contribute less than plans in non-ESOP companies or how many private firms set up an ESOP that would have set up a different plan had the ESOP option not existed.

Data on public companies provide a somewhat different picture. A recently completed study conducted by Michael Conte of the University of Baltimore and the NCEO made it possible to analyze the effect of ESOPs on employees' compensation in public firms. In a sample of twenty-one firms providing adequate, detailed data, the average contribution to an ESOP was $1,306 per year, or about 6 percent of participants' salaries and wages. This percentage is lower than the average figures given earlier because ESOPs in public companies tend to be smaller than ESOPs in private companies, and hence annual contributions tend to be smaller. When the return on the assets is calculated for the years the companies had plans, this figure increases to 12 percent per year. By contrast, the comparable figure for a matching sample of non-ESOP companies with profit-sharing plans and pension plans (using annual pension costs to the company) was only 3 percent of compensation per plan per year.[28] Moreover, it is likely that the public companies with ESOPs had other deferred income plans as well. Of course, the higher contributions to the ESOPs must be somewhat offset by the greater risk ESOPs entail.

In an analysis of how employees fared in forty-two public companies with ESOPs set up in 1988 and 1989, the NCEO showed that in twenty-two of these companies, the ESOP resulted in a net increase in employer contributions to all benefit plans, in twenty contributions remained the same, and in two contributions declined.[29] Susan Chaplinsky and Greg Niehaus, in another survey of public companies with ESOPs, came up with virtually identical results.[30]

It does appear that ESOPs have a positive impact on employees' financial well-being. Although further data are needed to determine to what extent ESOPs substitute for other plans, especially in private companies, the existing data suggest that for the large majority of participants, ESOPs represent a net financial gain, often of significant size. At the same time, if ESOPs are a company's only deferred compensation program, these participants are also assuming greater risk.

Why would companies be so generous? If they set up an ESOP, why should they not follow the economic dictum of "no free lunch" and take something away? Public companies often do, by using the ESOP to replace previous matches to employee contributions to savings plans. Because the ESOP borrows money to fund these plans, the company repays a fixed amount each year. But the amount employees save each year will vary. To be sure they can cover variations in patterns of savings, companies will often borrow more than they need to meet employees' savings in a normal year. The extra tax benefits of the ESOP pay for the difference.

Private companies are a very different case. A principal purpose of the large majority of ESOPs is to buy out an owner. If the ESOP did not buy out the owner, either the company would use its own cash to do so or someone else would buy the shares and expect the company to generate enough earnings to repay the investment. Either way, the sale of shares is an expense to the company employees would not normally be expected to pay. An ESOP transfers the benefit to employees, so the pressure to decrease other compensation for an ESOP is not so great as in public companies, whose shareholders demand to know why the company is paying more than it needs to pay to attract qualified employees. In fact, many owners of private companies want to put as much into the ESOP as they can in order to accumulate enough cash to buy out the target shares. The effect on overall compensation is a secondary issue.

Are Benefits Distributed Fairly?

Even if critics agree with the gross numbers gleaned from surveys, they charge that the distribution of benefits in ESOPs is unfair. Blasi, for instance, concludes that "widespread exclusion of lower and middle paid workers from the plans and stock allocations weighted in favor of more highly paid employees have meant that workers who are already stock owners are receiving the most ownership."[31] Has all this tax money supporting ESOPs simply replicated the pattern of ownership the system was designed to change?

The answer to this question depends on one's perspective. The data are fairly clear. The median participation rate for employees in ESOPs is 73 percent.[32] In other words, half the companies have more than 73 percent of employees participating and half have less. The larger the company, however, the lower the participation rate. Thus when Douglas Kruse looked at the actual percentage of all ESOP employees who participated in plans in 1984, he found it to be only 47 percent.[33] Kruse's data included many tax credit ESOPs, however, almost all of which were in very large companies. These plans would have accounted for a very large percentage of the total employees in his sample. It seems reasonable to estimate that in current ESOPs, about three-fifths to two-thirds of all employees participate.

The excluded employees fall about equally into three groups: part-time workers, workers who have not yet met the minimum one-year service requirement, and employees covered by a collective bargaining agreement. Those excluded because they have not worked for one year are a special case; they will be included if they stay. Employees covered by a collective bargaining agreement are excluded from some ESOPs, usually because the union has already negotiated other benefit plans. The ESOP would have to be in addition to or in place of these plans. In some cases, management may not want to add more costs to its existing contracts. In other cases, the benefit plans already provide close to the legally allowed maximum employers may contribute (normally 25 percent of pay), and the ESOP would not be possible unless something was sacrificed. In still other cases, the union opposes participation in an ESOP regardless of its benefits. Many companies do include union employees, although there are no reliable data on the frequency of their inclusion. Finally, part-time employees are usually, but not always, excluded from ESOPs.

The same pattern of participation would be evident in other benefit plans, such as profit-sharing and pension plans, because the rules governing who the employer can include or exclude are the same (details can be found in chapter 2). The patterns whereby benefits are allocated would also be exactly the same in ESOPs as in other benefit plans. Benefits can be, and usually are, allocated according to relative pay, although amounts over $200,000 are not counted and no one can get more than $30,000 in any year.

Looking at these patterns, Blasi and others have contended that the people who are excluded, other than union employees, tend to be the lowest paid—part-timers and new or transient employees—and that benefits are skewed to favor employees with the highest incomes. In fact, when the law that governs benefit plans, the Employee Retirement Income Security Act, was passed in 1974, the rules were set largely at the instigation of unions, which also wanted to give greater rewards to higher-paid, permanent, and more senior people.

It is difficult to know just what percentage of stock in ESOPs is owned by people making over a certain income, but in almost no ESOP is more than one-third of the stock owned by top management and people making over $75,000 a year because if they did, they would lose important tax benefits or be subject to stricter rules. This situation is vastly more egalitarian than the general economy in which people making over $75,000 a year own over 95 percent of the privately held stock.

ESOPs and Corporate Performance

The primary purpose of ESOPs is and always has been to widen the ownership base of substantial capital estates. No other goals are mentioned in any of the legislation governing ESOPs. Nonetheless, many advocates of employee ownership predicted that one of its benefits would be to improve corporate performance by linking the financial interests of employees and companies. Several early studies seemed to suggest that this was the case, but all looked at companies only after they set up their plans, then compared them to non-ESOP firms, and therefore could not tell whether the ESOP caused the change in performance or whether it was only that better companies set up such plans in the first place.[34]

The first effort to address the issue more systematically was a comprehensive survey undertaken by the NCEO of twenty-seven hundred employees in thirty-seven ESOP firms. The purpose was to discover whether ownership really did have an impact on employees' attitudes. The answer was clearly yes. The more stock employees owned in their company, the more committed they were to the firm, the more satisfied they were with their work, the less likely they were to look for other jobs, and the more they liked being owners. The positive effects of ownership were magnified when active programs were adopted for sharing information and soliciting employees' input into decisions at all levels of the company.[35]

But there is no automatic linkage between employees' attitudes and corporate performance. Just because people are more satisfied with their jobs and more interested in their companies does not mean they are working harder. And even if they are working harder, they may just be doing the same unproductive tasks more diligently. In most companies, labor is only about one-third of total costs. If a company can motivate two-thirds of its work force to work 10 percent harder (an impressive accomplishment, according to most managers), the total cost savings would only be $.33 \times .67 \times .10$ (one-third of the costs times two-thirds of the people working 10 percent harder). That comes to a 2 percent cost saving. It is significant but not dramatic. If employees do more than just work harder—if they contribute ideas and information about how their jobs and their company can perform better—they can make a difference. Do employee-owners make these efforts? Do managers listen to them? And is the result better performance? To explore this plausible but not inevitable chain of events, the NCEO compared before and after performance records of ESOP firms. For each of the forty-five firms included, the NCEO compared how the company performed for five years before the ESOP was set up and five years after. To correct for changes in the economy and individual markets, these numbers were indexed by comparing the ESOP firms to at least five competitors. For example, if ABC Company did 1 percent better per year than its competition in the five years before its ESOP, the company would have to do at least 1.1 percent better per year after the plan was started for the ESOP to have a measurable impact.

Overall, the ESOP firms grew 3 to 4 percent per year faster than they would have without the ESOP, depending on the measure used. Over a ten-year period, this growth would create almost 50 percent more jobs in the ESOP companies. A closer look at the data showed that most of the growth occurred in the most participative one-third of the companies, those that allowed for relatively high degrees of employee input into job-level decision making. These firms performed 11 to 17 percent per year better.[36] Participation was measured by asking managers to tell how much influence nonmanagement employees had over issues ranging from social events to corporate policy. Firms were considered to be participative if employees at least had the opportunity to share decision making with management on issues affecting the organization and performance of their jobs. Most often, they would do so through employee participation groups or ad hoc employee teams, although few of the companies limited participation to these forums.

One might interpret this finding to mean that it is participation, not ownership, that makes the difference, but that did not turn out to be the case. Many other studies have found that participation alone has only an ambiguous and generally very short-lived impact on performance.[37] Ownership motivates employees; participation gives them an opportunity to use this motivation to contribute their ideas, knowledge, and experience to help the company grow.

The General Accounting Office completed a study using a different sample but similar methodology about a year after the NCEO completed its study in 1986. The GAO did not find that ESOPs had any effect on performance per se, much as the NCEO had not. But in participative ESOP firms, the productivity growth rate was 52 percent per year higher than it would have been without ownership and participation.[38] Economist Patrick Rooney also found a strong synergy between employee ownership and participation in decisions affecting the performance of their jobs; neither factor had much effect on its own, but together they were strongly correlated with improvements in productivity. Rooney, unlike other researchers, also found evidence that voting rights were correlated with performance, although employee representation on boards was not.[39]

This relationship between ownership, participation, and performance has become the conventional wisdom, backed by a growing number of examples from companies that have used this approach. Both the critics of ESOPs and most of its advocates agree that participative management is essential to assuring that employee ownership will improve corporate performance. Chapter 4 looks at how companies are putting this management philosophy into practice.

It is important to realize that employee participation involves more than economic performance. In survey after survey, employees say they want more opportunities to participate in the work they do. Such opportunities rank high on their list of what makes work worthwhile. In the Gallup poll mentioned earlier, 61 percent of the people surveyed said they were not given enough say about how their jobs were performed. In evaluating employee ownership, therefore, we have to consider to what extent it encourages greater participation simply because that is a worthwhile end in itself.

Employee Ownership and Participation

The question then becomes, How many ESOP firms overall are participative? The GAO found that 27 percent of the firms sampled reported an increase in employee participation, generally over job-related issues.[40] Only 1 percent reported a decline. The GAO's study was based on survey data from early 1986. It was about this time that the research on ownership and participation was becoming public. Since then, three new surveys have suggested growing interest in the linkage. A 1989 survey of Washington State firms, for instance, found that 35 percent provided for joint worker-management decision making on job-related issues, and 54 percent sought workers' opinions. About one-third of the companies used formal groups to accomplish this level of participation.[41] Half the firms surveyed in an Ohio study met the researchers' criteria for being participative, generally by providing employees at least an opportunity to have significant input into job-level decisions.[42] Finally, in a study of large leveraged ESOP transactions in which the plan bought a majority of the company's stock, Chong Park found that sixteen of twenty-nine firms provided at least the opportunity for joint worker-management decision making on job-related issues. Ten of the sixteen companies started their participation plans after planning for the ESOP had started, and the nonparticipative companies tended to have relatively recent ESOPs.

Some of these companies may not have had time to get a program started.[43]

The record is not consistently encouraging, however. In his study of public companies, Michael Conte found no evidence of increased participation and even some indication that the ESOP companies might be less participative than non-ESOP public firms.[44]

There are no data on how many non-ESOP companies, public and private, are participative, but it seems that the non-ESOP firms are much less participative. Participation experts are also fond of pointing out that most participation programs last only a few years; no ESOP companies are known to have terminated their programs. Without ownership, employees may lack the motivation to continue to participate, and management may lack the sense of obligation to respond to owners, not "just" employees. Nonetheless, it is clear that a majority of ESOP firms are still not very participative, and even those companies that do have programs may have only scratched the surface of their potential. Although critics have many examples to decry, it should be kept in mind that employee ownership is still at a very early stage of development. As companies learn from the success and failure of other employee ownership firms, we can expect participation to continue to grow.

ESOPs and Corporate Governance

The following hypothetical conversation between an ESOP critic and the owner of a privately held business on who should have control over the business highlights one of the problems ESOPs create.

> CRITIC: You say that you want your workers to share in ownership and act as owners. Yet these "owners" have no say over how "their" company is run. You can do whatever you like, even things that may reduce the value of their shares. How can you call that ownership?
>
> OWNER: You have to understand that I have spent a lifetime building this business. It was my money, sweat, and ideas that made it a success. Right now, the employees only own 30 percent of the stock, so even if they could vote, it would only be a formality. But in a few years they will own a majority of the shares. Then they could decide to do what they like with the business I have built. I am not comfortable with that.
>
> CRITIC: Why are you so concerned? If you have treated your employees well and provided them with sufficient financial education, don't you think they would make good decisions?

OWNER: It seems to me that I have done enough in giving over financial ownership to the employees. Not many people are willing to do that. Why should I be criticized for not giving up control, too? After all, these people have no experience running a business.
CRITIC: You haven't really "given" ownership to employees. You have sold it to them out of the profits of the company they help earn, and the government has made the deal sweeter with substantial tax incentives. It seems only fair that employees get the full rights of ownership in return.
OWNER: Well, let's say that I did give them control, and they decided to act as rational business people. Once they had 51 percent of the stock, what would prevent them from selling the company out from under me, or firing me, or telling me that they would start issuing new shares to dilute my ownership interest and would never buy my shares back from me?

This debate has been going on since ESOPs were created. It is an issue only in private companies; public companies must pass through full voting rights for all allocated shares. Because employees in these firms typically own only 5 to 20 percent of the company's shares, however, they rarely have much influence at the board level.

Analyses of the importance of this issue have always been more ideological than empirical. Proponents believe that control is a right of ownership that employees should have. Most are convinced that control is also necessary for an ESOP to be an effective motivational tool. Opponents argue that employees are getting a financial benefit from ownership for which they generally pay nothing; if companies were required to share power with them as well, many fewer companies would set up plans. A recent membership survey from the ESOP Association, for instance, reported that 44 percent of the responding company officials said they would not have set up their plans if full voting rights were required.[45] Moreover, they contend that managers are the people who should manage.

To look at this issue more objectively, the NCEO's survey of employees correlated the presence or absence of voting rights and board representation with employees' satisfaction with their ESOP and their jobs. It also looked at whether employees' voting rights or board representation had an effect on corporate performance measures. No relationship, one way or another, was found.[46] The NCEO then surveyed sixteen ESOP firms that provided full voting rights, were majority employee-owned, and had employee-elected representatives on their boards. In each case, the NCEO found that employee control

made little actual difference. Managers said that the employees tended
to elect managers, qualified outsiders, or responsible employees to
the board and that board decisions were made by consensus. Rarely
did employee representatives vote one way and management or outsiders another. No one could point to a specific change in policy
direction attributable to the more democratic structure.[47]

Respondents in the Gallup survey affirmed these general findings.
Seventy-two percent believed management should be responsible for
deciding financial and strategic issues, and 71 percent said management should deal with hiring and firing. These results were a dis-
appointment to both sides in the dispute. Corporate democracy was
not a sure road to corporate anarchy, nor was it an essential element
of a successful ESOP.

But the issue remains unresolved. Critics such as Congressman
Fortney Stark (D-Calif.) argue that greater control is valuable in its
own right as leading to a more democratic society. Employee control
might also stem some of the abuses ESOPs have been subject to, as
will be discussed below. Stark's views have found some support in
both the media and Congress. Among ESOP companies, about 15 to
20 percent of the privately held firms pass through full voting rights;
4 percent have employee representatives on their boards (an unknown
number of others have employees elect people other than employees).[48] In large majority ESOPs (companies with assets over $10 mil-
lion), however, the trend is very different. Among these companies,
40 percent give employees both full voting rights and board representation.[49]

How one looks at these numbers is clearly an "is the glass half
empty or half full" question. Although only a minority of ESOP firms
are democratically structured, there are several hundred of them, and
many are substantial firms with thousands of employees. That is
several hundred more companies and tens of thousands more employees than in conventional firms, which very rarely exhibit any
form of corporate democracy.

At the same time, employees are gaining a potentially powerful
voice in hundreds of America's largest companies. Employees own
only a minority of shares in these firms, but they own enough to
block hostile takeovers, which is why half the ESOPs in public companies are created. Because voting power is so dispersed in public
companies, if employees could vote with one voice, they might be
able to influence other aspects of corporate policy or elect their own
representatives to the board. To date, this voting power has served
more to back management than to give employees a voice, but it is

not difficult to imagine circumstances in which disgruntled employees could at least make life difficult for corporate management.

ESOP Foibles: Abuses and Problems

No evaluation of ESOPs is complete without an analysis of the abuses that have occurred. Any time the government uses tax incentives to stimulate some development, people inevitably find ways to use the incentives for purposes that were not intended. The more lucrative the benefits, the more abuses are likely to occur. ESOPs have not been an exception to this rule.

Of course, one person's abuse is another's clever and appropriate application. With that precaution in mind, here is a list of potential areas of abuse:

The "What me worry?" abuse. No doubt the least publicized and most common abuse is the sale to employees of a company that has inadequate cash flow to cover the debt incurred. This situation occurs when an owner of a private company wants to sell and an ESOP looks very appealing. A valuation adviser sets a price for the shares, and the ESOP attorney or financial specialist does an analysis to determine whether the company can repay the loan. If the adviser really wants the deal but the numbers look questionable, there is a temptation to change them a bit to make it more appealing to the lenders. Eager to make a loan, the lenders may ignore their suspicions. Unfortunately, when the company cannot repay the debt, the employees are the ones who suffer and usually lose their jobs.

The "MESOP" abuse. The NCEO coined this acronym for management entrenchment stock ownership plan. It describes just about anything people do not like about ESOPs, though it was originally meant to focus on ESOPs set up mostly to protect managers from losing their jobs, even if the ESOP was not in the financial interest of employees. Dan River, for instance, set up an ESOP to ward off a hostile takeover by Carl Icahn in 1983. Contributions to a pension plan were stopped (but workers kept the benefits they had accrued) and an ESOP set up to replace it. Although employees owned 70 percent of the stock, management controlled the plan. No effort was made to give employees more involvement in the firm, and when the company tried to go public in 1988, employees were not allowed to vote on the issue. Normally, this would be a voting issue, but management found a way around it. Management also bought most of the rest of the stock but for 10 percent of the price the ESOP paid. Although there were some valid reasons for the substantial differential (management put up its own money to buy the stock, for instance, and the stock would be valuable only if Dan River's performance met certain targets), some of the reasons were illusory. Management had nonvoting stock, for instance, which is worth less than voting stock, but management controlled the voting shares of the ESOP and did not need voting rights on their own shares.

Dan River was a lackluster performer over the next several years and was sold in 1989. Employees got an average of a little over $7,000 each for their stock. Although that was not an especially poor showing, other ESOPs in similar circumstances had vastly better results.

Some critics of ESOPs believe that any ESOP used as a takeover defense is an abusive "MESOP." The government, they argue, should not subsidize management's efforts to save itself from the free operation of the market. This is, frankly, a silly argument. Taxpayers already heavily subsidize raiders, mostly by allowing them to deduct the enormous amounts of debt they take on to buy companies but through other tax rules as well. Raiders are also given access to vast amounts of government-required financial filings without which it would be much more difficult to launch their efforts. When a company is bought in a hostile takeover, management can provide itself with golden parachutes; employees are left working for a company with a heavy debt and a need to "reallocate resources" (close or sell operations), "maximize free cash flow" (try to cut labor costs), and "focus on productivity enhancements" (try to get fewer people to do more work). For all the risks foisted on employees, they get nothing in return.

Almost all ESOPs created as a defense against takeovers are structured to allow employees to make an independent decision about the takeover, based on the same information other shareholders get. Companies are not being charitable in this; it is what the courts believe is necessary to establish the ESOP as an independent party and not an arm of management. As long as they have these rights, however, the ESOP simply seems to give employees a well-deserved role in the outcome of events affecting their lives.

The "If you don't tell, I won't tell" valuation abuse. Until 1986, a private company did not have to have an outside valuation to determine the price of its shares. Most did anyway, and others used a formulaic approach that may have hurt the selling owners more than the employees. Not everyone was so up front, however. Managers at Hall-Mark Electronics (not related to Hallmark Cards) bought stock from the company's ESOP at $4 per share. Then its managers did a leveraged buyout of the stock and sold the company one year later for $100 per share. Employees sued and won. The company did not have a particularly outstanding year; management, the court ruled, manipulated the share price. In 1986, Congress required that an independent, outside appraiser set share prices. Abuses can still occur, but they are likely to be rarer and less intentional.

The "What's it worth to you?" abuse. No area of ESOP practice is more complicated than "multi-investor leveraged buyouts." For example, suppose two people want to buy a company. One is rich; the other works hard. The first one puts down $100,000 and promises to run the company. The second one says, "Have the company borrow my $100,000 and we'll repay it out of earnings. But I'll work hard, and we can get some tax breaks too. We'll each get 50 percent." Would they have a deal? Not likely. In real life, investors and managers might put up $10 million in cash, and an ESOP might borrow $100 million. How to decide what percentage of the shares each side gets, given the different risks and contributions each is making, is far too complicated to explore here, but the potential for abuse is clear. The investors and managers have sophisticated financial advisers to argue for their position to get the most they can. The employees generally are represented indirectly. The trustees of the ESOP are supposed to watch out for their interests, and the valuation people are supposed to be responsible to the trustee. But the company pays these people, so most will try to get the best deal they can justify, legally and maybe ethically as well, for the investors and managers.

In 1984, a deal along these lines was proposed for the Scott and Fetzer Company. The Department of Labor did not like the way the deal was structured, and because of its opposition the proposed ESOP collapsed. Since then, several similar transactions have taken place. Many of them seem fair to employees; others are not clear. There have been no guidelines from the courts or the government on how to proceed with buyouts of this type. To illustrate the ethical difficulties of the issue, however, consider Scott and Fetzer. ESOP opponents made a point for their side, but soon after the Department of Labor acted, the company was sold to someone else in a leveraged buyout. That buyer got all the equity, and the employees ended up working in a highly leveraged company with no return for their risk.

The "Let's hope for the best" abuse. When employees leave a private company, the company has a legal obligation to buy back their shares. That is a good law, but so far there has been no monitoring of just how companies are providing the funds to assure that employees are paid. According to an NCEO study, about 80 percent of the companies with a substantial obligation to buy back shares do have plans in place, but half these companies rely on future cash flow to supply the money. In other words, they hope they will have the money when they need it. So far, few firms have failed to meet these obligations, but the potential for serious problems grows as ESOPs become more mature and account balances grow.

The "Have I got a deal for you" abuse. Most ESOPs are funded by the company with nothing expected in return from employees. *Most* means *not all*, however. Sometimes the assets of profit-sharing plans are used to help fund an ESOP, and when an owner leaves, the company does not have sufficient cash flow to buy him or her out. If cash in a profit-sharing plan can be used for part of the purchase, however, the problem can be solved. Companies can either let employees vote on whether they want to transfer their assets, usually giving them an individual choice, or they can just transfer the assets. If they follow the latter course, the trustees of the profit-sharing plan and the ESOP are supposed to be able to show that the ESOP was a good investment choice.

Most of the time, they do just that, and most of the time these deals work out just fine. Employees get the company and keep their jobs, and the ESOP performs well. Sometimes, however, managers of a company will move assets when they know its stock is about to collapse. Lawyers file suits, of course, but usually there is not much left to sue for.

In other cases, employees give up their pension plan for an ESOP. Pension law guarantees that the accumulated value of their benefit must be paid out to them when they retire. Funds needed to cover that obligation cannot be put into the ESOP, although funds held beyond that can. The employee has to decide whether the ESOP is a better continuing benefit than the old pension plan. That depends on how the company does. South Bend Lathe, for instance, followed this route in 1975. It did well for a few years, then tailed off into bankruptcy in 1989. Had its five hundred employees continued to get pension contributions during that time, they would have been much better off. Yet the company probably would have closed in 1975 had it been forced to continue the pension plan.

There are other variations on this theme. Some public companies, such as Boise Cascade, Ralston-Purina, and Lockheed, are setting up ESOPs to pay for retirees' health costs. These costs have soared in recent years, and many companies are finding them impossible—$265 per month per employee at Lockheed, for instance. So Lockheed is gradually reducing the share of the benefit it pays and is setting up an ESOP that contributes a small amount more to the total benefit package than Lockheed had been contributing. Employees are told they can use the ESOP to help pay the medical costs. Is this an abuse? Is it better than requiring employees to pay more, as some companies are doing? As in many other areas, the answer is not clear cut.

The "It's a wonderful life" abuse. Most people who start ESOPs are committed to providing their employees with good jobs and benefits. Some people appear to have something else in mind. Thomson-McKinnon was a large national brokerage firm that used an ESOP to become majority employee-owned in the late 1970s. The company did well for a while, and the value of the ESOP increased to $220 million by 1987. As the company prospered, its executives prospered even more. Salaries and bonuses for the top executives were close to $1 million a year; by contrast, top executives at A. G. Edwards, a very successful ESOP firm of about the same size and in the same industry, made less than half that, although A. G. Edwards was more profitable. The ESOP made interest-free loans to executives (now a subject of a lawsuit), and the company paid for a ninety-seven-foot yacht used for entertaining clients and for executive vacations, posh resort apartments, and lucrative golden parachutes. While money was being lavished on these luxuries, Thomson-McKinnon was failing. In 1989, the company went up for sale, but its ESOP, once worth $220 million, now was worth only 25 percent of that, or nothing at all, depending on how pending lawsuits and other financial matters are settled. The company's assets were eventually sold, but its employees lost their jobs. The ESOP was their only retirement plan; now it is virtually worthless, and employees are suing.

Laws covering ESOPs provide specific remedies for these abuses; unfortunately, suing a bankrupt company does not produce much, and suing the executives who caused the problem is costly, time-consuming, and uncertain. These abuses are not common in ESOPs, however, and they occur in companies with profit-sharing and pension plans as well.

An Assessment: Abusing Abuses

The serious abuses described above rarely occur. Out of over ten thousand ESOPs, there have been only a few dozen court cases in this litigious society. Most of these involved improper valuations conducted before 1986, when Congress wisely addressed this issue by requiring outside appraisers. Most of the others come from raiders who oppose ESOP defenses or from the Department of Labor in multi-investor leveraged buyouts. Both of these situations could be eased or eliminated if Congress or the Department of Labor would issue clear guidelines on the use of ESOPs in these circumstances, which they have promised but never done.

The remaining areas of abuse can and should be addressed by legal reform. They are not inherent in the idea of employee ownership, and there have been many proposals to address them. Joseph Blasi argues that enhancing employees' bargaining rights in ESOPs could stem many of the abuses. Others have focused on clearer financial standards or independent counsel for the employees in larger, more complex ESOP transactions. These proposals have merits and problems, but the issues they address are not intractable.

Are ESOPs Worthwhile?

Current estimates of the annual cost of ESOPs to taxpayers run around $1.5 billion. That has provided an additional $6 billion to $24 billion in stock for employees over the last three years. Some of these tax "losses" are really deferrals; employees will pay taxes on their ESOP benefits when they leave the company, and owners selling to ESOPs will often pay taxes when they sell the new investments they buy with the proceeds of their ESOP shares. If our figures are correct, ESOP companies are growing 3 to 4 percent per year faster than they would have without their plans. That means that they probably produce more than $1.5 billion more in tax revenue a year. This comparison is simplistic, however. Perhaps the government could have invested that $1.5 billion in something else and made even more money.

How one judges the costs and benefits, therefore, depends more on values than numbers. The numbers could justify either side of the argument.

Conclusion: I Can Bake a Pie, but Not Yet

To their most unabashed advocates, ESOPs are the ultimate in capitalism. These people think Kelso's magic potion will bring wondrous results. Employees will work harder, capital will be cheaper, and the economy will boom. To their most unthoughtful critics, ESOPs are just another scam. Kelso's elixir is a fancy placebo tricking the taxpayer into lining corporate pockets.

Neither view is accurate. One of the problems ESOPs and other employee ownership plans have faced is that the claims for them have

A more sober set of expectations would ask that ESOPs improve employees' financial security over what they could realistically expect otherwise, that they make a positive contribution to corporate performance, and that they help make work more satisfying.

Why not be content with the first objective, as some ESOP proponents have argued? If all ESOPs are expected to do is make employees more money, the case for them could become very hard to make. Why not give extra tax benefits to profit-sharing plans that invest in a diversified portfolio of investments? Any sophomore economics major would say that is a wiser course than investing everything in one's own company if the only goal is to maximize risk-adjusted investment performance for employees. But ESOP advocates say that ESOPs have the unique ability to finance capital growth and employee financial security simultaneously. Indeed, they can. But they do not. ESOPs are almost never used to acquire new capital. They are used to buy existing shares. So it must be argued that there is value in ownership per se, that it is better for employees to own their companies than for someone else to buy the shares or the company and pay employee benefits based on competitive conditions.

What, then, is valuable about ownership? First, it does seem to improve employees' financial well-being. The data are persuasive that employees are usually, but not always, better off with an ESOP than they would be without one. Although the data are imperfect, it appears that ESOP employees get at least twice the average annual contribution from the company as non-ESOP employees. One reason companies can do this is because they are buying their own shares for the ESOP, which is better than the alternatives. If the company bought the shares and retired them, the dollars spent would have increased the percentage owned by the remaining owners. If someone other than the employees buys controlling interest, that person will want the earnings of the company to pay for the investment. If it does, the owner gets richer. If the ESOP buys the shares, the employees get richer. Part of the reason, of course, is tax incentives, but as long as they are only part (as all the surveys show), they are doing their job.

Second, ownership can prevent employees from losing their jobs or having to deal with new owners. ESOPs are most commonly used in private companies to assure business continuity when many of these businesses would otherwise be sold or closed. Free market economists say the new owner will keep employees at market wages or they will find other jobs. Maybe some companies will have a problem because of "labor market friction," but the buying and selling of companies is all part of the market's magic whereby resources get allocated to their highest use. Employees may have a less theoretical perspective. They may not want to look for other jobs or have other owners, and they place a value on their psychological costs, even if economists do not.

Third, people like being owners. Many, as the polls have shown, are even willing to give up a pay increase to get stock in their company. Ownership is a long-held, deeply rooted value in American culture. Being an owner means more than being a profit sharer. With fewer and fewer opportunities for Americans to own their own homes or businesses, ESOPs are important simply in that they help restore a basic value, one that imparts dignity and a sense of accomplishment to millions of people.

Fourth, ownership can improve economic performance. It may be unfair to expect ownership to make society more equitable and more productive, but people expect it to do so and it can, at least when combined with participative management. Management has a responsibility to its shareholders to act in their interests, just as it has an obligation to nonemployee shareholders to maximize their return. The record of employee ownership on this score is imperfect, but it is still impressive compared to the nonemployee ownership universe.

Fifth, employee ownership can make work better by giving employees a chance to have a say. The record of employee ownership companies on this score also leaves much to be desired, but it does seem that ownership is a significant spur to changing management style. Change is most common at the job level but perhaps more distinctive at the company level. Job-level participation programs are common in nonemployee ownership companies, but outside of employee ownership, participation at the company level is nonexistent. So, though employee ownership may not satisfy its harshest critics on this score, it is still a large step ahead.

Now I will explain the odd title at the beginning of this section. Some years ago, I met a three-year-old girl who told me proudly, "I can bake a pie, but not yet." Of course, she was right. She had the innate ability to bake a pie, but she had not yet acquired all the necessary skills. ESOPs are like that too. They have demonstrated an enormous ability to transform the way we think about and operate businesses. So far, their potential has only occasionally been fully realized, but it is there, and there are indications that as ESOPs mature, their potential will be realized more and more.

2 Employee Stock Ownership Plans in the United States

Darien A. McWhirter

An employee stock ownership plan is a type of deferred benefit plan. Many people have deferred benefit plans such as profit-sharing or pension plans that buy stocks and bonds and place them in a fund for the employees' use when they leave the company or retire. An ESOP does the same thing, only it buys stock in the company the employees work for. The shares belong to the employees, but they cannot sell them until they leave the company or retire. Until then a trustee holds the stock.

The Basic Rules of ESOPs

An employee stock ownership plan is first of all a trust. Trusts were invented in England during the time of the Crusades. A knight could turn his property over to a "trusted" friend. That friend would own the property for the benefit of the knight's wife and children and use the income to make sure they had the means to live while the knight was away fighting in the holy land. By putting the property in the hands of a trustee, with specific requirements that had to be followed, the knight was assured that his family would be taken care of. Technically, the trusted friend "owned" the property, but he was required by a contract (called the trust documents) to use the property and the income it produced to benefit the absent knight's family. If the trustee failed to live up to this requirement, the beneficiaries (the knight's family) could go to court and get the judge to substitute a new trustee for the incompetent (or immoral) one.

In an ESOP shares are purchased in the employees' names and held by the trustee until the employees retire or leave the company. The company may either put money into the trust to be used to buy stock for the employees or issue new shares and place them in the trust.

Two Types of ESOPs

There are basically two types of ESOPs, distinguished primarily by whether they have borrowed money. Accountants use the word *leverage* to describe the process of using borrowed money to buy a company. Just as a lever helps lift a load that otherwise would be impossible to lift, borrowed money helps buy a company that one would not otherwise be able to buy. With a nonleveraged ESOP, contributions of stock (or cash to be used to buy stock) are made on a regular basis to the ESOP. The amount of the contribution can vary from year to year and is strictly up to the employer. This is basically the same as many other pension and benefit funds except that the plan buys mainly stock in the employee's own company rather than in many different companies.

With a leveraged ESOP, shares are purchased with borrowed money. One major advantage of an ESOP over other benefit funds is that federal law allows it to borrow money. The money might be used to buy out existing stockholders or to invest in new plants and equipment. With a leveraged ESOP the company is usually required to make payments to the ESOP to pay off the loan.[1] Otherwise, banks and other financial institutions would not be willing to loan money to the ESOP.

How does a leveraged ESOP work from the employees' point of view? As an example, suppose corporation X has just been bought. The ESOP has borrowed money to buy half the shares, and the other half will be owned by a group of investors. When the ESOP has a loan payment due, the company puts cash into the ESOP trust, which is then used to pay off the ESOP loan. As the loan is paid off, stock is placed in the accounts of individual employees. The employees own these shares increasingly over time as they vest in the plan (the same way they would vest in any other benefit or pension plan). The money that goes into these plans is an employee benefit and is almost always paid in addition to regular pay. A typical company would contribute between 5 and 15 percent of an employee's pay into the plan each year.[2]

When the loan is first made, all the stock bought with the borrowed funds is placed in what is called a suspense account. It is not allocated to any particular employee's account. When a payment is made into the plan, a percentage of shares equal to the percentage of the loan that is paid off is released to each employee's account. Suppose the ESOP borrows $1 million to buy 1 million shares and the loan is paid off over ten years in ten equal payments. Suppose there are one hundred employees and they all make the same salary each year. During the first year 100,000 shares will be released from the suspense account into individual employees' accounts. A typical employee, Fred, would get 1,000 shares. If the number of employees remained the same, Fred would get 1,000 shares each year. How much the shares added to his individual account are actually worth will depend on how well the company is doing. If the shares are worth a dollar each the first year, Fred's account gained $1,000 worth of shares. If the shares are worth two dollars the second year, Fred's account gained $2,000 worth of shares. If the company is not doing as well, the shares could be worth less than they were originally. Of course, in most companies the employees make different salaries. The amount of shares put into their individual accounts will usually be proportional to the amount of money they make. If we suppose Fred's right to the shares vests 20 percent each year, when Fred has worked for the company for five years he owns all the stock in his account, but he cannot get it until he leaves the company or retires. Over the years Fred's account becomes more valuable as more shares are purchased and the value of each share increases (if the company is growing and the value of the shares is going up). In some companies that have had ESOPs for many years individual accounts are worth over $100,000.

Of course, the value of the stock could go down, and the company might even go out of business. In that case Fred's shares would be worth little or nothing. This is the extreme exception, not the rule, but it has happened and will happen again. That is why experts advise that an ESOP should not be the only retirement plan people have. About 80 percent of all ESOP companies do offer some other employee savings or retirement plan.[3] Companies that do not may be jeopardizing their employees' retirement.

Participation

The law requires companies to allow employees to participate when they have reached the age of twenty-one, have worked full time for one year with the company, and work at least one thousand hours a year for the company.[4]

A special rule covers employees who work under a collective bargaining agreement. Because unions have already negotiated special benefits as part of the collective bargaining agreement, the law allows companies to exclude these employees from the ESOP. Once the ESOP is established, these employees' participation becomes a topic for contract negotiation along with other issues regarding benefits and working conditions. This has caused some confusion. Some managers, in explaining ESOPs to rank-and-file employees, have given the impression that union members will never be eligible to participate in the ESOP. That is not true (and some managers have ended up in court for suggesting that it is). The law does not allow the exclusion of union members per se. It allows the exclusion at the beginning of the ESOP of any employee, union or nonunion, who is already covered by a collective bargaining agreement. Whether they participate in the future will depend on the negotiations at the next contract bargaining session. Any contract can be changed at any time, and the union could negotiate a change in the contract when the ESOP is established. It is not necessary to wait until the present contract expires. If these employees want to be part of the ESOP, the company has to bargain in good faith with them.

The law also allows (but does not require) exclusion of part-time employees (those working less than a thousand hours a year) and those under the age of twenty-one. Managers are included in the plan, but only up to a limit. Generally, no more than $30,000 can be placed in the ESOP for one employee in any one year, and salary over $200,000 a year does not count for the ESOP allocation. This puts a limit on how much stock highly paid managers can accumulate in the ESOP. An executive earning $250,000 a year and working for a company that contributes 10 percent of salary to the ESOP would have $20,000 placed in the ESOP, not $25,000.

One of the advantages of an ESOP is that, under some circumstances, the company can put a much greater amount into employees' tax-free accounts than is possible under other retirement and benefit plans. Generally, federal law limits the amount that can be put into these plans to 15 percent of payroll. For ESOPs this limit is raised to 25 percent if the ESOP is part of a money purchase pension plan. In a money purchase pension plan the company must contribute at least 10 percent of payroll a year in cash, although the cash can be used to buy shares. The limit is also raised to 25 percent if the ESOP has a loan to pay off. If an ESOP borrows money to buy shares, all of the principal portion of the loan is deductible up to 25 percent of the annual payroll of the ESOP participants and all of the interest is deductible, provided that more than one-third of the ESOP benefits do not go to "highly compensated" people. Reasonable dividends paid on the stock held by the ESOP can also be used to pay off the loan, and the additional shares are placed in employees' accounts. These dividends do not count toward the 25 percent limit. All of this can add up. If a leveraged ESOP is used and a significant dividend is paid on shares already in the employees' accounts, average employees might find that an amount equal to a third or more of their annual salary is being put into their individual accounts every year, tax free. Although the amount cannot exceed $30,000 a year for each employee (this figure will be adjusted for inflation over time), dividends do not count toward that total.[5]

Vesting

Employees vest in an ESOP the same way they vest in any other employee benefit or pension fund. Federal law requires full-time employees over age twenty-one to begin vesting after at least their third year of company service and to be fully vested by the end of their seventh year. In a typical plan employees would vest 20 percent after the third year, 40 percent after the fourth, and so on until they would be 100 percent vested after seven years. Companies that do not wish to have a gradual vesting schedule can vest 100 percent after the fifth year and nothing before then. Companies can also vest more quickly. For example, many companies begin vesting 20 percent the first year so that employees are 100 percent vested at the end of five years.[6]

Employees who are vested have a nonforfeitable right to the shares in their account (although they cannot sell them or use them until they are released from the ESOP). An employee with three years of company service and 20 percent vesting might have an account worth $3,000 but only own $600. Three years later, that same employee may have an account worth $8,000 and at 80 percent vesting would own $6,400.

Although it might seem that it would be to employees' advantage to vest as quickly as possible, employees as owners might want to have a slow vesting schedule to prevent experienced employees from leaving the company. The issue of how to deal with vesting when an ESOP is first introduced is particularly difficult. Should employees who have worked for the company for many years be 100 percent vested in the new plan from the beginning or should they have to vest over time like new employees?

The Right to Vote the Shares

Once it is clear which employees will participate in the ESOP, it must be decided if they will be allowed to vote like other stockholders, even though they technically do not own any shares (technically, the trustee owns the shares). Federal law has set minimum voting rights for employees. If the corporation's shares are traded on the open market, the employees can vote the allocated shares in their accounts just like any other stockholder. They vote for major decisions such as whether to merge with another company and for the members of the board of directors. The same is true if the shares in the employee's account were purchased with a loan made after 1989 that qualified for a special tax deduction for the lenders.[7] In privately held companies the employees must be allowed to vote their shares only on major corporate decisions such as mergers, acquisitions, and sale of the corporate assets.

An ESOP plan may give the employees more voting rights than those required by federal law. A study conducted by the General Accounting Office suggests that about 15 to 20 percent of privately held ESOP companies pass through full voting rights even though they are not required to do so.[8] To the extent employees have been given voting rights, they vote the shares in their individual accounts whether they are fully vested or not.

When ESOPs were first introduced, the question of whether employees should be allowed to vote the shares in their accounts evoked a great deal of controversy. Some supporters of voting rights believed that owning shares they could not vote would make workers cynical about the ownership concept and would defeat the purpose of employee ownership. Opponents of voting rights argued that workers might vote for outrageous wages and destroy the long-term economic viability of the company. To try to discover the effect of full employee voting rights, the NCEO did a survey in 1986 of sixteen private firms in which the majority of stock was owned by the ESOP and the employees had been given full voting rights.[9]

In the average corporation stockholders seldom vote on much more than who will sit on the board of directors. The same was true of a majority of the ESOP companies surveyed in 1986 that passed through full voting rights. Some of the other companies extended voting to issues such as how many people would sit on the board of directors and who would constitute the ESOP committee. In two companies the stockholder-employees voted on a wide range of issues usually reserved for management.

Voting for the board of directors is the most important decision stockholders make. Thirteen of the sixteen firms studied held direct elections for the board. Eleven of these thirteen voted for a preselected slate, and in two other cases the board was elected by written ballot of all the shareholders. In most cases the boards chosen consisted mainly of managers. Six consisted entirely of managers or managers and outsiders. Of the remaining seven firms, nonmanagement employees sat on the boards with varying percentages of control. The percentages did not matter on most boards because decisions were made by consensus.

This study suggests that allowing employees to vote has less impact on the decisions made than on how managers and employees feel about those decisions. Only two of the sixteen companies could point to concrete policy changes that resulted from allowing employees to vote. Several managers talked a great deal about how voting rights affected attitudes. They believed that allowing employees to vote for the board of directors made them feel more like owners, even though employees' choices for members of the board were similar to those who would otherwise have been elected.

In a survey conducted by the NCEO during 1982–84 of thirty-seven hundred employees at forty-five companies, it was discovered that employees were not very concerned about voting.[10] There was no relationship between voting rights and employees' attitudes about ownership, their jobs, or their companies. Nor were their attitudes about the company affected by whether or not employees sat on the board of directors. The real issue for most employees was the extent to which they had some say in how their individual jobs were structured. The more influence they were allowed to have on their own work situation, the better they felt about the companies they owned.

Dividends

Employees have the right to receive dividends like other stockholders, although in a leveraged ESOP the trustee may use the dividends to help pay off the loan. Most private companies do not pay dividends. Instead, they reinvest the money that would otherwise go to dividends in the company so that the value of the company's stock increases over time.

The payment of dividends raises an interesting problem. Money paid to employees either as direct compensation or into a benefit plan like an ESOP is usually tax-deductible for the corporation, but dividends paid to stockholders are not. If the corporation pays dividends on the stock held by an ESOP, those payments are tax-deductible for the corporation if they are used to repay the ESOP loan or if they are passed through to the employees as a cash payment.[11] If they are used to pay off the loan, additional shares worth the value of the dividend must be moved into individual employees' accounts.

Social Security taxes do not have to be paid on dividends paid to employees on shares held in an ESOP (Social Security taxes are due only on wages). This tax saving could be another reason to pay employees dividends through their ESOP stock instead of paying them a bonus, which would be subject to Social Security taxes.

One way to provide the shares in the ESOP with a higher dividend is through the use of convertible preferred stock. Preferred stock is paid a fixed dividend, which is usually higher than that paid to regular common stock. Convertible stock is convertible to common stock; usually one share can be converted into one share of common stock at some future date. Convertible preferred shares can be issued to an ESOP as long as the shares can be converted to common stock later and the conversion premium is fair. A conversion premium is the difference between the price of the common stock and the higher price of the convertible preferred stock at the time the latter is issued.

Many of the larger companies that have formed ESOPs such as Procter & Gamble and Ralston-Purina have used convertible preferred stock.[12] Preferred stock not only gets a higher dividend than common stock, but if there is not enough profit to pay a dividend to both, it goes first to the preferred stock. That is why people are willing to pay a premium for preferred stock. The company likes convertible preferred stock because it can pay a higher dividend and use that to help pay off the ESOP loan or to pass through tax-deductible money to employees that is not subject to Social Security taxes. The employees like it because it is safer than common stock. If the company goes bankrupt, the preferred stock is paid off before the common stock. To increase this safety feature, many companies have promised to buy back the convertible preferred stock for at least the price the ESOP originally paid for it.

Suppose, for example, that a company has common stock worth $80 a share and it sells convertible preferred stock to the ESOP at $100 a share with an 8 percent dividend and the right to convert one share of preferred stock into one share of common stock. The ESOP borrows

$100 million on a ten-year loan to buy the preferred stock, and the company uses the money to buy $100 million worth of its common stock. The company may be paying a higher dividend on the preferred stock, but it is not paying a dividend on the common stock it bought back with the money paid by the ESOP, and the dividend to the ESOP preferred stock is tax-deductible, whereas a dividend on common stock to regular stockholders is not. Because of this tax advantage, a company can pay a higher dividend on the ESOP preferred stock and still save money.[13]

Diversification

As employees near retirement they may wish to diversify the stock in their accounts. The law allows them to require the trustee to use 25 percent of the value of their account to buy a diversified portfolio of investments when they have participated in the plan for at least ten years and reached the age of fifty-five. Five years later, employees can ask that 50 percent of the account be diversified. Companies have the option of paying the employees the required percentage of their accounts and letting them choose their own investments.[14]

Getting the Money Out

There are general rules covering when employees get their money and special rules that apply in some situations. In most plans, employees get their money when they become disabled or reach retirement age, or their heirs get the money when the employees die. If the ESOP is still paying off a loan that was used to purchase the shares, employees do not receive the shares in their accounts when they leave the company. If the ESOP loan has been repaid, or if the stock was not acquired by a loan, employees are entitled to receive the stock in their accounts no later than the close of the sixth calendar year following the year they left the company. Companies can then pay the money out over five years, with interest.

Retirees can choose to delay distribution of the money, but not past the age of seventy and a half. Retirees can also choose to take the money in installments, but generally not over more than a five-year period.

Employees who receive the money in their ESOP account before retirement age must either place the money in a qualified retirement plan such as an Individual Retirement Account or pay income taxes and a 10 percent penalty tax.

Repurchase Liability

When employees leave a company whose stock is publicly traded, they can take the stock from their ESOP account and do whatever they want with it: keep it, sell it, or give it away. If they work for a private company, there is no market for their stock, and the law requires that the company buy it back at the fair market value. That means the company must repurchase the stock if requested to do so within sixty days of the distribution (or within another sixty-day period a year later).[15]

This requirement that private ESOP companies buy back the stock of retiring or departing employees is a liability from their point of view. It is a payment they must make. In some cases the ESOP trust can buy the stock of retiring or departing employees to put in the accounts of other employees. That way new employees can receive stock even if the company is not acquiring any additional shares for the ESOP. Ultimately the company is obligated to buy the shares if the ESOP does not.

Companies can prepare for this eventuality in several ways. They may set up a special fund to pay the future liability or go public so employees can sell their shares on the open market when they are ready to do so. Companies may also purchase life insurance on employees who have large ESOP accounts and use the proceeds to buy back their shares.[16]

Combining ESOPs with Other Retirement Plans

An ESOP may provide an employee with a handsome nest egg, but it may also be a loss if the company goes bankrupt. That is why many experts suggest that employees have some additional plans for retirement. Many companies combine their ESOP with another retirement plan that buys a wide variety of stocks and bonds.

There are two general categories of retirement plans, defined benefit and defined contribution. A defined benefit plan pays a fixed amount when the employee retires based on the number of years with the company and the salary the employee was paid. This is what most people think of as a standard pension plan. A defined contribution plan places a fixed amount of money into each individual employee's account every payday. That money is then invested in stocks and bonds. Over time the account balance grows. The money will be used to provide the employee with income upon retirement, and this income will be higher or lower depending on how well the stocks and bonds in the individual employee's account have done. An ESOP is a kind of defined contribution plan except that it invests mainly in the stock of the company the employee works for instead of in a large group of stocks and bonds.

In some cases a company converts an existing benefit plan into an ESOP. If the existing plan is a defined benefit plan, the Pension Benefit Guaranty Corporation (PBGC), a federal agency that insures defined benefit plans, considers that the plan has been terminated and replaced. This means that the participants become fully vested in the old pension plan. Employees must be assured that they will get the benefit they have earned when they retire. The company might have to place more funds into the old plan if the PBGC determines there are not enough securities to assure payment of benefits. In many cases there are excess assets in the plan (the securities in the plan are worth more than is necessary to pay the expected benefits upon retirement). In that case the excess assets may be used to buy the company's stock and those shares allocated to fully vested accounts in the ESOP.

If the company wishes to convert an existing defined contribution plan, it can usually change the documents that control the plan. Employees may then be given the option of taking their money out of the plan and placing it into Individual Retirement Accounts instead of having the money put into the new ESOP plan. Alternatively, the company can freeze the old plan and contribute in the future only to the ESOP. Or it can ask employees to decide whether they want to move part or all of their accounts into an ESOP, although this may require an expensive registration with government securities agencies. Finally, a company can put the assets of the old plan into the ESOP. If the employees are not given any options, however, and the ESOP turns out to have been a bad idea because the value of the company's stock went down, the employees may be able to sue the trustees of the old plan for not investing their retirement funds prudently. Despite these potential problems, one-third of all ESOPs use at least some funds from another defined contribution plan when they are introduced.[17]

Role of the Trustee

The ESOP trustee has a great deal of responsibility and must be mindful of both the legal requirements that apply to all trustees and special rules that apply to ESOP trustees. The ESOP trustee has what the law calls a fiduciary duty to make sure all decisions are made with only the best interests of the employees (the beneficiaries of the trust) in mind. The trustee must act for the sole and exclusive purpose of providing benefits for employees and must act prudently.

In most situations an ESOP trustee should have no trouble meeting these requirements. In some special cases, such as when a corporate raider is trying to buy stock, the trustee may be in a difficult position. The employees as beneficiaries may be better off in the short run if they sell out (because of the high price being offered for the stock) but worse off as employees if the takeover means drastic cuts in employment.

The managers of the company appoint the trustee to hold the shares in the company's retirement plan. Although this makes sense in most situations, there are times when the desires of those who run the company do not coincide with the best interests of the beneficiaries of the retirement plan. The trustee is required by law to do what is in the best interests of the beneficiaries, not the company. In some cases, outside legal and financial advice will have to be sought by the trustee to help ensure that only the interests of the employees are being considered. There are times when the trustee must say no to management, such as when the company wants the ESOP to buy shares at an unfair price or to refuse to sell to an outside buyer at a very good price.

Companies are usually bought when a buyer (often called a raider if current management opposes the buyout) offers to buy shares only if enough stockholders are willing to sell their shares at the price offered. Stockholders are asked to "tender" (offer for sale) their shares. In some cases, whether the shares in the ESOP are tendered will determine whether the buyout is successful or not. Employees vote on some issues related to the shares in their account, but whether to sell those shares is usually considered an investment decision that the trustee should make. Some plans, however, call for the trustee to pass through to employees the vote on whether to tender shares held by the ESOP. Federal law is not clear concerning how this pass-through vote should be accomplished and when a trustee is authorized to overrule the employees' vote when the trustee feels it would be in their best interests to do so.[18]

Disclosure Requirements

The Employee Retirement Income Security Act (ERISA) mandates that the participants in an ESOP be given basic information about the plan and how it will affect them. Employees (or anyone receiving benefits under the ESOP) must be given a summary description of the employee stock ownership plan and a summary of the annual reports. Annual reports must be filed with the Department of Labor and the Internal Revenue Service and must be made available to any employees who wish to see them. Employees are also entitled to receive an updated summary if any major changes are made in the plan. They should also receive an annual summary of the balance in their personal account, showing the current value of the stock and how much stock is in the account. Employees also have the right to see (and copy at a reasonable cost) all the plan documents, reports, bargaining agreements, contracts, and trust agreements that relate to the ESOP. Most experts believe that employers are wise to provide even more information to employees than the law requires so that employees can understand how the plan works and how it will affect them.[19]

Why Employees Want ESOPs

ESOPs are attractive to employees because through them their employer buys stock for them with borrowed funds while the employees do not have to put any of their own assets at risk. The assets of the company serve as collateral to secure a loan that allows the employees to buy all or part of the company. Though the loan has to be paid back, using an ESOP allows the company to make this payment with pretax dollars. Companies can afford to buy significantly more stock for employees this way than if it were purchased with wages after taxes have been removed.

Most employee benefit plans can put only 15 percent of wages into the plan. With a leveraged or money purchase ESOP, 25 percent of wages may be placed in the plan. This allows a company putting in the maximum to buy a great deal of stock quickly. Dividends may also be paid to employees through the ESOP without having Social Security taxes taken out. This money may also be used to pay off the ESOP loan faster and put even more shares into employees' accounts.

In other words, with an ESOP, companies can buy more stock for their employees faster and at a lower cost than with any other plan. The company can also borrow money to buy the stock without the employees having to be personally liable if the loan is not repaid.

All this presupposes that the employees want to own a significant stake in the company they work for. Putting a large sum of money into buying the stock of one company entails risks if the value of that stock should fall. If the value should rise because of their joint efforts, however, they could achieve a significant increase in wealth.

Why Owners and Corporations Want ESOPs

To Leverage or Not to Leverage

In purchasing stock, ESOPs may use leverage (borrowed money) to buy a large block of stock all at once or buy the shares slowly over time as money is placed in the ESOP fund. One reason an ESOP might wish to borrow the money is because of a federal law that says if the ESOP ends up owning at least 50 percent of the company and the employees are given the right to vote the shares in their account like other shareholders, the bank can deduct half the interest income it receives from the ESOP loan. In most cases, that means the corporation (through its ESOP) is paying interest rates 80 to 85 percent of the market rate. This is known as a "133 loan" because Section 133 of the Internal Revenue Code provides for this tax break.

There is another, more important reason an ESOP might borrow money to buy shares. Usually, when a corporation borrows money and then repays the loan, it can deduct the interest payments but not the principal. When the loan is through an ESOP, the payments are technically being made to an employee benefit plan so the entire amount is deductible. This means that the corporation has borrowed money for expansion or buyout purposes and can deduct both the principal and interest payments, provided that no more than one-third of the ESOP stock is going to highly compensated employees.

Buying Out a Departing Owner

An ESOP can borrow money, which no other benefit plan can do. This means an ESOP can be used to buy out a retiring owner or even to do a leveraged buyout. The theory is fairly simple, although the legal and financial procedures can be very complex.

Suppose Mr. Founder has worked for forty years building up a small company. He does not have any descendants who wish to run the company, and he would like to sell out. His options are limited. He could sell to a large corporation, but the needs of the local community and his employees may not be uppermost on the minds of that corporation's leaders when decisions are made in corporate headquarters. He could try to find another individual owner, but that is difficult in today's economy, or he could sell to his employees. In this case an ESOP may be the answer. Federal law allows a departing owner to sell to an ESOP, use the money to buy securities (stocks, bonds) issued by other American corporations, and not pay any income taxes until those newly purchased securities are eventually sold. To qualify, the seller must be selling stock in an American corporation that has no tradable stock outstanding; the seller must have owned the stock for at least three years; the ESOP must end up owning at least 30 percent of the corporation; the seller must buy the replacement securities between three months before the sale and twelve months after the sale; and the securities purchased must be those of corporations that are engaged primarily in active business, not the reception of passive income (such as rents). Also, the seller must file the proper forms with the IRS the year of the sale. To maintain all of these tax advantages, the ESOP must not sell the stock purchased for at least three years after the sale to the ESOP. This is called a "1042 rollover" because Section 1042 of the Internal Revenue Code allows for this special tax treatment.[20]

This rollover tax provision was necessary because if departing owners sell to a larger corporation by trading the stock in their small companies for stock in the giant corporation, the tax law does not consider that a sale has taken place until the new stock is sold. Until departing owners were given the same tax advantage when selling to the ESOP, sales by such owners required a real sacrifice on their part. If, however, they sell out to another corporation and trade their small company's stock for shares in the other corporation, they are still stuck with all their eggs in one basket. That is something most retiring owners would just as soon avoid. Under the present law, selling owners can avoid this problem by selling to an ESOP because they can use the money to buy a diversified group of stocks and bonds. Also, sellers have to sell only 30 percent of their company to an ESOP to get this tax advantage instead of having to sell all of their company in a merger. If Mr. Founder dies without having sold the replacement securities, his heirs inherit them free from normal income tax (they may still have to pay estate taxes). Accountants say the heirs get a "step up" in basis, which means they inherit the stock at its value on the day of Mr. Founder's death. If the value of the stock has gone up over Mr. Founder's lifetime, no income taxes are due on that increase.

An example of a major ESOP buyout of a departing owner is Wyatt Cafeterias. In 1931 Earle Wyatt opened a small cafeteria inside a Piggly Wiggly grocery store he had purchased in Dallas, Texas. After World War II he began building freestanding cafeterias. In 1988 the shareholders, consisting primarily of Wyatt family members, sold out 100 percent to the sixty-five hundred employees. The ESOP paid $173 million for the shares of the company.

This ESOP borrowed the money to buy the entire company all at once, though it could instead have purchased shares over time as money was placed in the ESOP fund without borrowing money. Or it could have borrowed enough money to buy 30 percent of the stock (so the seller could get the rollover tax advantages) and then bought the rest of the stock slowly over time once the initial loan was paid off.

That is exactly what the founder of Connor Spring and Manufacturing did. The ESOP borrowed enough money to buy 30 percent of the stock, and the founder planned to sell more once the initial loan was paid off. The tax advantages make this a sensible way to conduct a gradual sale to an ESOP.

The company does not have to be a giant for selling out to an ESOP to be advantageous. Reflexite was founded in 1970 by two brothers who were both engineers. The company, located in New Britain, Connecticut, makes reflective devices. By the early 1980s the brothers wanted to get some of their equity out of the business and to move out of management and into more entrepreneurial roles. They received handsome offers for the company, but they felt a strong commitment to their community and their employees and were reluctant to sell to outsiders. The ESOP provided them with a way to sell part of the company, retain a controlling interest, and reward their employees. In 1985 they used a leveraged ESOP to sell 30 percent of their stock to 130 employees. During fiscal year 1988 the company increased sales by 27 percent with profits up 43 percent over the previous year. By the end of 1989 the ESOP owned 32 percent of the stock and the company had grown to 160 employees.

Some company owners find they can sell part of their shares to the ESOP and, because the company grows and productivity increases, their remaining shares are worth more than the entire company had been worth when they began to sell shares to the ESOP.

Buying Out a Minority Owner

In many American corporations a small family group starts a company, but as it grows the various family members drift apart. At some point one or more of the family members would like to sell out, but most investors are not willing to buy a minority interest in a small, closely held corporation. The family members usually receive compensation by paying themselves salaries, not by declaring dividends. With little hope of having any real voice in the corporation or of realizing any financial gain through dividends or the sale of the stock, these minority interests are often difficult to sell. This purchase might not be very good for the average investor, but it can be good for the employees, through an ESOP, because federal law requires the company to repurchase their stock when they leave, and this repurchase must be based on an objective outside appraisal of the value of the company.

An example of an ESOP that was used to buy out a minority owner can be found in Yellow Springs, Ohio. Yellow Springs could be considered a hotbed of ESOP activity because all four of its major employers (except Antioch College) have ESOPs. Yellow Springs Instruments was begun in 1948 by three people in the basement of an Antioch College science building. By 1989 the company had 370 employees making a variety of measuring devices. In the mid-1980s two of the company's founders were ready to retire, and each owned a minority interest in the company. The ESOP borrowed money to buy 25 percent of the company. That interest had grown to 30 percent by the end of 1989.

Some of those who helped create ESOPs in the 1970s did so in the hope of keeping American companies in American hands. They hoped the owners would sell to an ESOP instead of to a foreign company. In 1989 Syncor Corporation put a new twist on that scenario. Syncor provides radioactive materials to hospitals and physicians for use both as drugs and in imaging devices. In December 1989 Syncor used an ESOP to buy back 1.5 million shares (15 percent of the company) from a French shareholder, Companie ORIS Industrie. One million of these shares were placed in the ESOP, and five hundred thousand were retired.

Divesting from a Parent Corporation

Several large corporations have sold major divisions to employees using an ESOP. Divesting to the employees can be advantageous to a large conglomerate because the ESOP may be the only buyer willing or able to meet the parent's price. In some cases the parent company loans some of the money for the purchase and retains the right to buy stock in the new company at a set price if the spinoff is successful.[21]

By 1987 Avis had changed hands five times in ten years and the employees were tired of being someone's stepchild. The 12,500 employees used an ESOP to buy the entire corporation. The company introduced a new employee participation program and began to run advertisements that emphasized that the employees owned the company. It must have worked. The value of the stock tripled over the next two years.[22]

Avis is a recent example of using an ESOP to buy a division of a large corporation. BCM Engineers may have been one of the first. In 1977 it was a division of Betz Laboratories of Trevose, Pennsylvania. Betz Laboratories wanted to get out of the engineering business, and two Philadelphia banks were willing to finance a leveraged ESOP. The ESOP purchased 75 percent of the new company using a $3.8 million loan at a fixed rate of 8.8 percent for seven years. The remaining 25 percent was purchased by a group of corporate officers for $1.3 million, 80 percent of that with bank financing. James Jablonski, president and chairman of the board of the new company, thought that interest rate was very high, but it turned out to have been a smart move because the prime rate rose into double digits soon after. The stock fell from $10 a share to $2.40 soon after the ESOP buyout because of the high debt level of the new company. This might have been discouraging, but by 1989 the stock was valued at $38.50 a share and revenues had tripled over the previous five years to $64.5 million. BCM had twenty-two offices nationwide with over a thousand employees by the end of 1989. A dividend of sixteen cents per share was declared in 1990 and passed through as cash to the ESOP participants.

Buying Out a Large Public Company

An ESOP can also be used in a leveraged buyout of a large corporation. In a leveraged buyout, an individual or a group of individuals borrows money to buy out the stockholders of a corporation. A group of employees can form an ESOP trust and have the trust borrow the money to accomplish the same purpose.

As this book is being written, the employees of United Airlines are attempting to accomplish the largest employee buyout in history. The story of the United buyout begins in April 1987, when the Air Line Pilots Association (ALPA) offered to buy the company for $4.5 billion. This offer was ultimately rejected. At the same time, the International Association of Machinists (IAM) signed a new three-year contract with an 11 percent wage increase over the life of the contract. It was suggested at the time that the company had "bought" the machinists to keep them from joining the pilots in trying to take over the company. After rejecting the pilots' offer, the company sought another buyer. Ultimately this effort failed and the stock of the company, which at one point had risen to $294 a share, fell to $140 a share. Finally, the company's board of directors accepted an offer of $4.38 billion made by the three major unions: ALPA, IAM, and the Association of Flight Attendants. This offer amounted to $155 a share plus notes and other securities worth $35 a share. The employees agreed to wage and work rule concessions that could save $300 to $400 million a year. Only time will tell if the employees are able to obtain the financing they need to complete the buyout and if they can then pay off the loans and end up owning one of the largest airlines in the world (seventy-one thousand employees).[23]

Financing Corporate Growth

An ESOP can also be used to inject new capital into a corporation for the purchase of land or equipment for expansion. Suppose the outstanding shares are worth $100 million and the corporation needs another $100 million to expand. The ESOP can borrow the money and buy newly issued stock from the company. Overnight the employees have become half-owners of the corporation (if the ESOP ends up owning over half the company and employees are given full voting rights, the interest rate on the loan will be lower because the bank making the loan does not have to pay income taxes on half the interest income). If the land and machinery are used wisely, the corporation will grow, its profits will grow, and both the old stockholders and the new stockholders (the employees) will have a company worth more than the original $200 million.

When Louis Kelso developed ESOPs in the 1970s, he imagined that bringing in new capital for expansion would be their major use. In fact, very few ESOPs are set up solely for that purpose, but borrowing new capital for expansion can be one of many reasons for implementing an ESOP. Speedy, Inc., a trucking firm based in the Midwest, formed an ESOP at the end of 1989 to perform a variety of functions: it purchased a majority interest in the company by buying out the founder; it refinanced existing debt; and it financed an expansion of office and warehouse facilities.

Although few ESOPs are set up for the sole purpose of financing corporate growth, many are used for that purpose once the original ESOP loan is paid off. For example, BCM Engineers paid off its original ESOP loan in 1984. In 1986 it acquired a New Jersey engineering firm using a $1.5 million ESOP loan. In 1987 another ESOP loan of $1.1 million was used to refurbish one of its laboratories. Because the ESOP owns over 50 percent of BCM, half the interest on these loans was tax-deductible, allowing BCM to finance expansion at approximately 85 percent of prime rate.

Building a Takeover Defense

An ESOP can be used as a takeover defense. To understand how requires some understanding of how corporations operate in the United States. Many of America's largest corporations are incorporated in Delaware. For a takeover to succeed, in most instances, the target company must be merged into another company that has been set up to accomplish the takeover. A recent Delaware law allows stockholders holding at least 15 percent of a corporation's stock to block a sale of the company for three years. In 1989 dozens of giant American corporations that had incorporated in Delaware placed 15 percent of their stock in ESOPs. Many of these plans require decisions on whether to sell to be passed through to the employees. The law also requires that decisions on whether to merge be passed through to employees in both public and private companies. This means that most takeover artists will have to convince the employees that the takeover is in their best interest, a task few corporate raiders have been able to accomplish in the 1980s. Corporations believed to have formed ESOPs at least in part to defend against takeovers include Polaroid and Lockheed.[24]

In the summer of 1988 Shamrock Holding, Inc., announced its bid to buy controlling interest in Polaroid eight days after Polaroid had announced its intention to increase the amount of stock held by its ESOP to 14 percent of the total shares. During the takeover battle that ensued, there was little doubt how most Polaroid employees felt about the possible takeover. They signed petitions and demonstrated in favor of the current management. Shamrock Holding sued Polaroid in Delaware court, but the judge upheld the ESOP.[25] Important to the judge's decision were two facts: the ESOP was in place before the takeover battle began, and the company claimed other reasons for setting up the ESOP. Because the employees could vote their shares confidentially, there was little chance of management coercion in the vote. The court was also impressed with research studies conducted throughout the 1980s that show that ESOPs can have a positive effect on productivity when combined with participatory management.[26] Faced with this and other obstacles, Shamrock Holding eventually gave up and negotiated a settlement with Polaroid that ended its bid to take control of the company.

In early 1990 few people could ignore the takeover battle for Lockheed because both sides bought full-page advertisements in major newspapers around the country. Dallas investor Harold Simmons was trying to win control of Lockheed by putting up a slate of candidates for the board of directors to compete with the candidates supported by management. This is called a proxy fight because each side tries to get the proxy votes of as many stockholders as possible for its slate of candidates. It is believed that each side spent between $6 and $8 million on the proxy battle. When the smoke cleared, the candidates supported by the current management had won easily, in part because the ESOP owned 19 percent of the stock and 90 percent of the employees voted with current management against Harold Simmons.

The assumption that employees will usually vote against a hostile takeover is supported by a 1990 Gallup poll commissioned by the Employee Benefits Research Institute that found that 65 percent of the employees surveyed said they would not sell their stock to a hostile investor even if they were offered 50 percent more than the current market value of their shares. This may not be the case with every company, however. Some employees may feel that they will do better with new management than with the current management. Also, the corporate raider may offer the employees instant 100 percent vesting and termination of the ESOP so that they can receive the money in their accounts immediately. Although these employees would have to pay income taxes on this money (and a 10 percent penalty if they are under the age of fifty-nine and a half), they might still want to get the cash if the balance is significant. They can roll over the money into an Individual Retirement Account and avoid the taxes and penalties. Employees in a new ESOP with small account balances would find this offer easy to turn down, but it might be attractive when the ESOP is older and account balances represent a large sum of money.

Trying to Save a Failing Company

Weirton Steel, perhaps America's best-known employee-owned company, was a division of National Steel in 1982 when the parent company decided it would no longer invest funds in an apparently losing proposition. The company had once been profitable, but since 1974 it had either lost money or earned little in profits. Because Weirton Steel employed more than eight thousand people in a West Virginia community of twenty-six thousand, the union, management, and the community were willing to work together in an effort to save the company. An ESOP was formed that purchased the company from

National Steel for $386 million. Most of the money needed for the buyout was loaned to the ESOP by National Steel. Wages were lowered and productivity improved. Weirton Steel was the only American steel company to show a profit every quarter during the last four years of the 1980s.[27]

Such "distressed buyouts" do not always work out so well. In January 1988 the 485 employees of Chase Brass Sheet Division were about to lose their jobs to a plant closing because the parent company had decided it was not worth the millions of dollars necessary to improve the productivity of the plant. The employees bought the plant and became 100 percent owners of their new company, North Coast Brass and Copper. But they did not save their jobs. In 1990 the company went bankrupt, at least in part because labor-management relations, which were bad before the buyout, did not improve.

Many people think trying to save failing companies is the major use of ESOPs because of the media attention such attempts often receive. Actually, only 2 or 3 percent of ESOPs are formed for this purpose. Although most such attempts failed in the 1970s, the record for the 1980s was better: over half these attempts resulted either in corporate survival or the eventual sale of the company for a profit.

Trading Stock for Wages

In some cases employees have accepted lower wages in exchange for an ESOP and keeping their jobs. One of the most successful of these was Columbia Aluminum in Goldendale, Washington. The plant, which the Australian owners had never been able to make profitable, closed in March 1987, putting three thousand people out of work. The plant was then purchased by local investors and an ESOP. In exchange for lower wages and an ESOP investment, the employees were promised a salary increase of 8 percent if the company showed a profit. Because the ESOP was combined with participatory management, the company made an amazing turnaround (aluminum prices also rebounded from a slump). Columbia Aluminum shares worth less than 50 cents a share in 1987 were worth over $150 a share by the end of 1989. At that time Columbia Aluminum could claim to be the most efficient aluminum plant in the world.

Another case involved Eastern Airlines, which in 1983 sold 25 percent of its stock to an ESOP-like trust in exchange for wage concessions from the employees. By August 1985 Eastern had rebounded from a loss of $183 million in 1983 to post operating profits for six consecutive quarters. The company introduced a new management system in the machine shop which saved $35 million in the first eighteen months. Employees were given the power to restructure jobs and buy parts from the cheapest source. By 1985 cost cutting and wage concessions appeared to spell recovery for the airline. We will never know. Though there was an operating profit, because the cost of servicing the company's debt was high, the bottom line was still printed in red ink, not black. On December 31, 1984, CEO Frank Borman decided to renege on a provision in the original contract that called for a restoration of wage cuts. This saved the company $22 million per month, but it made the union leaders furious. Because of what some observers called the inability of both management and labor to restructure their relationship after a decade of animosity, Eastern was sold to Frank Lorenzo and his Texas Air Corporation in 1986 and wound up in bankruptcy court soon after.[28]

Western Airlines had similar difficulty but a happier result. In 1983 management felt the company could not survive to the end of the year without wage concessions. The concessions were made in exchange for 32 percent of the company and representation on the board of directors. Two years later Western was sold to Delta. The value of the stock had tripled and the employees had saved their jobs.[29]

In general, wage concessions in exchange for a small percentage of the company have not had a record of success, though wage concessions for a majority interest in the company have worked out in many cases. There are so many variables—the type of business, attitude of management, attitude of union leaders, degree of foreign competition, percentage ultimately owned by the employees, and so on—that it is difficult to predict in any particular case whether a wage concession will have the desired result.

Restructuring Benefits

Some companies that already have a benefit or pension plan may wish to combine it with or replace it with an ESOP. An ESOP might be attractive because of its ability to borrow money. If the company believes its stock is going to go up over time, it makes good sense to buy a lot of it while it is at a bargain price.

Suppose the stock sells for $10 a share when first purchased and the ESOP buys 10 million shares on a ten-year loan. Every year a million shares are released for distribution to the employees. Suppose, for the sake of illustration, that the loan is for 10 percent and $10 million of principal is paid off every year. The first year, costs might be $10 million in interest and $10 million in principal. If at the end of the year the shares are worth $12 each, the employees have received a benefit worth $12 million and the company has spent $20 million. Because the interest payments were deductible, the company saved (if the company pays 34 percent) $3.4 million in income taxes, so it is out only $16.6 million. Suppose in the fifth year the stock is worth $20 a share. Then when a million shares are released, the employees receive a benefit worth $20 million. In that year the company spent $10 million to pay off that amount of principal and $5 million on interest (which cost only $3.2 million because of the tax savings). The company has spent $13.2 million and provided $20 million in employee benefits. If in the tenth year the stock is worth $30 a share, the employees receive a $30 million benefit and the company is out less than $11 million. Of course, if the stock does not appreciate significantly in value, this plan is not very advantageous.

Some companies that already have a 401(k) benefit plan may wish to combine it with an ESOP. In a typical 401(k) defined contribution plan, employees put a percentage of their salary, up to some maximum, into the plan and the company matches their contribution, often by putting in fifty cents for every dollar contributed by the employee. By combining the 401(k) plan with a leveraged ESOP a company may be able to increase the percentage matched at no extra cost to itself. The company can borrow money to buy inexpensive stock, deduct the interest and principal payments along with the cost of any dividends paid on the stock, and then use the stock to match employee contributions to the 401(k) plan. The employees get more in their pension accounts and the company has not spent any more money after the tax savings and stock appreciation are taken into account. The advantages to the employees include a higher match on their contributions, a commitment by the employer that some match will be provided (many 401(k) plans provide matching funds only if the company is profitable), and if the participants take their stock when they leave the company, instead of cashing it in, they only pay income taxes on the price the stock was at when the ESOP purchased it. They do not have to pay income taxes on any increase in value until they actually sell the stock.[30]

Setting Up an ESOP

Once the employees have decided they want to buy and the sellers have decided they want to sell and an ESOP looks like the best way to accomplish their mutual goals, there are still issues to consider before deciding to use an ESOP.

Cost

Setting up an ESOP is much less expensive than taking a company public or using a broker to negotiate a private sale, but it still is costly. Consultants, lawyers, and accountants will have to be paid. A typical ESOP transaction involving a private company and no complex stock issues generally costs between $12,000 and $30,000. The valuation might cost between $5,000 and $10,000. Legal and accounting fees associated with setting up the plan may run between $7,000 and $15,000. A lender will require an enforceable promise that the company is bound to do everything possible to repay the loan. In many cases the loan is to the company and the company loans the money to the ESOP.

Lawyers, accountants, and bankers now have two decades of experience with ESOPs. A once new and legally questionable process is now routine at many large law firms and banks. As ESOPs have been embraced by even the giant companies of the Fortune 500, the business community has come to see them as an acceptable way both to finance a buyout and to provide an employee benefit. The ability to accomplish both these functions is certainly one of the major advantages of ESOPs.

The cost of an ESOP should be compared with the alternatives if the current owners are determined to sell out. The costs of a private placement or a sale of stock to the public could easily run between $100,000 and $200,000.[31]

Feasibility

Before an ESOP is set up, an outside expert should be brought in to determine whether it is feasible. This expert will study the corporate structure, the industry, and the company. Subchapter S corporations do not qualify for the special tax treatment the ESOP provides, so a subchapter S corporation would have to consider whether it wants to change to a different corporate structure (a subchapter S corporation has few owners and does not pay corporate income taxes). The company must have a large enough payroll and be making enough profit to be able to make the payments to the ESOP to pay off the loan. The business should be stable. Not only must the ESOP loan be repaid, but the employees will not be encouraged to work harder by their stock ownership if the stock goes down very far in value after the introduction of the ESOP. Finally, the managers of the company must be committed to making employee ownership work.[32]

The feasibility study will include a preliminary estimate of the value of the company's stock. An ESOP can pay a "fair" price under federal law. The first question is whether the ESOP can pay enough to satisfy the sellers or outbid other potential buyers. The study will also analyze how the introduction of an ESOP will affect the value of current stockholders' shares and the financial health of the corporation. It will propose how the ESOP should be structured and what effect the repurchase liability will have on the company in the years to come.

When an ESOP is being designed there are dozens of decisions that must be made: what vesting schedule will be used, who will participate, whether the ESOP will be the only retirement plan, what will be done with existing pension plans, and so on. Because the ESOP is often both a benefit plan and a way to finance a corporate takeover or the introduction of new capital, both goals have to be taken into account.

Valuation

Before the ESOP buys its shares, the value of the company must be decided. In a publicly traded company that is easy. The value of the shares is the price quoted on the open stock market. The stock of most smaller companies is not openly traded. An outside valuation of the corporation must be done to decide the value of the shares the ESOP will be buying.

The appraiser, who must be independent and qualified, will look at a variety of factors: the history of the company, its earning capacity, the potential future of this type of business, the value of tangible assets such as buildings and equipment, the price similar companies have sold for in the recent past, and the amount of control the ESOP will have. The value of owning a controlling interest in a company is difficult to determine in ESOP transactions. It is very common for someone buying more than 50 percent of the stock in a company to pay a premium for the controlling interest. In some cases this premium has been twice what the shares would have cost without this control feature. When it is reasonable to expect an ESOP buying more than 50 percent of the stock to pay a premium is often the main question when ESOPs buy a majority of the stock in a company.[33]

Besides the problem of control, there are many intangibles that must be taken into account. Is the management good, and do the managers intend to stay with the company? Are there new products in development that might contribute to increased profits? Are the employees trained, or will they require expensive retraining? Have products been sold in the past (such as the Dalkon shield) that might result in expensive litigation and large damage awards?

Historically, the more risk someone was willing to take, the more reward would be garnered if the company proved to be profitable. When an ESOP and others, perhaps an outside investor or a group of managers, decide to buy out an ongoing business, the ESOP will be providing borrowed money, which will at least in part be protected by the ability to foreclose on company assets. The outside investors will be putting up their own money, and they may lose it all if the company fails. When the risk factor is combined with the degree of control and marketability of the stock, deciding how much each group should pay for the stock becomes very difficult indeed.

There is another factor that may also affect the value of the stock. When employees leave or retire, the company must buy back their stock. This repurchase liability may cause the company's stock to be valued lower than it might otherwise be. If the company is growing, the ESOP may be able to buy the stock of retiring employees for placement in the accounts of new employees. The originators of ESOPs imagined that as older employees retired new employees would buy their shares through the ESOP. But if the ESOP is unable to purchase all of the departing employees' stock, the company will have to buy the stock as required by law. This can have a negative effect on both cash flow and the valuation of the company stock.

Financing an ESOP

Many ESOPs involve borrowing money to buy all or part of a company. The money comes from a variety of sources. Each lender will have a different degree of risk and will ask for an interest rate that reflects that risk. Part of the funds will be secured, meaning the lender can foreclose if the loan is not paid. Because there is collateral backing up the loan, this lender will charge a lower interest rate. Some of the funds will be unsecured, meaning the lender will be left with nothing except the interest earned and principal repaid if the loan is not paid back. Lenders require a higher interest rate to take this higher risk. What have come to be called junk bonds are bonds that have been sold by companies in which the risk is high and therefore the interest is also high. While junk bonds have been used by takeover artists to buy giant corporations, they have also been used to finance ESOPs.[34]

For example, someone taking over a large corporation might have to pay $3 billion. The plants and equipment the corporation owns can secure $1 billion, but $2 billion must be borrowed with an unsecured loan. The lenders will have to believe the new company will have enough cash flow to repay the loan. This belief will depend on the confidence the lenders have in the people buying the company and the ability of the managers and employees to make the necessary profit. If the employees are participating in the buyout through an ESOP, lenders may have more confidence that everyone at the corporation will work hard to repay the loans.

At the end of the 1980s, Greyhound Lines, Inc., the bus company, was bought through a leveraged buyout. The employees were asked to take a wage cut and make other concessions. They were not given an ESOP as part of the deal. Early in 1990 the employees of Greyhound went on a strike that turned out to be violent and destructive. The lenders should have considered demanding that the employees participate in the deal. Employees who are part-owners through an ESOP can go on strike against their company, but they seldom do. If the employees of Greyhound had been told that they were making wage concessions at the beginning to allow a loan to be paid off that would result in their stock being worth a great deal of money five to ten years later, they might have been much more willing to accept the wage and benefit package offered by the company.

Accounting for ESOPs

During the 1970s and 1980s there was some confusion in the accounting community about how to treat the debt owed by an ESOP when the ESOP borrowed money to buy stock. In 1990 the accounting community decided that because the company is the sole source of the funds needed to repay the debt, the ESOP debt must show up as such on the company's financial reports.[35]

This can have an adverse effect on the valuation of the stock. If the stock is publicly traded, the price may go down, reflecting the new debt the company has taken on. This is often a surprise to everyone, but it should not be. Obviously, a company with a large debt is worth less than a company with little or no debt. As the debt is paid off, the value of the stock usually goes back up.

Plan Administration

After the ESOP has been created, it becomes an employee benefit plan with legal, accounting, tax, and human resource ramifications.

The participation and vesting rules of the Internal Revenue Code must be followed. The plan may not discriminate in favor of highly compensated employees. A great deal of information must be compiled about the employees to make sure stock is allocated to their accounts correctly, and a variety of reports must be filed with the Department of Labor and the Internal Revenue Service. All of this will take time and cost money and must be considered by anyone contemplating the installation of an ESOP.[36]

Getting Help from State Agencies

During the 1980s more and more states saw the wisdom of encouraging employee stock ownership plans. There are many ways a state agency can help. Often a feasibility study is needed, and a state agency can either perform the study or help pay for the cost. There is often a need for help in explaining ESOPs to employees and in paying for a valuation of the company. Again, the agency can either pay for these services or provide them.

Possible Abuses of ESOPs

Imagine that the current owner of a company establishes an ESOP and learns that because he is the trustee of the ESOP no one else, including the employees, will have to be given access to the company's financial records. There is no labor union and no direct employee representation concerning the ESOP. The owner then proceeds to pay high salaries and bonuses to himself and his relatives who work for the company. The employees could file a complaint with the U.S. Department of Labor if they knew, but they never find out.

Imagine that the owner of a very capital-intensive business has learned through real estate investing that it is possible to shop around for the desired valuation. He finds a valuation company that is willing to set a value on his company significantly higher than previous valuations. A bank is still willing to finance the ESOP because it believes the assets of the company could be sold if necessary to pay off the remaining balance on the loan. The result is that the employees have an ESOP whose worth is predicated on the breakup value of the company, which can be realized only if the company is liquidated, forcing the employees out of their jobs.

Finally, imagine a company in which the employees do not vote for the board of directors and the CEO appoints the ESOP trustee under the rules of the trust. The CEO wants to buy another, smaller company in a nearby town in order to expand. The trustee does not believe this would be a smart move for the company in the current economic situation. The trustee's opinion counts because the ESOP owns a majority of the company's stock. The CEO fires the trustee and appoints another executive in his place who believes the purchase is a good idea.

These stories are fictional, but they are all inspired by reality. Other abuses, real and theoretical, were discussed in chapter 1. While these examples are disturbing, they raise important questions. What if there would have been no ESOP if the owner had not been allowed to be the trustee, if the owner could not sell for the high valuation, or if the CEO had not been given control over the ESOP trustee? Is a less than perfect ESOP better than no ESOP at all? Does it make a difference that in each case the company prospered and the value of the ESOP shares increased?

In some cases, abuses like these have led to bankruptcy and the employees have ended up with nothing in their ESOP accounts after years of hard work. Slick operators have used ESOPs to acquire a low-interest loan to engage in what could only be called speculation, especially in the savings and loan industry. During the 1980s many of these speculations failed, leaving employees holding the bag. We can all hope that the Department of Labor and federal bank regulators will be more diligent in the 1990s to prevent some of these abuses.

Summary

From the employees' perspective, an ESOP is a benefit plan with advantages and disadvantages. The advantages flow from the fact that, unlike other benefit plans, the employees have a chance to make a difference. Although many employees own stock in a wide variety of companies through their pension funds, there is nothing they can do to improve the financial health of those companies and thereby increase the value of the stock in their accounts. With an ESOP, employees can work to improve the profitability of the company they work for and thereby increase the value of the stock in their individual accounts.

Because in some cases 25 percent of one's pay can be placed in an ESOP account every year and dividends on shares already in the account can also be used to buy stock, employees can build up money in their ESOP accounts at a much faster rate than they can with the usual defined contribution benefit plan. But ESOP companies have gone bankrupt in the past and will certainly do so in the future.

Whereas the standard benefit or pension plan buys stocks and bonds in a wide variety of companies, the ESOP has most of its eggs in one basket.

The incentives for investors and corporations to introduce ESOPs are many and varied. An ESOP enables the company to borrow money and deduct both the interest and the principal as the loan is paid back. A departing owner can sell shares to the ESOP, roll over the proceeds into other securities, and not pay any income tax until those securities are sold. The ESOP can provide the company with a take-over defense (assuming the employees vote with current management) and reduce benefit costs. If the ESOP is combined with increased participation and communication, it can improve productivity and product quality while helping to attract and retain high-quality employees.

Beginning with the passage of ERISA in 1974, Congress has attempted to balance the needs of society for a more productive private sector, the needs of the federal treasury for more revenue, the desire of employees for a stake in the ownership of the companies they work for, the desire of departing owners and stockholders to realize a return on their investments, and the desire of managers to maintain the long-term profitability of the companies they manage. Over a decade and a half, tax incentives have come and gone in an effort to balance all these interests. Although each side in this equation could quibble with some aspect of the current system, the fact remains that by the end of the 1980s, with more than ten thousand employee stock ownership plans and over 11 million ESOP employee-owners, America had a healthy and growing employee-owned sector.

3 Non-ESOP Alternatives

Sue Steiner

ESOPs, with all their advantages, are not the answer for all companies. No serious effort to encourage widespread employee ownership can concentrate solely on ESOPs. For many companies, other approaches are more appropriate. In the enthusiasm for ESOPs, many companies whose needs have called for other plans have been neglected. Let us look at a few hypothetical situations.

The first example concerns someone starting a company in an exciting new market. Investors are lining up to participate in the venture. But equipment, leases, advertising, payroll, and so on will make start-up costs extremely high. Good people are needed, but even with many potential investors, it will not be possible to pay them what they deserve. One way to attract the right people is to offer them a share in the company.

ESOPs have been in the news lately, but an investigation of their potential indicates that they are not the right answer in this situation. The tax advantages they offer will be useless because taxes are not due unless the business makes a profit, and this one will not make a profit for several years. And the allocation rules are too strict. Eventually perhaps all employees will be included as owners, but the initial goal is to offer key people large amounts of stock to encourage them to join the firm. And maybe most important is the need to keep costs down. The tens of thousands of dollars it would cost to establish an ESOP do not fit well with that plan.

A second case could be that of a business that is already established. The problem is not in attracting good people but getting them to stay. Perhaps if they shared in the company's ownership, they would be more committed and would work harder and stay with the firm longer. ESOPs look promising, but they are not practical for a company with only eight employees and $30,000 in profits after taxes. Surely there must be a less expensive way to include employees as owners while retaining control of the business.

A third situation is that of an established, midsized, successful business whose owner wants to bring employees in as owners. ESOP fees do not pose a problem, but the myriad regulations governing them do. The owner is uncomfortable with the idea of employees becoming owners with no financial commitment and does not want to give all employees at the same salary level the same amount of stock, regardless of other pertinent factors. There must be a more flexible way to offer employees a part of this business.

This chapter explores alternative ways of increasing employee ownership. For those seeking practical information, it provides a primer on non-ESOP approaches to ownership. For those with a more academic interest, it discusses the basic philosophy behind the choice of a plan, as well as providing a look at some of the creative ways companies are sharing ownership with their employees.

A variety of alternatives are open to companies searching for a method of sharing ownership. Companies can choose between existing employee stock ownership plans or a combination of several plans. These options include stock bonus and purchase plans, stock option plans, 401(k) savings plans, and profit-sharing plans that give bonuses in the form of the employer's securities. A company can also create its own plan to fit its specific needs and goals or establish itself as a worker cooperative. The various plans differ in the amount of administration and expense they require and in the regulations that govern them.

The plans also differ in their purpose and focus. Some plans can give employees a stake in ownership without being specifically designed for that purpose. Unlike an ESOP, which must invest in employer securities, profit-sharing and 401(k) plans are allowed but not required to do so. Trustees of these plans must show that using company stock in their plans is a prudent investment. If the investment is shown to be unsound, the employees may sue.

Plan Classification

There are three categories of ownership plans:

1. **Qualified or nonqualified.** A qualified plan must follow numerous regulations and in return receives special tax benefits. A

nonqualified plan is not subject to the same stringent regulations but does not receive the special tax benefits available to qualified plans.

2. **Purchase or bonus.** Employees can either purchase stock within a plan or receive it free as a bonus.

3. **Stock held in a trust or held directly.** The stock in the plan can either be held for the employees in a trust or employees can own the stock directly. Stock held in a trust is generally not available until an employee leaves the company. It is also frequently subject to a vesting schedule. When stock in an employee's account is vested, it becomes nonforfeitable. This process generally happens over time, with the employees gaining the right to an increasing number of shares the longer they are with the company.

Purpose of the Plan

The philosophy behind the establishment of an employee ownership plan can have a bearing on the type of plan a company chooses. A company can adopt a plan with the intention that it will become a central part of the company's culture and that ownership will be a major theme reflected throughout the company. This was the case when Harry J. Grant, the chairman of the board of the Journal Company, instituted a stock purchase plan. The Journal Company, headquartered in Milwaukee, is a diversified communications company with sixty-three commercial printing, publishing, broadcasting, and telecommunications operations in fourteen states. Among its companies are Milwaukee's two daily papers, the *Milwaukee Journal* and the *Milwaukee Sentinel*. Grant believed that "it is the right of men and women whose lives go into building a newspaper to have a share in the ownership."[1] Thus the employee stock trust agreement he established in 1937 was meant to turn the company into an employee-owned firm, with ownership playing a major part in every aspect of its business.

A company can also adopt a plan that gives employees a share in ownership as a means to stimulate productivity but not as a core theme or a way to relate to employees. In this case, employees will own stock, and they should realize that their performance at work affects the value of their stock, but there will be no substantial changes in the way the company is run. A company can also give employees an ownership stake as part of a retirement plan, unrelated to operating philosophy. An employee ownership plan can also be a blend of all these. For example, a company can set up a plan as a retirement benefit with the hope that it will stimulate productivity.

The type of plan a company chooses and its design also depend in part on whether the company is new or established, public or private, large or small. New companies often have a pressing need for cash, and this can affect whether they give or sell stock to employees. New firms also need to retain capital, so paying high wages is not always practical, which can pose a problem when trying to attract good people. For this reason, offering stock to all employees may be more important to new firms than to established firms.

Public and private companies also have different considerations when deciding on an ownership plan. Registration under federal or state securities laws may be required if a company sets up certain plans and is much more of an issue for private than for public firms. Private firms also have to consider the need for stock valuation, whereas stock in a public firm is already valued by the market. Finally, private companies have to consider the question of repurchase liability, that is, if and how they will buy back employees' shares when they leave the company.

Many small companies do not have a large enough payroll or enough employees to justify spending a large sum of money to establish or maintain a highly regulated or extremely complicated plan. They may have no profits or only limited profits taxed at a low rate so that tax incentives are not a key concern. Larger companies, by contrast, may be extremely concerned about the tax consequences of a given plan. They may also have the resources to establish large, intricate plans that provide flexibility or to combine several different plans.

Basic Plan Requirements

The Internal Revenue Code stipulates that all qualified profit-sharing and stock bonus plans must meet the same basic requirements, principally the following: (1) there must be a formal written plan that is communicated to all employees; (2) the plan must be established with the intent of being permanent; (3) the plan must include employees in general, not just a select group; (4) plan contributions and benefits may not discriminate in favor of shareholders, officers, and highly paid employees; (5) the plan must be for the exclusive benefit of the employees or their beneficiaries; (6) forms must be filed with the IRS to request an IRS determination on whether a plan is qualified and to give a yearly report on the plan; and (7) the plan's assets must be kept separate from general company assets.

The Employee Retirement Income Security Act of 1974 and the Tax Reform Act of 1986 established standards for all pension, profit-sharing, and stock bonus plans. These are *minimum* standards, and employers may institute plans with more liberal provisions.

Vesting gives employees a gradually increasing right to the shares contributed to their accounts. For all plan years beginning after December 31, 1988, employer contributions must vest according to one of two schedules: (1) 100 percent after five years of company service, or (2) 20 percent after three years and 20 percent in each subsequent year until 100 percent is reached at the end of seven years. Complete vesting also occurs at regular or early retirement.

Employers do not need to offer these plans to all employees. If the plan is available to a certain category such as all salaried employees, however, all persons in that category must be included if they meet certain age and service requirements; usually the employee must be twenty-one years old and have completed one year of service. Plans that offer immediate vesting may require three years of service. Categories cannot be set up, however, to include only highly paid people.

Other Plan Considerations

Repurchase of Departing Employees' Stock

Because there is generally no outside market for shares in private companies, these firms should make provisions for buying back employees' shares when they leave the company. Clear and fair rules must be established to govern this repurchase. Unlike an ESOP, there are no laws requiring employers to repurchase departing employees' stock in some of the plans described below. If a company does not establish a repurchase plan, however, the stock employees receive may be worthless because there is no one to buy it.

Shares should be repurchased within a reasonable time after an employee leaves the company, or ownership will be seen as too distant or uncertain a reward. At the same time, a company should allow itself some flexibility in buying the shares. Most repurchase plans are written to allow the company enough time to buy back shares if it is short on cash, say five years. Payments can also be made in installments.

Although a company should agree to repurchase the shares, it should protect itself by having a right of first refusal, which requires employees to give the company or an incoming employee-owner the option of buying their shares before selling them to someone else, thus eliminating the risk of an outsider gaining control.

In addition to establishing repurchase rules, a company must provide funds to buy back shares. Repurchasing shares can be a serious cash drain and must be planned for. A company should make projections of how many people it expects to leave and put aside a reserve fund to cover a worst-case scenario.

Valuation

Private companies need to establish a value for their stock. The stock price must reflect the value of the ongoing business, which involves a variety of considerations, including earnings, future cash flow, the reputation of the company, market conditions, assets, and liabilities. Valuation for an ESOP must be done by an outside consultant. The law does not require an outside valuation for the plans discussed here, but it is probably best for most companies to have one.

A formal valuation of an ongoing business usually costs at least $3,000 to $5,000. Some firms avoid this process by relying on book value, which is the net value of the assets over liabilities. As an initial appraisal, this method will work for many, particularly smaller, companies, but it will undervalue the shares if part of the company's worth is intangible, such as its reputation or participation in a growing market. Book value can overvalue shares if, for example, a market is declining. For these reasons, a formal valuation is advised for most companies as soon as it is feasible to undertake one.

Philosophical Questions

Before selecting a plan, a company should address several philosophical questions.

First, which employees should be eligible to participate in the plan? Should all employees be included, and if so, should they all receive equal amounts of stock? Should some employees be compensated more than others? Is the goal to motivate or reward one sector, plant, or store exclusively or at a higher level than others?

The answers to these questions depend, in part, on whether a goal of the plan is to create an "ownership culture" with a "we're all in this together" attitude. Obviously, if a limited number of employees are included in a plan, it will be difficult to build an overall ownership culture. Rather than bringing employees together and encouraging teamwork, the plan may cause divisions between those included and those excluded.

A central consideration here is whether it is important to motivate all employees or, as some believe, only those at the top, who are in the position to effect substantial change. If a company believes the latter, an inclusive plan may not be desired, and this would rule out plans that require widespread participation, such as 401(k) plans. If, however, there is a belief that teamwork is necessary and that each member of the team makes an important contribution, a plan that includes all employees may be appropriate.

Second, how much control of the company, if any, should be shared? Should employees have voting rights?

If the present owners or management are not comfortable giving up any control of the company, a plan in which employees hold stock directly and have voting rights may not be a good idea. A deferred plan, in which stock is held in a trust for employees and the stock can be nonvoting shares, may work better.

Third, is stock being conferred as a benefit, or should employees purchase stock? Is employee ownership to be used as a means to raise capital?

The decision whether to give or sell employees stock depends on the individual circumstances of each company and its employees. If employees have little disposable income, requiring them to buy shares may pose a hardship. Lower-income people are unlikely to have purchased stock before and may be hesitant to buy stock in the company, even if it is offered at a discount. Furthermore, if a company's future is uncertain, having employees purchase stock would be asking them to share a risk they may not be able to afford.

Conversely, some people believe that it is important to have employees purchase stock rather than be given it as a gift. This belief is based on the theory that stock will mean more to employees and their commitment to the company will be stronger if they have actively invested their money. Also, there is the belief that it is only fair for all "owners" to invest something. Additionally, a company may need to raise capital, a purpose more easily achieved by selling than by giving shares.

Fourth, should ownership be based on performance or on salary or other factors? If it is based on performance, should employees receive stock or the opportunity to purchase stock based on individual, departmental, or companywide performance?

Some of the plans discussed below impose no restrictions on how stock can be allocated; others have strict regulations that must be followed. Many contend that performance-based incentives are the most effective motivator. If an employer believes this, a plan should be chosen that allows flexibility in allocation. A company should also try to determine whether employees are most effectively motivated by individual or group performance standards.

Fifth, is long-term or short-term employee ownership intended? Should employees be able to sell their stock at will, only when they leave the company, or at some time in between?

It is good for employees to make money from their company stock. But if they earn this money by selling their stock soon after they get it, it is questionable whether the company will gain the benefits that longer-term employee ownership can produce. This situation can also create short-term cash flow problems for the company.

The requirements of some plans promote long-term employee ownership. For example, certain types of contributions to a 401(k) plan cannot be withdrawn or distributed before an employee reaches age fifty-nine and a half, retires, dies, or leaves the job. If these contributions are invested in company stock, long-term ownership is pretty much guaranteed. Other plans allow employees to sell their stock at any time, which may mean that employees make a profit but long-term ownership is not achieved.

If an employee owns stock for several weeks or months and then sells it to make a profit (as is frequently done in stock option plans), will that employee ever really feel like an owner? Will it be possible to develop an employee ownership culture? Here it may be useful to consider whether the goal is simply to have employees become stockholders or to encourage employees to see a connection between their work, stock prices, and the money they can make if their stock goes up over the long term.

Finally, is the intention to build an ownership culture with a feeling that the employees are all owners and all in the venture together?

Some plans may include employer securities in their investment portfolio but not stress ownership. Because a 401(k) plan, for example, is essentially a savings plan, its foremost purpose must be to provide a safe vehicle for employees' savings. Its purpose is not to make employees owners. Other plans, such as ESOPs or stock bonus plans, have the express purpose of making employees owners.

Some believe that more company stock is held for employees in trust as a part of profit-sharing plans than in ESOPs.[2] There is, however, some question as to whether profit sharing is an effective means of making employees owners. Some employees who have stock held for them within their profit-sharing plan may not even be aware that they are owners. In this case, any positive effects from ownership are doubtful.

In plans that do not make ownership a central focus, employees may not feel like owners or see any connection between the stock that is held for them and the company's, or their own, performance. If a company makes a specific effort to fulfill both the original intent of the plan, such as providing for employee savings in a 401(k) plan, and to stress the employee ownership features of a plan, it may be an effective employee ownership vehicle. This, however, takes serious commitment from the employer.

Simple Stock Bonus/Stock Purchase Plans

The easiest and most flexible way to start an employee ownership program is with a nonqualified stock bonus/stock purchase plan. *Nonqualified* simply means the plan does not qualify for any of the special tax benefits available to ESOPs, profit-sharing plans, qualified stock bonus plans, and the like. Nor is it subject to the same stringent and costly regulations. Such plans can be designed to meet whatever objectives a company has. Because of their simplicity, they work well for newer and smaller companies, but they can be and are used in more established firms and companies of all sizes.

Unlike ESOPs or cooperatives, there are no standard guidelines or rules for these plans. Companies choose them for many different reasons and set them up in a variety of ways. After choosing a nonqualified plan, a company first needs to decide how to bring employees into ownership. This can be done by selling them stock, giving them stock, or some combination. The pros and cons of each of these options were discussed earlier.

The Bureau of National Affairs (BNA) decided to bring its employees in as owners by selling them stock in the company. BNA, founded in 1929, is in the publishing and electronics information business, reporting and interpreting government activities and laws for professionals in a variety of fields. BNA's founder, David Lawrence, sold the company to its employees in 1947 through a stock purchase plan. Today about 73 percent of the firm's sixteen hundred employees own 100 percent of the company. Employees have the option to buy stock through payroll deductions or by making an offer to buy stock. There is a limit to the number of shares employees may purchase per pay period, and once they buy stock, they hold it directly, rather than it being held for them in a trust.

America West Airlines also decided to sell stock to its employees, but its plan differs from the BNA plan in that it is mandatory. Upon beginning employment, employees are required to buy stock equivalent to 20 percent of their first year's base pay at a 15 percent discount from the current market price. An exception is made in California and Canada, where mandatory stock purchase is prohibited by law. The stock may be financed through payroll deductions over a period of five ye 1rs or paid for in cash. Mandatory stock purchase fits well with America West's goal of developing an ownership culture within the company by ensuring that all employees will be owners. This goal is further ensured by an emphasis on employee participation.

If a company decides to sell shares, the employees can pay cash or buy shares gradually through salary deductions. As the above examples show, buying stock can be a condition of employment or voluntary. Some companies require employees to purchase a minimum number of shares upon employment, with an option to buy more. Buying shares through salary deductions has important advantages for employees. First, many will not have the cash to buy the shares any other way. Second, the company does not have to pay payroll taxes on the wages it does not pay, although the employee must count the shares as income.

To make the purchase of shares more attractive to employees, they can be sold at a discount as is done at America West. A discount of up to 15 percent requires no special tax treatment; if employees get more than a 15 percent discount, however, they have to pay tax on the discount they receive just as if it were income. Another way to encourage employees to purchase stock is for the company to contribute stock each time an employee buys stock. This is done at the Kentucky Medical Insurance Company, which provides liability insurance to Kentucky physicians. All of the stock that the firm's fifty employees purchase is matched dollar for dollar by the company. A company can match stock dollar for dollar, or, more typically, it can contribute a percentage of the employee's purchase. For example, if an employee purchases ten shares of stock, the company could make a 50 percent match and contribute five additional shares.

If employees are given shares, they must pay tax on their value. This may prove difficult for some lower-paid employees, who are receiving something that is not providing them extra cash. The company can deduct this contribution from its taxes, however. Giving employees shares is one way to pay a bonus without paying cash. Some shares can be given as a bonus, allowing or requiring employees to buy additional shares. Of course, giving away new shares will dilute the ownership share of existing owners.

Vesting and Allocation

There are no vesting rules for nonqualified plans, but for them to be effective, a company should develop a fair vesting schedule. A good vesting schedule will give employees an incentive to stay with the company and will make the benefits of ownership seem within reach.

A company should then decide how to allocate shares and determine eligibility for participation in the plan. When determining who will participate, a company should not only consider the usual eligibility requirements, including length of service, age, and number of hours worked, but also whether all employees will be owners or only one group, such as managers. It is good to keep in mind that when only some workers are owners, it is difficult to build a shared sense of ownership.

Stock Option Plans

In 1989, PepsiCo was looking for a way to provide its employees with an ownership stake. ESOPs and a variety of other ownership plans were investigated but did not fit the company's needs. Stock options have traditionally been almost exclusively a benefit for senior executives, but PepsiCo implemented a "SharePower" plan, which offered stock options to all of the company's roughly one hundred thousand full-time employees.

Before examining stock options, it is helpful to understand several basic terms and concepts unique to them:

Grant date: The date at which an option is offered to employees.

Offering or purchase price: The price of the stock on the day an option is offered.

Exercise an option: To act on the option and purchase shares of stock that have been offered.

Exercise date: The date an employee purchases the stock.

Exercise period: The time period between the offering and expiration dates when an employee has to exercise an option.

Vesting: The percentage of the total options offered that an employee can exercise in a given year.

Stock option plans give participants the right to purchase shares of their company's stock between certain dates for a price fixed by the company at the time the options are granted. The amount of stock each individual may purchase is generally tied to a percentage of compensation, and the employee is under no obligation to act on the option. As an example, in PepsiCo's SharePower plan, each July 1, employees are granted options totaling 10 percent of their previous year's compensation, including bonuses and overtime. The options give the employees the right to purchase PepsiCo stock at the July 1 price at any time during the next ten years. The employees can exercise each annual grant at the rate of 20 percent per year. As an example, employees who made $20,000 last year would be granted $2,000 in options this year, exercisable over the next ten years. They could exercise up to 20 percent, or $400, the first year. If the offering price was $20 per share and one year later the stock price had risen to $25 per share, the employee could purchase ten shares, which at the offering price of $20 per share would cost $200 and would now be worth $250.

Types of Plans

The Internal Revenue Service distinguishes between three types of stock option plans: nonqualified stock options (NSOs), incentive stock options (ISOs), and Section 423 qualified employee stock purchase plans. The majority of established plans are either NSOs or ISOs, in part because participation in both of these plans is extremely flexible, whereas in a Section 423 plan, participation must be broader based. The requirement of widespread participation would make it difficult for companies to follow their traditional path of offering options to a select group of executives.

In an NSO, the duration of the option and the exercise period, as well as participation in the plan, are flexible. Additionally, the price of the option can be set at, below, or above the current market value. PepsiCo's SharePower plan is nonqualified, as is a plan established in 1989 by the Birmingham Steel Corporation through which Birmingham offered nonqualified stock options to all its nonunion employees who had not previously been granted options under the company's executive stock option plan.

Under the plan, all nonunion, full-time employees were granted options equal to 10 percent of their salary. Each option has a term of ten years, extending from July 18, 1989, through July 17, 1999, and a purchase price of $21.125 per share. Employees can exercise the options at a rate of 25 percent of their total options the first year, adding another 25 percent for the next three years, at which time all of their options may be exercised.

At the time employees decide to exercise all or part of their options, they pay the company the purchase price of $21.125 per share. Because the plan is nonqualified, employees owe income tax on the difference between the offering price and the price on the day the option is exercised. The plan stipulates that employees must pay the company the amount of all the taxes that the company must withhold at the time they buy the stock.

An incentive stock option plan has more restrictions than a nonqualified plan. The option price in an ISO must be at least 100 percent of the fair market value on the date it is granted. This figure increases to 110 percent of the fair market value for owners of 10 percent or more of the company's stock. The life and exercise period of a plan may not exceed ten years, and there is a $100,000 maximum on the amount to be vested in any one year. In other words, an employee can exercise up to $100,000 worth of options per year. Finally, for the plan to qualify as an incentive stock option, the stock must be held for at least one year from the exercise date and two years from the grant date. For example, suppose the ABC Company grants its employees the option to purchase stock anytime between July 1, 1989, and July 1, 1999, at the July 1, 1989, price. An employee, Simon Oner, exercises his option and purchases ten shares of stock on July 1, 1992. Simon would have to hold the stock until at least July 2, 1993, which would be one year from the exercise date and more than two years from the July 1, 1989, grant date.

Although Section 423 of the Internal Revenue Code is titled "Employee Stock Purchase Plans," its text describes the transfer of stock to employees through the granting of options. Under a Section 423 plan, options must be granted to all persons who have been employed by the company for at least two years and who work more than twenty hours per week and a minimum of five months in a calendar year. Highly compensated employees may be excluded from a plan, however. Employees who own or after the granting of options will own 5 percent or more of the company's voting shares may not participate in a Section 423 plan.

In a Section 423 plan, options may be granted proportional to pay. The price of the option may not be less than the lesser of 85 percent of the fair market value of the shares at the time the option is granted or exercised, and an option cannot be exercised more than twenty-seven months following the granting date. If, however, the plan stipulates that an option must be exercised at 85 percent or more of the fair market value at the time the option is exercised, the expiration date may be extended to five years from the grant date. Finally, no employee may be granted an option worth more than $25,000 in a single year.

Plan Rules and Requirements

Drafting and implementing a stock option plan tends to be relatively easy and inexpensive, although as plans get larger, they get more costly. A company first needs to determine whether it wants a qualified or a nonqualified plan, how the plan will be structured, and who will be eligible to participate. A company can use any class of stock in an option plan, and the stock can, but does not have to, carry voting rights.

After stock is purchased in an option plan, it is usually fully vested. It is possible, although uncommon, to impose additional vesting requirements for a period of time after an option is exercised. Many companies also have vesting on the exercisability of the stock option itself. This means that employees may be granted options totaling 10 percent of their previous year's salary, but they can exercise only a given percentage of those options per year. As was described above, this is the case at both PepsiCo, whose employees can exercise up to 20 percent of their options per year, and Birmingham Steel, for which the figure is 25 percent per year.

Advantages of Stock Option Plans

Stock option plans are attractive to companies for several reasons. They are relatively inexpensive for companies to institute and maintain, although administrative costs will increase as the number of participants grows. Depending on the number of shares authorized under a plan and the source of the shares, they can generate capital with relatively little dilution of stock price. If the number of shares authorized is moderate or the plan uses shares that are purchased on the open market, a plan will have little dilutive effect. If, however, a company uses authorized but unissued shares and offers a significant number of shares in relationship to those outstanding, substantial dilution is possible. Stock option plans can serve as a reward for employees, while at the same time providing an incentive for them to see that the company does well. Finally, these plans help companies attract good people.

Some companies like stock option plans because they believe that having employees purchase stock, rather than receiving it free, motivates them because they have made a decision to invest in the company's future. Stock options obviously serve this purpose. Furthermore, although traditionally reserved only for key people, options can be accessible to employees at all income levels because they can be set up so that employees do not need to have cash available to purchase them. A plan can give employees the opportunity to use the appreciation in the stock value over time to buy stock.

Problems with Stock Option Plans

Stock prices can go up, but they can also go down. When employees pay for stock, they will be harder hit when stock prices fall than if they have been given the stock. Furthermore, stock price drops can be influenced by factors outside the individual or collective employees' control. Thus, when stock prices go down, particularly when they drop sharply, employees can be hurt financially and morale can suffer. Employers need to be sure that employees understand the risks involved in stock purchases before they participate in plans.

Dropping stock prices have somewhat less of a negative effect in a stock option plan than in a general stock purchase plan because employees do not have to exercise an option. Those not exercising their options lose an opportunity to make money if the price goes up, but do not lose money if the price goes down. An employee granted a ten-year option can wait and see how the stock price changes during that time. If after, say, six years, the price has gone up considerably, an employee can decide to exercise the option. If the stock price has dropped, the employee can simply not exercise the option, thus losing no money. Of course, as with any plan under which an employee purchases stock, there is the risk that the stock price will fall after the employee exercises an option and purchases stock.

From the employer's perspective, if the company's stock price rises dramatically during an option period and many employees exercise their options, purchasing shares at a severely reduced price, the plan becomes expensive for the company. Because stock prices cannot be predetermined, a company cannot know what price employees may be paying for stock in future years.

What options are and how they work is confusing to many people. Because employees have to participate actively in acquiring stock through options, as opposed to having the stock given to them, it is essential that they understand the process and the potential gains and losses. Thus to have any success with a stock option plan, a company must be committed to putting time into developing and implementing an ongoing education program about the plan.

PepsiCo has developed such a program. Its comprehensive communication plan includes substantial involvement by senior management as well as line managers throughout the company. Meetings introducing the concept of stock options and giving a detailed explanation of the administrative aspects of the plan were held with all employees soon after the plan was instituted. Additionally, each division incorporates communication plans linking the SharePower program to business performance through special meetings, articles in in-house employee materials, and various other means. According to PepsiCo, its overall objective is to "integrate the concept of ownership and empowerment into the fabric of our entire management process."[3]

Stock Options for
Increased Employee Ownership

The answer to the question, Are stock option plans a good way to transfer a lot of stock into employees' hands? is an emphatic maybe. On the positive side, stock option plans that are offered at market rate do not cost the company anything. With nonqualified options, companies receive a tax deduction for the difference between the purchase and market prices when the option is exercised and receive cash when the stock is purchased. Thus, other than the possible dilutive effect discussed earlier, they have little negative financial impact, which means the company can offer employees a large number of shares. Conversely, a stock bonus plan costs the company more and may limit the amount of stock it can transfer to employees. Of course, though the exercise of options does not directly cost the company anything, it does cost the shareholders, whose stock price is at least somewhat affected by purchases of new shares at below market value.

In a stock option plan, however, the employer has no control over whether employees exercise their options or keep their stock for an extended period of time once they purchase it. Employers can want to place a large amount of stock in employees' hands and offer them large numbers of options, yet no stock will actually be transferred unless employees exercise their options. And in a nonqualified stock option plan, companies rarely require employees to keep their stock after they exercise their options, even though they may do so. The result is that stock option plans can offer employees large amounts of stock but cannot guarantee employee ownership.

Stock options can be more effective in increasing employee ownership if the company communicates well with employees about it. Merely giving employees an option will not make them owners. Options are complicated, and without extensive, ongoing communication about what they are and how they work, employees may be unlikely to exercise them. There is a telling story about a CEO who offered a large number of options to a truly exceptional shop foreman in his company when company stock was about $2 a share. The stock was selling at about $135 a share at the time the options expired, unexercised. When the CEO asked the foreman why he had never acted on the options, he responded that it was an honor to get them but he did not know how he would ever come up with more than $20,000 to buy them. He had turned down almost $150,000 in stock because he did not realize any bank would have loaned him the $20,000 to exercise the options.

A strong ownership culture in a company can encourage employees to keep their stock for a period of time after they exercise their options. This can be done more effectively through actions than words. When top management at a company holds a lot of stock, employees will realize that the stock must be worth holding on to. When top managers sell their stock quickly, employees' faith in the value of holding the stock may be weakened.

401(k) Plans

The rules and regulations for 401(k) plans are spelled out in Section 401(k) of the Internal Revenue Code, thus the name. The plan, which is also known as a cash or deferred arrangement, is a feature of a qualified profit-sharing or stock bonus plan that gives employees the opportunity to elect to receive part of their salaries in the form of employer contributions. 401(k) plans were established as savings plans, and they generally give employees several investment options from which to choose. By making one of these options stock in the employer's company and/or matching employees' contributions with stock, 401(k) plans can be used to create employee ownership as well.

Types of Contributions

There are four possible types of contributions to 401(k) plans:

1. **Elective contributions.** Also known as a salary reduction feature, these allow employees to elect to receive a portion of their salary as

deferred compensation in the form of a contribution to the 401(k) plan, rather than as current income in cash.

2. **Voluntary after-tax contributions.** In some plans, employees may make additional contributions of a fixed percentage of salary through payroll deductions. These contributions are included in an employee's gross income, but money earned in the plan is not taxed until distribution.

3. **Matching contributions.** Some employers make contributions to their 401(k) plans for every dollar employees contribute. A plan may make a dollar-for-dollar match, but the more typical contribution is fifty cents on the dollar. An employer may match only elective contributions or both elective and voluntary after-tax contributions. Matching contributions are frequently included in a plan to encourage enough lower-paid employees to participate so as to meet nondiscrimination requirements discussed below.

4. **Nonelective contributions.** Employers may make contributions to their 401(k) plans independent of any election or contribution by employees. These may be determined by profits and are usually allocated according to salaries.

Of the four types of contributions listed above, only elective contributions are necessary to constitute a 401(k) plan. The others are optional features that are frequently added to make a plan more attractive and to encourage participation.

Employee Coverage and Nondiscrimination Requirements

Like other qualified plans, a 401(k) plan must not discriminate in favor of highly compensated employees. In addition to the usual nondiscrimination requirements, 401(k) plans are governed by other rules. There must be no discrimination in contributions or benefits. Although a plan formula may be set up in a nondiscriminatory fashion, such as according to an employee's compensation, the majority of the benefits may still be going to highly compensated employees because lower-paid employees may elect to take their compensation in cash. To avoid unintentional discrimination, the law requires that a plan be nondiscriminatory with respect to actual deferrals and actual contributions.

After a plan is established, if an employer is having difficulty meeting the minimum deferral requirement, there are several ways to increase participation by lower-paid employees, such as offering or increasing matching contributions for these employees. According to a study by the General Accounting Office, employee participation in plans that provided matching contributions was 88 percent, whereas in plans without matching contributions participation was less than 50 percent. A company may also add a loan provision that allows employees to borrow against the plan. This can help reduce employees' fears that they will not have money available if they need it. Finally, a rapid vesting schedule can encourage younger employees, who are not sure of their future with a company, to participate in a plan.

Vesting Requirements

The vesting requirements in 401(k) plans differ depending on the type of contribution. Both elective and voluntary after-tax contributions and their earnings must be fully vested at all times. This means that the accrued benefits are nonforfeitable and belong to the employee regardless of how long he or she has been in the plan. Any other contribution that is included when computing the employees' annual deferral percentage to meet nondiscrimination requirements must also be fully vested at all times. All other employer contributions may be subject to a deferred vesting schedule. This schedule may be determined by the company within certain legal limits. The portion of a participant's account made up of employer contributions in plans established after 1988 must be fully vested in at least five years or 20 percent vested after three years, increasing 20 percent per year until the employee is 100 percent vested after seven years.

Contribution Levels

Employers who plan to make matching or nonelective contributions need to determine the level of their contributions. These contributions are limited not only by what an employer can afford but also by the law. The aggregate amount that an employee who is participating in a 401(k) plan may defer is $7,000 adjusted for cost-of-living increases. The adjusted $7,000 limit does not apply to employer contributions or to after-tax employee contributions. The total of elective and other contributions to an employee's 401(k) plan presently cannot exceed the lesser of 25 percent of compensation, of which only 15 percent of the total compensation of plan participants for the year is deductible by the employer, or $30,000. These limits include contributions to other defined contribution plans, as well as pension plan contributions based on a complex formula. In other words, if a company has a profit-sharing and a 401(k) plan, the total contributions to both must be within these limits.

An additional point to consider is that matching contributions are a cost an employer cannot control. After a matching formula is set, the cost is determined by employees through elective contributions. If employer contributions are determined through profit sharing or an employer-determined bonus system, employers have more control over the level of contributions.

Plan Costs

The cost of establishing a 401(k) plan varies greatly. A simple, elective contribution-only plan costs very little because contributions are provided by a reduction in employees' salaries, and a basic plan is relatively inexpensive to administer. As other options are added, however, costs can rise dramatically. A simple plan for a small company can cost less than $1,000 to draft and implement and roughly the same per year to administer. Setting up and maintaining a more complicated plan for a large company can cost anywhere from $20,000 to $50,000 per year.

Investment Options

Employers need to decide whether to allow employees to control the investment in their 401(k) accounts. They also need to determine how broad a range of investment options to offer employees. These options can include stocks, bonds, mutual funds, and investment in the employer's stock, among others.

In general, a company that offers a plan that gives employees a choice between receiving compensation in cash or in the employer's securities must register with the Securities and Exchange Commission (SEC). This means that if any employee's money, whether from salary deferrals or from after-tax contributions, goes to purchase the employer's securities, the company must register. This should not be a problem for public companies, which are already registered, because they need to complete only one additional form. But it can be a tremendous burden for private companies that are not registered because registration with the SEC generally costs a company in the six-figure range. There are registration exemptions that allow small amounts of company stock to be purchased by employees, but this severely limits the amount of stock that can be involved, and even if a federal exemption is granted, a company may still have to fulfill state registration requirements.

SEC registration also has strict financial disclosure rules, which poses a problem for some private companies that are not used to, or do not wish to, share information with their employees or with their competitors. Even if a company receives an exemption from SEC registration, it must still comply with the strict disclosure requirements, and preparing adequate disclosure documents is expensive.

It is possible to give employees stock in a 401(k) plan and not register with the SEC if a company sets up a plan in which the employees' money is not invested in the employer's securities. In such an arrangement, stock is given to an employee as a matching or nonelective contribution by the employer, and the employee's money is used to make other investments.

The American Woodmark Corporation, headquartered in Winchester, Virginia, has such a 401(k) plan for its employees, although because it is a public company SEC registration was not an issue. The company matches 25 percent of each employee's savings, up to 4 percent of salary, in company stock. American Woodmark also makes a nonelective contribution, based on profits, in company stock. The profit-sharing contribution is determined and distributed quarterly. It is determined by taking the company's total profits, dividing that figure by the total number of employees, and then multiplying by 3 percent. All employees receive an equal profit-sharing distribution, and because of this nonelective contribution, all are owners, regardless of their participation in the 401(k) plan. For their elective contributions, employees choose between four outside investment funds, which vary in risk.

401(k) Plans and Employee Ownership

There are a variety of ways that an employer can use a 401(k) plan to encourage employee ownership. An employer can include company stock in the 401(k) plan's portfolio, offering it among other options from which an employee can choose to invest. Or company stock can be used as the employer's matching or nonelective contribution. Companies can also agree to contribute company stock to an employee's account when that employee purchases stock through the plan.

Square D of Palatine, Illinois, uses the latter approach. The company had been giving cash to employees who invested part of their salary in the firm's 401(k) plan. In 1989 the plan was changed with the express purpose of increasing employee ownership. The new plan contributes stock to an employee's account if the employee buys stock through the plan.

Public companies already are making about two-thirds of their matching contributions to employees in the form of their own stock. Although we do not know exactly how much employee ownership of these companies has been produced, it is probably in the tens of billions of dollars.

It is also possible to combine ESOPs with 401(k) plans as a means of increasing ownership. Both an ESOP and a 401(k) can be written into one plan document, known to some as a KSOP. In the most basic merging of these plans, employees can elect to have a portion of their salary go into the 401(k) plan in addition to their ESOP allocations, and that amount can be invested in a diversified portfolio. This lessens the risk that employees face when all of their retirement funds are in their employer's stock. Another option in a KSOP is to use the ESOP stock contribution as the company's 401(k) matching contribution.

Pros and Cons of 401(k) Plans

401(k) plans can be attractive for both employees and employers. They allow employees to save for retirement with pretax and tax-deferred dollars. Plan participants can also receive rollover treatment if they reinvest their plan funds after retirement; that is, they can put their money into other investments and defer tax on the gain made from the sale of stock.

The plans are advantageous for employers as well. If an employer cannot afford to make substantial contributions to a retirement plan, it can establish a 401(k) plan in which the only contributions come from employees' salary deductions. This way the company has a retirement plan, and the only costs to the employer are those of setting it up and administering it. Additionally, a profit-sharing feature can be written into a plan that allows a company to contribute to employees' retirement accounts when the company has a good year. In general, 401(k) plans offer employers a great deal of flexibility and discretion.

As a method of increasing employee ownership, 401(k) plans can be used if they are carefully designed. Employers must remember that they are savings plans, meant to help employees save a part of their salaries, and try to help them understand the principle of savings. Investing savings in stock can be risky. If stock prices drop drastically or a firm goes bankrupt, it may defeat the purpose of these funds, which is to ensure that the employees' money will be available to them at a later date.

Employers should also keep the company's goals and the various related laws in mind when deciding on or designing a 401(k) plan. Private companies that are not registered with the SEC and do not wish to register need to set up a plan in which no employee money is used to purchase company stock. If a plan is set up properly, a company can transfer stock to employees by giving all of its matching contributions and any nonelective contributions in its own stock, while offering a variety of other investment options for employees' contributions. This can also help address the concern of offering a safe investment vehicle for employees' savings. Such a plan can give employees a diversified portfolio in which some but not all of their savings or retirement income is invested in the employer's securities.

Because of the strict employee coverage and nondiscrimination rules governing 401(k) plans, they will not work well in companies that want to reward one group of employees either exclusively or at a much higher rate than other employees. These rules can, however, ensure that a large percentage of employees will participate in a plan. High participation helps a company build a sense of team spirit.

Likewise, a 401(k) plan can work well for a company that wants long-term employee ownership. Because withdrawals from a plan are either not allowed or discouraged by penalties, participants in a 401(k) plan keep their stock until they retire or leave the company. Therefore, long-term ownership and the motivational benefits that come with it can be achieved by giving stock in a plan.

Problems sometimes arise for companies that want to transfer a large amount of stock to employees through a 401(k) plan. The majority of the investment in a plan is based on employee contributions, and many employees do not have much excess money, nor do they want to contribute large sums of what they do have to a retirement plan. Thus the actual amount of stock purchased can be low. One way to correct this problem would be to make nonelective contributions to an employee's account. These bonuses could be a flat percentage of salary, or, if a company's aim is to increase employee motivation, they could be based on profits.

Because 401(k) plans are complex, they can be difficult to explain to participants. There are ways to explain a plan effectively, but they take time and commitment by the employer. Small group presentations are a good way to explain a plan, particularly if they are coupled with individual counseling sessions either for all employees or for those who request them. The American Woodmark Corporation has developed a presentation for its employees in which a prepared script and slides are used to explain the plan in depth in small group sessions. The presentation was put in a written form so that it could be given uniformly in all of the company's twenty-one locations.

Profit-Sharing Plans

Profit-sharing plans are essentially what the name suggests: they share a portion of company profits with employees. If company profits are high, the employer's contribution will be large. Conversely, if profits are low, the employer's contribution will be smaller. ESOPs and stock bonus plans can also be based on profits. But unlike these plans, which must invest primarily or exclusively in the employer's securities, a profit-sharing plan is only allowed to do so.

Profit-sharing plans can generally be broken down into cash, deferred, and combination plans. Cash plans give all eligible employees a share in the bonus pool as soon as profits are determined. These plans basically give employees a bonus based on current profits. Their primary goal is to create an employee incentive. The profits can be given to employees in cash, in employer securities, or in a combination of both.

Deferred plans are basically pension plans based on profits, with the aim of providing retirement income. In a combination plan, employers give employees both a current bonus and deferred compensation. According to the Profit Sharing Council of America's 1989 Profit Sharing Survey, only 4.2 percent of the companies surveyed have cash-only plans. Over 79 percent of those surveyed have deferred plans, and 16.6 percent have combination plans.[4]

Only deferred and combination plans can be qualified plans, and they are subject to participation and vesting standards but are not required to comply with the most stringent ERISA rules. Profit-sharing plans are also the only benefit plans that are exempt from legislation requiring minimal voting rights in plans with more than 10 percent invested in employer securities.

Participation and Contributions

Deferred profit-sharing plans must include all employees who are at least twenty-one years old, have worked for the company during part of each of the last two years, and have worked at least one thousand hours per year. An employer can contribute up to 15 percent of an employee's compensation per year to a deferred profit-sharing plan.

These contributions can be determined in several ways. In fixed formula plans, an employer agrees to contribute a predetermined percentage of the company's profits to employees'accounts. This amount can be based on total company profits, profits above a certain amount, or a percentage of the operating profits. In discretionary plans, the employer determines the percentage of profits to be shared each year. This type of plan is most often used by smaller companies, whose profits and capital needs are not always stable from year to year.

Profitability can be based on corporatewide earnings or on profits earned within a specific operating unit, plant, or store. Recent changes in the law allow companies to make contributions even when there are no current profits. Additionally, a plan may allow employees to make after-tax contributions to their accounts or pretax contributions if the plan is qualified as a 401(k) plan.

In most profit-sharing plans the allocation of funds is determined on the basis of relative compensation. As with other plans, however, allocations can be based on length of service or any other nondiscriminatory formula an employer chooses. Allocations can also be divided equally between all eligible employees.

Vesting, Distributions, and Forfeitures

The funds in a profit-sharing plan are subject to the same minimum vesting requirements as qualified pension plans. As of 1989, an employee's account must be fully vested in at least five years or 20 percent vested after three years, increasing 20 percent per year until the employee is 100 percent vested in seven years. Because these are minimum requirements, an employer can establish a schedule that vests employees' accounts more quickly.

In general, minimum distribution in a profit-sharing account must begin when the employee is aged seventy and a half. All vested funds in an employee's account must also be available for distribution when an employee leaves the firm. Distribution can be made in a lump sum or in installments over a number of years, with the choice to be made by the company or the employee. Payments are usually made in cash but can also be made in company stock, if the company has stock in the plan. Additionally, a company may allow an employee to take a distribution before employment is terminated in the event of financial hardship or after a specified period of time. A plan may also loan money to participants.

When employees leave a company before their profit-sharing accounts are fully vested, they forfeit the unvested portion in the account. These forfeitures cannot go back to the employer. They must be distributed among the remaining employees, either to reduce future contributions or to increase benefits to plan participants.

Profit-Sharing Plans and Ownership

Profit-sharing plans have been around for a long time. Procter & Gamble used a cash profit-sharing plan as early as 1887, and the Eastman Kodak Company instituted a plan in 1912. Nor is using profit-sharing plans to increase ownership through the distribution of company stock a new idea. Most of the original profit-sharing plans established in the early 1900s used stock rather than cash. In fact, most of the profit-sharing plans in existence before 1973 used employer stock.

During the 1973 downturn in the economy, many profit-sharing plans that used company stock as a primary investment lost a great deal of money. This had a negative effect on employees' retirement income, not to mention morale. As a result, many companies cut back on their use of employer securities, generally by diversifying their investments, though larger companies still commonly use their stock in these plans.

Profit-sharing plans have the advantage of allowing flexible contributions and are clearly tied to a company's performance. They are also easy to explain to employees and easy for employees to understand. There is some question, however, as to whether profit sharing is an effective means for creating a company culture based on employee ownership. For many companies the plan is merely one of many investments, not an explicit means of increasing employee ownership. It may also be difficult to justify investing profit-sharing funds in employers' securities. The trustees of the plans are obligated to administer them for the exclusive benefit of participants. Any investments they make must be prudent. If the use of company stock is deemed not to be prudent compared to other investment alternatives, employees can sue.

A distinction must be made between the use of company stock in a profit-sharing plan in public and private companies. For private companies to use stock in any plan, they must have the stock valued, which is usually an expensive process. For this reason, the use of stock is more common in, and may make more sense for, public companies.

If profit-sharing plans are to be effective in making employees owners, they must stress the ownership aspect of the plan, not just the shared-profits aspect. Because there are no rules, employers can choose how much stock they want to transfer to employees and what rights, such as voting, will be given along with the stock. Therefore, it is possible for a company to turn its profit-sharing plan into an employee ownership plan if it is designed and explained effectively.

Hallmark Cards, Inc., is an example of a company that has a large portion of its profit-sharing funds invested in company stock. Hallmark, a privately held company headquartered in Kansas City, Missouri, is the world's largest manufacturer of greeting cards. Hallmark set up a profit-sharing plan in 1956, and today, through that plan, 15,500 of the 19,000 full-time employees own about one-third of the company. Hallmark is rated as "one of the best 100 companies in America to work for" by authors Robert Levering and Milton Moscowitz.[5] Many employees who have left the company have had hundreds of thousands of dollars in their accounts.

Contributions to Hallmark's profit-sharing plan are determined yearly by the board and can be in cash or stock. These contributions have traditionally been generous, ranging from 8.5 to 11.5 percent of employees' pay. Employees can draw out up to 25 percent of the fund to buy or renovate a home, cover expenses during an illness, or finance children's college expenses. Hallmark offers employees other exceptional benefits, and it has a no-layoff policy. The management style is highly participative, and managers are said to foster a family atmosphere.

Worker Cooperatives

Worker cooperatives have been vehicles for shared ownership since the nineteenth century. They are unique among means to employee ownership because of their legally mandated "fairness." Every member of a worker cooperative owns one membership share and must have one vote in the election of a board of directors. In other employee ownership plans, workers vote their shares, or not, only to the extent the plan allows, and if they are allowed to vote, they rarely vote on a one-person, one-vote basis.

Many cooperatives have been founded as tools to aid in community economic development, especially in low-income communities. (For more information see chapter 5.) Others have been established in the desire to create an egalitarian workplace, to avoid a plant closing, or to provide a market for a departing owner to sell a business when no outside buyer could be found. In this last instance, the cooperative structure is particularly useful for small companies for which the cost of establishing and maintaining an ESOP is prohibitive. Cooperatives have low start-up costs and thus are a good structure for beginning an employee-owned company.

Sahag and Elizabeth Avedisian, founders of the Cheeseboard in Berkeley, California, turned their business into a worker cooperative because of their desire for economic equality. The Avedisians opened the Cheeseboard, a retail store specializing in fine cheeses, in 1967. As their business grew they hired employees whom they treated and compensated well. But they wanted to provide more than just fair treatment, and in 1971 they suggested that their six employees join with them and repurchase the business as a worker cooperative. The Avedisians and the other employees had fifty cents per hour deducted from their wages over two years to gather the funds needed to purchase the business.

As is the law for worker cooperatives, the Cheeseboard is completely owned by its employees. No one who is not a member of a cooperative firm can be an owner. (Cooperatives can, however, hire nonowning workers.) People pay to become members of a cooperative. The share price is generally fixed low and is essentially a membership fee rather than representing the value of the cooperative. At the Cheeseboard, new members work a forty-hour probationary period, during which they work with all the rest of the members. If the members decide to let them join, their forty hours of work constitutes their membership fee. If they are not accepted, they are paid in cash for the forty hours.

Participation is built into the cooperative system in part by the one-member, one-vote rule. Most worker cooperatives develop other highly participative structures. The Cheeseboard is no exception. All members are involved in the operation of the business. People oversee their own work in the areas that do not involve other members. Small decisions can be made by a majority vote at a monthly meeting, or a proposal can be placed on the bulletin board where members can sign their votes. For larger decisions consensus must be reached at monthly meetings.

Worker cooperatives can be structured in many different ways. A cooperative can be set up as a sole proprietorship, partnership, association, joint venture, corporation, not-for-profit corporation, and, if state law allows, a cooperative corporation. The structure a company chooses will determine how profits are taxed and distributed, the legal liability of members, and the activities the firm may engage in, among other things.

Worker cooperatives receive some federally regulated tax advantages, such as a rollover provision for owners selling to a cooperative, similar to the provision that applies to ESOPs discussed in chapter 2.

They are also regulated by state law, which differs greatly from state to state. Some states have laws providing for cooperative corporations; others make it difficult for a firm to establish itself as a cooperative.

Worker cooperatives are attractive because of their low set-up and maintenance costs and their lack of regulation. They are also attractive because of their simplicity. Each member owns one share and has one vote. The structure is generally easy for members to understand and conducive to encouraging worker-owners to be aware of their ownership responsibilities. Their primary drawbacks are the one-share, one-vote requirement and equality in the distribution of profits. Many owners do not want to give up that much control of their firms.

New Ideas in Ownership

In addition to the established plans discussed previously, companies have the option of creating their own plans to expand ownership. They can combine a variety of existing plans or develop something new that suits their "personality" and goals. The array of ways to transfer stock into employees' hands is limited only by a company's imagination and certain federal and state laws. What follows is a description of a variety of new ideas that may stimulate thought about employee ownership possibilities.

Sale/Lease Agreements

For many smaller businesses, ownership continuity presents a very difficult problem. Even when these firms are profitable, finding buyers may be impossible because the companies are too risky to be attractive to investors. Some competitors may want to buy the firms, but often merely to acquire their assets or locations, not to maintain them as operating businesses. Current owners may want to sell to employees, but rarely will employees have the cash or assets to make the purchase. As a result, many smaller firms end up being sold for the market value of their assets or going out of business.

A promising option that has not been well explored yet is to lease the business's hard assets to employees and sell them the nonhard assets such as goodwill, receivables, and patents on an installment basis. In this way, the current owner can realize an income from the assets of the company without being forced to liquidate them under what may be fire sale circumstances. At the same time, employees can become owners of the company without having to put up their own money.

It would be possible to give the employees the stock in the corporation, then lease them the assets on a long-term basis, but this
may not be practical if the company has substantial liabilities or legal
obligations because the employees would inherit them with the company. Before giving employees the stock, the ownership of the hard
assets would have to be placed in the name of the owner. That would
substantially reduce the value of most smaller firms. Employees may
be able to pay for any value that is left, such as the company's name,
in installments.

The lease could be structured so that it ended after a certain number
of years, with the employees then being given title. At some future
time, these assets will either have been used (such as inventory to
sell or receivables) or fully depreciated (equipment, land, and buildings). One (but not the only) significant exception, of course, is real
estate, which could appreciate in value. In this case, the lease could
specify that the employees will gain title to all assets that are depre-
ciable or expiring other than real estate and will have an option to
buy the real estate at an appraised price at the end of the lease.

A second alternative would be to sell the company on an installment
basis. In this case, the owner would have the business appraised,
then sell the business in installments, with interest, over a period of
years. The employees would then gain ownership out of the earnings
capacity of the company. The sale could be structured so that in the
case of default, the title would revert back to the owner.

In either case, the seller would pay ordinary income tax on the
payments received, but the employees would not have to use after-
tax dollars to finance their purchase. Decisions would have to be made
about how to distribute ownership to the employees, much along the
lines described earlier in this chapter. Shares of the company could
be given to employees on whatever basis was decided. Initially, the
structure of the transaction would probably leave the employees with
stock with very little value so that they would have a minimal tax
obligation. Rather than the employees earning a direct equity interest
in the company, a share of the company's profits could be placed in
a fund to be distributed to them when they left. This could be in the
form of a tax-qualified profit-sharing plan or a nonqualified deferred
plan on which the company would pay tax and the employee would
pay tax only on receipt of the funds. When the company was sold,
the value of the shares, if any, could be distributed to current and
former employees, according to rules set up by the corporation. Anyone considering this type of plan should be aware that securities
registration could be an issue, and legal advice is definitely called for.

Ownership at Life USA:
Buying Stock with Wages

Five partners founded Life USA, a Minneapolis-based life insurance company, in 1987 with the express purpose of being an employee-owned firm. After examining existing stock plans, the company decided to create its own route to ownership. When people decide to work at Life USA, they agree to take 10 percent of their compensation in company stock. This stock compensation is deductible to the company, but the employee pays tax on it. For field agents this means 10 percent of commission, and for home office personnel it is 10 percent of salary. In the company's early days, home office employees worked for a straight salary for a probationary period of six months. If both parties were satisfied after this period, the employee received a 5 percent raise, which was given in stock, and agreed to have another 5 percent of salary paid in stock. This process was discontinued, however, because employees wanted to participate in the stock plan as soon as they began working.

All employee-owners at Life USA own stock outright. The stock comes with full voting rights and is vested immediately. Between 80 and 85 percent of the company is owned by employees (30 to 35 percent is owned by employees other than the five co-founders). The company is issuing new shares to pay its employee-owners. The remaining stock is owned by Life USA's lender, Transamerica, and several other investors.

From the beginning, the founders of the company envisioned an employee-owned firm. They decided not to establish an ESOP because they wanted the stock to be directly in the hands of all the employee-owners. According to Life USA president Robert McDonald, ownership permeates the entire company. For example, they have an "owner services department" rather than a personnel department, and people come to work through the "owners' entrance."

In two years Life USA has grown to 150 home office people and more than 10,000 agents. In 1989 it will have more than $300 million in sales, and profits should top $3 million. The company now writes more policies per year than 90 percent of its competitors.

Captive-Aire Systems, Inc.:
Ownership of Assets

Robert Luddy, the founder and CEO of Captive-Aire Systems, Inc., a kitchen ventilation equipment business headquartered in Raleigh,

North Carolina, wanted to offer his employees ownership but not give up equity. He wanted a plan that would let him reward certain employees more than others and that did not need much cash up front. He came up with the idea of having employees own something that was closely related to the business but not the business itself. What he decided on was real estate.

In the fall of 1983 the production facility that the company had been leasing came up for sale. Luddy created a limited partnership that bought the plant and arranged for a 100 percent mortgage for ten years. He then offered all the employees who had been with the company for more than one year the right to buy a 0.5 percent share of the partnership for $250 and offered key employees additional shares. Fourteen of the company's nineteen employees purchased shares. Since that time Captive-Aire has offered more shares at a higher price.

To take full advantage of their investment, employees must remain with the firm for ten years. If they leave before that time, they get back their investment plus 10 percent but lose their full share of the equity and appreciation. The way the plan was set up, there is little risk to employees of losing their investment. Even if the value of the shares should drop by 25 percent, a $250 share would still be worth $1,500, because of all the leverage.

Captive-Aire has been doing extremely well in recent years, and Luddy attributes at least some of the company's success to his ownership plan. He feels that the plan has made people work harder and stay with the firm because it showed them that they were important to the company. He also sees it as a recruiting tool because it offers potential employees a stake in something, and it is a benefit other companies do not offer.

Windsor Factory Supply:
Using Multiple Classes of Shares

Windsor Factory Supply is a Canadian distributor with 106 full-time and 30 part-time employees. The company's co-owners created their own plan to share ownership with their employees. In addition to their salary, employees get a bonus and shares of company stock based on profits. Employees who participate in the plan are required to put in 10 percent of the cost of the shares from their salaries. Although not all employees are required to participate in the plan, about 90 percent do. Those who chose not to participate receive an equivalent amount in a pension plan.

By 1995 the company will be completely bought out by its employees. The co-owners, Jerry Slavik and Joe Sobocan, can either cash in their shares for a lump sum or receive periodic payments. After the buyout is complete, no shareholder will own more than 6 percent of Windsor stock.

There are five levels of company stock, "A" through "E." "A" shares are old shares that are held by a few long-term employees. "B" shares are those held by the two co-owners. "C" shares are given to employees as their end-of-the-year bonus. "D" shares are acquired with the employees' 10 percent contribution, and "E" shares are those acquired by employees with a contribution above the required 10 percent. The company will buy back all "A" shares as people retire. If employees leave the company before the 1995 buyout date, they forfeit "C" shares, which go back to the company to be redistributed to other employees. The money for "D" and "E" shares is returned to the employees with interest. If employees decide to cash in their "D" and "E" shares before 1995, they forfeit their "C" shares.

Windsor's entire corporate structure is as unusual as its stock plan. Employees at Windsor start as truck drivers or counter or warehouse workers. Most employees do not stay in their initial positions, however. As openings come up within the company, they can move into those positions. Employees have the opportunity to try out different jobs by filling in while others are on vacation. And even if people do stay at their starting job, they are not penalized financially. Salaries at Windsor are not categorized by job title. People are paid according to their contribution to the company. Both profit-sharing funds and salary are based on employee performance, which is determined by other employees.

Both employees and the company are doing extremely well financially. As a sign of employee contentment, the average tenure at the company is ten years. There is almost no short-term turnover.

Reprographics:
Giving Employees Ownership

Arnold Abrams, the founder and president of Reprographics in Palo Alto, California, has a unique way of transferring the company to his employees: he is giving it to them. For some years, Abrams had been considering what would happen to the company when he was no longer around. He had no family who wanted the business or needed the money that its sale would bring. He decided that he wanted his employees to have the business.

After examining a number of employee ownership plans, Abrams decided to give the company to his six employees. He plans to divide the stock according to how many months each employee has worked, giving out 100 percent of the shares. Before beginning the stock distribution, Abrams is taking care of any liabilities that the company has, ensuring that the employees will have a clean start and a good chance of keeping Reprographics going. Although he will receive no money for the company, Abrams can deduct the stock from his taxes as a gift, and he is happy the firm will be continued by those who helped build it.

Summary

Of the plans discussed, stock bonus, stock purchase, and stock option plans were obviously designed to provide employees with an ownership share. For this reason, they may prove to be the most effective ways to build ownership, particularly when a company wants to transfer a large amount of stock to employees. Profit-sharing and 401(k) plans were established for different purposes, which may make it more difficult to use them to build employee ownership. Worker cooperatives obviously were designed to share ownership, and they work well for that purpose. Their major drawback is that they require a thorough sharing of ownership and decision making.

There is no one correct way to build employee ownership. It is important to remember that each company's needs, goals, and circumstances are different. What works well for one company may be a disaster for another. Companies need to consider carefully what they want to achieve and then put a plan together that will fit their needs. As can be seen from the companies that developed their own plans, the only barrier to finding the perfect plan is lack of imagination.

4 Theory O: The Ownership Theory of Management

Karen M. Young

Arthur King, the owner of the Xcaliber Company, does not trust his employees. "Basically people do not want to work," King says. "For this company to be effective, we need to have very clear rules about exactly what people have to do. Supervision is strict, but the employees get a good deal here. 'A good day's pay for a hard day's work' is what I always say. And though we haven't set any records, we have managed to keep this company afloat."

At Yeasted Products Company the attitude is almost the opposite. "Everybody is just rarin' to go. They come in the morning just bursting with enthusiasm. Jane wants to do this; Bob wants to do that. So we just let 'em go at it," says CEO William Baker. "Of course, we are concerned that personal needs are met by the company. Supervisors focus on helping and sympathizing rather than seeing that work rules are followed. And we're doin' all right; not as well as I would like, you understand, but we gotta keep these people happy here."

At Zero Refrigeration, still another management style prevails. "Just treating people well is not enough," says President Ralph Coldwell. "We look out for our people because we hope they are going to be here all their lives. But what keeps them in line is peer pressure. It's like a clan here; everybody pretty much has to agree about decisions, but individuals are responsible for their personal behavior in the context of being responsible to the 'clan.' We have all the traditional rules around here, and people don't usually deviate from them. If they do, the other workers bring them back into line pretty quick; especially if the younger ones stray, the older workers are like stone walls of disapproval. We are also very concerned to get employees' ideas about how to do things, not just management's ideas. We think nothing works better."

These companies are not real, of course, but the management attitudes they embody are. During the last forty years three theories of management have emerged: Theory X, Theory Y, and Theory Z. Theory X argues that people work mostly because they have to. To get a good day's work out of them requires a clear set of rules and procedures and strict supervision to enforce the rules. Theory X assumes that only managers and technical experts can, will, or should contribute ideas for running a company.

Theory Y takes the more positive view that how people are treated dictates how they will respond. If they are given free rein and responsibility, they will behave with self-control and be motivated to do a good job. Theory Y, however, maintains conventional distinctions between management and nonmanagement functions.

Theory Z accepts much of Theory Y but considers it only the first step. Employees have useful ideas and information that they do not, indeed usually cannot, share with management. Getting people to work harder is only a small part of the battle. People working smarter, doing what is most sensible in the most efficient manner, is the key to success. Part of this process must be a constant reevaluation of how the company does everything.

In practice, most companies combine some of each of these approaches, although Theory X, as unfashionable as it is among organizational development professionals, seems to be the one most accepted by business management. In part, the changing theories of work reflect how work has changed. Assembly line production lent itself well to Theory X. As technology became more complex and more people entered the service sector, more individual judgment and initiative were needed at all levels. The current economy is driven by information. Even production work, whether making cars or hamburgers, is readily subject to computer-based design, implementation, and performance. The best companies are those that can process the most information and ideas in the most efficient way.

Major changes have taken place in the way people perceive work. Early in this century, for most people, work meant survival. A stable job was considered sufficient reward. As workers became more sophisticated, they came to expect more than survival. They began to want to be treated and acknowledged as thinking, feeling individuals. Today, more and more people want their work to provide some personal fulfillment. It is as if the work force, as a group, has begun to move up Abraham H. Maslow's hierarchy of needs from survival, to security, to belonging, to esteem, toward self-actualization.

For a growing number of companies, however, Theories X, Y, and Z are not encompassing enough. These companies add another dimension: ownership, the ultimate expression of respect for an employee's contribution. Rather than talking about creating a *sense* of ownership, these companies provide the *essence* of ownership, by providing equity. Other rewards are fine, they say, but employees will be much more willing to share what they know if the company is willing to share the gain that results. These companies are characterized by Theory O, for ownership. Their experience can and should light the path to the next management revolution.

State of the Research Ten Years Ago

Ten years ago a few researchers were studying a few employee ownership companies to try to determine whether they were more profitable and/or more productive than conventional firms and, if so, why. Richard Long at the University of Saskatchewan considered two direct employee buyouts in Canada in which workers bought shares individually and determined that both the workers' motivation and product quality were higher after the employee buyout. Employees wanted a say in their companies and contributed to increases in productivity if they were allowed to participate.[1] About the same time two researchers at Cornell University, Tove Hammer and Robert Stern, reported that employees wanted to participate in the decision-making processes at their companies.[2] Stern and Hammer also looked at a direct employee buyout as Long had done. Based on information obtained from about a dozen worker-owned plywood cooperatives in the Pacific Northwest, Katrina Berman at Washington State University found that they were substantially more productive than comparable conventional firms.[3] Cooperatives are inherently democratic so it makes sense that people working in them want to participate in company affairs and that the employees would work harder if they did.

The ESOP was legislated at the federal level in 1974. By 1980 there were five thousand such plans in place, making the ESOP by far the plan of choice. A study published in 1978 by Michael Conte and Arnold Tannenbaum found that thirty employee ownership companies, mostly ESOPs, were 150 percent more profitable than comparable conventional firms.[4] The percentage of profit increased with the amount of stock owned by the employees. In an article in the spring 1981 issue of the *Journal of Corporation Law*, Thomas Marsh and Dale McAllister reported that companies with ESOPs had twice the annual productivity growth rate of comparable conventional firms.[5] In the late 1970s, William Foote Whyte, a renowned sociologist at Cornell University, had testified before the U.S. Congress about the usefulness of ESOPs for saving jobs and firms in distressed industries.[6] He was convinced that employees wanted to and must participate in the governance structures in employee buyout situations, as they came to be known, in order for them to function properly. And proper functioning was desperately needed at that time. The U.S. productivity growth rate was at an all-time low. The United States had fallen from the position of world economic leader to a nation in which *layoff* was a household word and fewer and fewer people could buy their own houses.

Whyte's views were echoed by most employee ownership experts at the time. The key to making employee ownership work, they were persuaded, was employee input into or control of company policy making. For employees such control would be the most important part of ownership and would most distinguish employee ownership companies from their conventional counterparts. These researchers would readily acknowledge, however, that the studies on which these impressions were based relied on too few and too idiosyncratic companies to reach firm conclusions.

Although the researchers believed corporate control was critical if employee ownership was to succeed, most ESOP professionals argued that the keys to success were communication and the value of a company's stock. If an ESOP provided a good financial benefit and a company did a good job of explaining to employees how the ESOP worked, people would be more motivated. And if they were more motivated, the company would perform better. Both these theories seemed intuitively correct. But in social science, what seems obvious is not necessarily true.

In 1981 the National Center for Employee Ownership was founded to try to learn more about employee ownership and to make that information available to those who might use it. In some ways, this research seemed almost unnecessary. Why, for instance, justify employee ownership by finding out if and under what circumstances it contributed to employee motivation or corporate performance? Wasn't it obvious that ownership would motivate people, and if they were motivated, their companies would perform better? And whether the companies did better or not, was not employee ownership justified because it was inherently more fair?

The answer was that plausible but unproven arguments were not enough. Employee ownership might seem inherently more fair, but Congress, the public, and corporate managers wanted to know if it was also more effective. If, as the early research indicated, employee ownership companies were more profitable and productive, then increased employee ownership could help pull the United States out of its economic doldrums. The early research was far from conclusive, however, and did not tell nearly enough about when employee ownership worked best. Perhaps employees did not really care much about being owners; perhaps even if they did, this attitude would not translate into better performance or would only do so under certain circumstances. More answers not only would give a better indication about whether this concept was worth taxpayer support but would help companies make their plans work better.

From the outset, it was clear that no matter how well employee ownership did in general, it would never become widespread unless executives of companies were persuaded that it could contribute to their bottom lines. Though that contribution would be made in part through tax incentives, it could make employee ownership very costly to the taxpayer. The taxpayer would want better corporate performance in return and therefore more profits to tax, more jobs, and a better competitive position internationally. Americans are a pragmatic people, and we want a return on our investments. Pragmatic managers would also be more likely to adopt an employee ownership program if they believed it would make their companies perform better—and if they knew how to implement successful programs. Similarly, although allowing employees to share in the gains accrued by a business seemed to be a much more just approach than the extremely skewed compensation arrangements being practiced in most corporations, whether employees themselves would see things this way was unknown.

Reconciling our value system of a political democracy with our economic system has been a dilemma since the industrial revolution at the turn of the nineteenth century crowned capitalism king. Investment is necessary to stimulate businesses, but it returns capital to those who already have it and locks out those who cannot invest. To help support those in need, the owners of capital must (often by law) transfer some of their earnings to those without, which lessens the amount investors can invest, thereby depressing economic activity.

Employee ownership seems to help address and ameliorate these injustices. Altruism and ideology, however, only got Congress's attention regarding employee ownership. To keep a supportable presence there and to win converts among business and union leaders, as well as employees, more practical reasons were needed.

Further Research Efforts

This chapter addresses questions asked by business and union leaders: How can employee ownership work for us? Can it make our companies better performers and, if so, how?

The early data cited above, though not conclusive, suggested that employee ownership might contribute to improving corporate performance. But it was unclear how employee ownership could be used to achieve the best possible results—what management styles work best, whether employee control is necessary, whether a certain amount of ownership is required. What about company and plan characteristics? These were all reasonable questions.

A few studies based on limited data do not prove a point, especially in the social sciences. Profits and productivity are elusive terms. Getting consistent, reliable data and enough of it to be useful for a study to be meaningful is not an easy task. For example, two companies each take in $1 million in revenue. One pays $500,000 in salaries; the other pays $300,000 in salaries. "Profits" are $200,000 more in the second company than in the first. But the additional $200,000 in the second company still goes to the owner(s) in some form. So what really constitutes profit and how it can be measured are questions researchers have to recognize.

Productivity is the other variable that concerns company decision makers and public policy makers. Company A may measure and keep very good records of the number of widgets produced per hour per employee. Company B measures the dollar sales per hour of employee input, and its records are not so precise; they are not always adjusted for inflation or for market-driven changes in the price of the product, for instance. The companies may be producing comparable numbers of widgets. But if the methods used to keep accounts are different and the record keeping is sporadic, there is no way to obtain solid, dependable data.

Another stumbling block to getting adequate information is getting companies to cooperate and provide the data needed to do profitability and productivity analyses. Privately held companies are not called private without reason. They usually hold their cards close to their collective chests and do not play them frivolously. They sometimes have good reasons for doing this, but it makes the researcher's task difficult.

A further problem in collecting and analyzing data is the subjectivity of assessing people's behaviors and attitudes. Unlike the physical sciences, in which variables can be separated fairly easily and theses can be proven to a fine degree, the human psyche involves many variables that are irrevocably intertwined. Cause and effect cannot always be determined; we can only look for correlations between or among variables.

Despite these difficulties, the task when the NCEO was founded in 1981 deserved a serious effort. If enough researchers attacked it, perhaps we could emerge with some consensus on how well employee ownership worked and under what circumstances it worked best. Theoretically, the issue was clear. Being an owner should make employees more satisfied with their jobs, more likely to stay with their companies, and more willing to make a greater effort at work. If all this was true, companies should perform better.

These simple hypotheses, however, masked considerable underlying complexity. Perhaps employees would respond to being owners only if, as earlier researchers suggested, they could vote their shares and control their companies. Otherwise, they would not really feel like owners and would not be motivated to perform better. Or perhaps the critical question was how much of a financial reward ownership provided, or what percentage of the company the employees owned. Maybe the effectiveness of the company's efforts to promote the ownership plan were crucial, or perhaps the company's size, line of business, or age of the plan were critical. Individual employees might respond differently as well, based on educational, income, seniority, or other considerations. All these hypotheses seemed plausible.

And even if employees were responsive to ownership, did that automatically mean the company would perform better? Maybe employees would work harder but as ineffectively or inefficiently. Or maybe they would like being owners but would not translate ownership into the sharing of ideas and information that could keep companies competitive. It is possible to try harder or care more but not make more progress. And even if employee ownership did contribute to performance, when would it contribute most? When employees owned the most? When they voted their shares? In smaller companies in which their efforts were most visible? The list of reasonable possibilities went on and on but provided no answers.

The NCEO created a questionnaire to give to employees at employee ownership companies nationwide and devised an interview form to be administered to a management official to obtain information about the company, the employee ownership plan, and employee influence in the company. Although specific productivity and profitability data were requested, not enough information was collected to be of use for analyses. The data were collected from 1981 through 1984 from more than fifty ESOP companies because an ESOP is the most commonly used employee ownership plan and from a dozen companies with other plans. Data from nearly three thousand employees in thirty-seven of the ESOP companies were usable in the analyses.

The employees in these companies indicated that there were four distinct circumstances that made them satisfied with their jobs and committed to their companies, happy with employee ownership, and unlikely to leave the company. The highest correlate with these factors was the amount of money being contributed to their accounts each year. The more ownership employees had, the more likely they were to feel like owners. Ownership in this sense does not mean ownership of a percentage of the company. As the NCEO had found, this is not in itself important in motivating employees. The other important factors that made employees feel like owners were management's commitment to the idea and practice of employee ownership, communication about the plan and the company's situation, and employee involvement, especially at the job level. All the seemingly reasonable hypotheses listed above, along with others, proved to have no independent effect. In other words, the percentage of a company employees owned was ostensibly important but only as an artifact of the tendency for companies where employees owned a high percentage of the company to be the ones where employees got the largest annual contributions to their ESOPs. Employees' individual attributes such as age, seniority, or income were not related to attitudes toward ownership.[7]

By 1986, four years after this project had begun, the NCEO had the most comprehensive information available about the attitudes of employees in employee ownership companies. Now that we knew how employees felt about certain issues in their companies, we still did not know whether these attitudes translated into improved corporate performance. We thus started on the second part of our search to try to find out whether employee ownership companies perform better, worse, or the same as their counterparts.

Eight companies were added to the thirty-seven in the original NCEO survey. The investigation focused on sales growth rates and employment growth rates. These data could be obtained from public sources and were good indicators of a company's performance. Employment growth was an important end in itself, arguably the most important one. After all, public policy makers are not interested in profits per se but in the ability of profitable companies to provide more good jobs for people. We also needed to know whether the ESOP was the "cause" of better performance. All previous studies had looked at companies only *after* their plans were established so we did not know whether the ESOPs had helped the companies do better or whether already successful companies set up ESOPs.

Using the measures mentioned above, the performance of the forty-five ESOP companies was analyzed for the five years before and the five years after their plans were established. These companies were then compared to five non-ESOP companies on the same measures for the same ten-year period to determine whether the ESOP or some other factor might be determining the growth rates or if it was the "ESOP effect." Generally, the ESOP companies grew faster than their competitors before setting up the ESOPs. After setting up their plans, however, their performance relative to their competition was even better, by a margin of an additional 3 to 4 percent each year. We had a 0.95 confidence level for these findings, meaning we were 95 percent sure these results were not just an odd coincidence. Some of the companies did much better than others, however. What particular factor or set of factors might be related to this growth was the next area to be investigated.

The performance measures were then tested against variables that logically might be related to corporate performance. In companies where management had a positive belief in the concept of employee ownership, rather than just in the tax benefits, and employees were involved in decision making primarily at the job level, the growth rate differentials increased to between 8 and 11 percent per year. The significance on these correlations was between 0.95 and 0.99 levels. These two facts were very strongly related to each other, and to a large extent they measured the same thing: the degree to which management wants to treat employees as owners, normally by seeking their input. These findings were remarkably strong for the social sciences; not many variables have been shown to have such a dramatic impact on company performance.

You might well respond, "That's pretty obvious." But consider the variables that were not related to corporate performance: the annual contribution; structural features related to performance (i.e., percentage owned, plan features, voting, and board representation); a change in management; and the ESOP tax preference. Any of these variables could be expected to have an effect on corporate performance, but participation was the only one that did.

Subsequent researchers found much the same relationship between ownership, participation, and performance. The media started writing about employee ownership companies that followed this path, and managers of these companies consistently showed up as keynoters and panelists at ESOP meetings to extol what they had done. As the results of the research became generally known, other companies knew the NCEO and, more important, their successful ESOP colleagues were proving the case. Participation had been something of an ignored entity in the ESOP community until the mid-1980s, a nice thing to do but peripheral to the "real" issues of taxes and account balances. That began to change dramatically. But companies wanted more than persuasive data or inspiring stories. They wanted to know how to do it themselves.

Putting Theory O to Work

When looking at the data collected for the work reported in *Employee Ownership in America*,[8] I compiled a list of the traits common to companies with the most committed, satisfied employees. Independently, Corey Rosen, director of the NCEO, put together a list of the features consistently occurring in financially successful employee ownership companies based on the corporate performance study. Our two lists were nearly identical. We called that list "Theory O" for the ownership theory of management.

Theory O

The person at the top of the organization is committed to the concept.

There is a written set of values embodying the commitment to employee ownership.

Attention is given to symbols indicating the importance of employee ownership.

Decisions are made at the level where there is the most relevant expertise.

Training in technical and participative skills is necessary.

The sharing of information from the bottom up as well as the top down is practiced.

There is a realization that participative decision making takes more time but is often more effective.

The combination of methods used to implement Theory O is unique to each company.

Commitment from the Top

The most successful employee ownership companies in the survey group were doing more than just instituting a new participative practice here or there. They were changing the expectations of both managers and nonmanagers. Managers were now expected to seek employees' ideas and input; employees were expected to provide them. This could be good news to many people, but it would be threatening and unsettling to others. Everyone had to understand that this new approach was a personal priority of the top person, not just another experiment.

There is no manager more committed to Theory O than Bob Fien at Stone Construction Equipment Company in Honeoye, New York. When Fien became president of Stone Construction in 1982, he firmly believed employees should be involved in the management of the company. In 1986 the employees took out a loan to purchase the remaining outstanding shares of the company through an ESOP. The plan had been set up in 1979 as a means for the Stone family to sell, but the plan held only a minority of the stock until the family decided to sell it all. Fien and other executives contemplated briefly but rejected the idea of a management buyout. "We realized that if we were to compete worldwide, we needed to treat all of our employees as partners," Fien said.[9]

Five years later Fien is still living up to that affirmation. Before the 100 percent buyout, employees showed some interest in the company's overall well-being, but after the buyout Fien noticed an "almost overnight change in the sensitivity to productivity and quality control by the employees. Having the plan helps keep the employees focused on the need for cost containment, automation, and quality because they reap the benefits also. And having employees share in the wealth makes them more interested in participating in the running of the company." There is a lot of talk about "allowing" people to participate in decision making at their companies. Fien says there is a problem getting people to participate but that the ESOP provides the incentive for them to do so. Fien also notes that participation does not mean consensus decision making but does mean that management makes an effort to seek and *to listen* to information from employees.

Fien recognizes that people will not suddenly start participating when told they are owners. They have to be provided with the means for participation, and they must be made aware that one person can make a difference in the success of the overall operation. Some of the avenues used at Stone are (1) the Partnership Personality, a company philosophy that executives will not receive special privileges; (2) SCOPE groups, made up of employees who meet to discuss ways to improve productivity and solve problems; (3) quality process control, which allows people on the floor to stop production if there is a quality problem; (4) an annual shareholders' meeting, at which employee-shareholders are given information about the company's finances and competition; (5) department meetings, held four times a year at which employees can ask the CEO questions; (6) stock certificates, issued annually; (7) dividends, paid twice a year depending on profitability; (8) monthly employee newsletters geared to employees' perspectives; and (9) a bulletin board on which advertising and feedback from customers are posted.

Revenues have increased by 50 percent since the buyout in 1986, and the employees are obviously proud to be part of Stone. Sales coordinator Penny Schultz says, "It's like having your own business." "If we make 'em, we can fix 'em," assembler Randy Zea says enthusiastically. And the employees sign the products, making a personal commitment that the machine the customer gets is the best they can provide. Bob Fien says, "It's a real honor and genuine pleasure for me to be associated with the employee-owners of Stone."

A Statement of Values

Many businesses have value statements; some businesses practice them. It is unclear why value statements seem so common and important in employee ownership companies. Perhaps people simply want to know that what they do matters in other ways than just making money. Whatever the reason, values, whether providing a high-quality product, assuring stable, good jobs, giving people a chance to participate, or some other objective, seem to matter. Yellow Springs Instruments (YSI) is a particularly value-driven company.

To be part of the business mainstream in the five-thousand-person town of Yellow Springs, Ohio, a firm has to have an ESOP. In one such business, Yellow Springs Instruments, the plan holds 25 percent of the stock and individual employees hold another 30 percent. Antioch College, long recognized for its concern with social issues, provided a basement room in a science building for the three-person fledgling company in 1948. YSI is now a leader in environmental quality measurement instruments and produces other instruments that measure environmental temperature and the amount of glucose in blood cells. YSI was able to put up its own building in 1951 and has expanded seven times since then. There are now 350 employee-owners, whom the company credits with "accepting responsibility for continuing our success. As we move into our second generation of leadership, we carry with us a heritage of human values and a commitment to meet the challenges of our rapidly changing markets."[10]

Malte von Matthiessen, an Antioch graduate and member of the board of Antioch Publishing, became president of YSI in the mid-1980s when the founders decided they were ready to retire. Antioch Publishing was one of the first firms in Yellow Springs to set up an ESOP. Lee Morgan, its president, suggested that YSI set up an ESOP in the 1980s. Von Matthiessen liked the ESOP idea, and before he accepted the position of president he convinced the departing founders to expand employee ownership at the company. That they did. Von Matthiessen went about getting the employees ready to be involved and then getting them involved. To von Matthiessen, ownership and employee involvement made good business sense, but, just as important, they were the right thing to do. They reflected not only his own strongly held values but the values of the unusual and tightly knit community of Yellow Springs.

To begin, a group of workers was trained by professionals in problem solving and in how to do the training. They now run the program for their co-workers. A concerted effort was begun to upgrade skills, again using in-house mentors to pass along their knowledge and experience to others.

Committees were set up to handle ongoing concerns, and ad hoc teams were formed as needed. The ESOP Task Force was instrumental in organizing events for Employee Ownership Week in 1989, a national event to encourage employee ownership companies to celebrate their employee ownership. In one part of the week's program managers and those in other areas of the company exchanged jobs in the morning, then had lunch together in a downtown restaurant. Employees of YSI and two other local employee ownership companies toured each other's facilities during the week to find out what their neighbors actually do and how employee ownership works at other companies.

Almost 100 percent of Yellow Springs Instruments' worker-owners participated in an employee ownership T-shirt day at which they wore their "We're Minding Our Own Business" T-shirts to work. There was also an essay contest on "What Employee Ownership Means to Me" and an Ownership Sweepstakes in which the employees submitted answers to questions about employee ownership. Participation in both events was high.

Although the committees and task forces concentrated on social events, the ongoing work at YSI focuses on employee involvement and responsibility. Ad hoc teams are expected to deal with most job-level problems, and employees are regularly surveyed to find out their concerns. The company plans to pass through voting rights and add an employee to the board. The plant's physical layout is open, and offices are separated by flexible dividers rather than walls. As von Matthiessen put it, "We would have an open door policy here, except we have no doors."

All of this creates the culture that is the "normative glue" holding YSI together. This culture is represented by the following statement:

1. We cherish the customer.
2. We foster trust and participatory team process.
3. We are a company of individuals.
4. We foster effective leadership and communication.
5. We reward performance.
6. We encourage risk taking.
7. We are a dynamic organization.
8. We are proud of our company, products, and services.[11]

Symbols Are Important

Companies communicate with employees through brochures, reports, meetings, letters, and in many other ways. These efforts may be regular or sporadic, but they are never as ever-present as a company's symbols. When key management people get perquisites and pay increases at the same time that workers are being asked to sacrifice, for instance, the company is communicating very clearly just how little employees matter. But symbols can also be used in a positive way to reinforce the value of ownership. The following example illustrates particularly effectively how a company can reinforce this message.

"This young woman is an owner of a major U.S. corporation," says a voice as a picture of a smiling woman waiting on a customer at a rental car counter flashes on the TV screen. What does this say to the viewer? That the owner is working at the counter, that the owner is young, and that this message is a hoax are three likely assumptions. In fact, the major U.S. corporation is Avis, Inc., and the young woman is one of the employees who, along with all the other employees at Avis, is also an owner. This advertisement is a symbol, a symbol of trust. Trust is a key word at employee ownership companies. The commercial, like the rest of Avis's advertising campaign, tells the world and the employees that the company trusts that the new worker-owners at Avis, Inc., will live up to the image being portrayed—that of an owner; someone who cares; someone who will go the extra mile; someone who will do what it takes to make the company a success; someone who will make the other owners proud.

The decision by Avis to focus its advertising campaign on employee ownership was a bold one. Avis's advertising agency did not think it would work until the agency surveyed car rental customers and found that 75 percent of them would prefer to rent from owners. But the decision was simply one of many that Avis executives *and* elected employee representatives throughout the company made to put a symbolic and practical emphasis on ownership. The symbols of the advertising campaign have been backed up in several other ways.

Do you remember the slogan "We try harder"? "Owners try harder" replaced it for a while after the ESOP buyout at Avis. The slogan was thought up by an employee. After Avis's advertising campaign had been running for several months, it was changed to its current form, "Now we're trying harder than ever." It reinforces the idea that ownership matters.

As important as symbols are, they will be meaningless unless they are backed up by practice. Avis created an environment in which employees are encouraged to think harder for *their* company and are provided with avenues to present their ideas. This last part is crucial. Suppose an employee had thought of that new slogan in a conventional firm. Perhaps she would have told the person working next to her or a friend. But she would not have been able to mark out "We" and write "Owners" above the marked-out word on every button being worn. At Avis, however, there are regular meetings at which employees can bring up ideas and get feedback about them, and this idea was introduced and accepted at one such meeting. Though this structure for employee input serves very practical functions, it also symbolizes that employees are partial owners and are valued as such.

One of the best anecdotes about Avis concerns a woman who rented a car from an Avis competitor. She had a flat tire while driving away from the rental site. The agency from which she had rented the car ignored her plight. An Avis employee went out and changed the tire for her. Fortuitously for Avis, the woman was married to the chairman of another major U.S. corporation. The business account went from the non-employee-owned agency to the employee-owned Avis Corporation. Joseph Vittoria, chairman of Avis, is convinced that the Avis employee was willing to help because, as an owner, if the company prospers he prospers.

To date, Avis's trust in its employees and the employees' faith in the company have not been misplaced. The divestiture by Wesray Corporation of the 12,500-employee company took place in the fall of 1987. A participative management style was introduced along with the new ownership. Many employee suggestions have been made and implemented in the last couple of years. Among them are a policy of having cars available for walk-ins, an effort to have bilingual employees available for non-English-speaking customers, a policy of notifying customers about lost articles, and the reshaping of curbs to avoid tire damage when filling cars with gas.

Avis's stock prices increased 300 percent the first year after the spin-off and 15 percent in the second year, despite considerable softness in the rental car market. The operating profits increased from $16 million the year before the ESOP to $79 million the year after to $93 million in 1989. The gap in the airport market share between Avis and the former number-one profit-making rival is virtually closed, and complaints about service are way down. Avis may have to adopt the motto "We're #1 because owners (we) try harder."

Decisions Should Be Made Where the Expertise Is

Few things seem so obvious as ensuring that decision makers are the people who know the most about the issue. Few things are also so rare. Most companies assign decision-making authority based on a pyramidal organizational chart in which people assume more and more authority as they rise in the company. Yet common sense, and many executives, tell us that the best people to make a decision are likely to be those lower on the organizational chart who know the most about a particular issue, such as how to run a machine or serve a customer, but have no say in policies or broad decisions affecting that issue. Although most executives realize this, they also know that to make decision making consistent with expertise would disrupt the chain of command. The awkwardness and ambiguity that would result, not to mention the difficulty of identifying experts for every decision, does not seem to them to justify the effort.

The best employee ownership companies have a different view. The costs of making less than optimal decisions, they believe, are far greater than the costs of undermining the organizational chart. Connor Spring and Manufacturing, headquartered in San Francisco, with plants in Dallas, Portland, San Jose, and Los Angeles, for instance, hired a systems/human resource manager in 1989. His job was not to make and see to the carrying out of all decisions in his areas of authority but to get those decisions made and carried out by the people most familiar with the area in question. Connor Spring manufactures metal stampings and industrial springs. The company established an ESOP in 1984 as a way to motivate employees and to reward them for any increases that resulted. This ESOP was begun at the same time the most extensive research about employee attitudes was being conducted.[12] At the time no one could know that that research would play an important role in the future of Connor Spring. Michael Quarrey, who followed up this initial research as a National Center for Employee Ownership staff member and found the first evidence that employee ownership contributed to corporate performance only in the presence of employee participation programs, was the manager later hired by Connor.

The management at Connor was interested in involving employees in corporate affairs but found that preparing to do so takes time. Sometimes the will is there but the way is hard to come by. Connor's management thought Quarrey could help them find a way. Quarrey found some other people eager to expand on the already existing participation programs at Connor.

Because management is committed to the idea of employee participation, it has used various techniques for facilitating employee input. These have met with varying degrees of success. Monthly non-management committee meetings are held at some of the plants to solve problems; there are also ad hoc meetings, such as those at which people who make the product can be told about customers' needs. One successful innovation has been to have workers on two shifts overlap for one and one-half hours each week to try to improve production.

The longest-standing employee-involvement method at Connor Spring is the Statistical Process Control System, a method of using statistics to help identify what factors contribute most to quality and what needs to be changed. Every employee is equipped with the necessary information to help determine these factors and stop production if necessary. Now Quarrey is developing a computer model to help all employees assess production performance in their areas.

Some of the questions and comments that arise at the meetings have to do with whether there are too many meetings and how to have a good meeting. After all, meetings are time away from production, and production is what puts broccoli on the table and money in the bank. But meetings are a way of life at participative employee ownership companies. An employee at Herman Miller (another employee ownership company) said that the company is sometimes referred to as Herman Meeting because there are so many meetings involving so many people. Despite the qualms and problems, both at Connor and Herman Miller the meeting mode is working. At both companies, managers report that employees frequently present valuable ideas that ultimately save a great deal more time and money than is spent on meetings.

Employees at Connor are also involved in hiring. They are, after all, among the best judges of what it takes to do the job. After candidates are narrowed down to a select few, employees with whom the new hire will be working hold a group interview. Employees sometimes come up with questions that a supervisor does not think of. Including employees in the hiring process gives them a sense of belonging.

Bob Sloss, president of Connor Spring, refers to the employees as partners and is totally committed to convincing them he means it. He is willing to share the rights if they are willing to share the responsibilities. The results seem to bear Sloss out. Sales were up in 1989 and skyrocketed in early 1990.

Training Is Necessary for Participation to Be Effective

Giving employees increased responsibility sounds reasonable, but both management and employees will be frustrated if the effort is not supported by training to ensure that employees can do the job. Even if employees already can handle the extra responsibilities, training can help them take on more.

Weirton Steel Corporation may be the best-known employee ownership company in the nation. When National Steel announced in 1982 that it would downsize and possibly close its West Virginia subsidiary, Weirton took the first steps to becoming the largest employee-owned company in the nation at the time. First, of course, there was a stunned silence followed by a lot of soul-wrenching discussion. Weirton would become a ghost town without the mill, and the social fabric of the valley and the economic structure of the entire state would be affected. An ESOP seemed to be a workable solution. Steel, in general, was in trouble, but Weirton was marginally profitable; it just no longer fit into its parent company's strategic plans. National agreed to sell to the employees, and a labor-management committee was formed to help draw up the agreement.

The Independent Steelworkers Union was the primary union at Weirton and was a major negotiator throughout the transaction. Much calling, reading, and talking ensued to investigate the best way to proceed. Lawyers, bankers, and accountants were hired. There were some dissenting groups, including some retirees, who thought there was too much secrecy about the transaction; some who felt that union members had no business owning a company; and some who did not want to make the 20 percent wage and benefit concessions agreed to. In September 1983, however, one and one-half years after the announcement by National, the employees at Weirton voted by nearly 90 percent to become an employee-owned company. The actual agreement went into effect in January 1984.

From the beginning, people agreed that to survive Weirton had to be both owned and operated by employees. How to meet this objective effectively became the next question. These people were steelmakers, not policy makers. But the people who were in the best position to know some of the policies to be implemented were those who dealt with the mass of molten lead being poured and coming down the line day after day. Making critical information available to the appropriate people was vital for the company's functioning.

Yet employees and managers alike had little experience in solving problems in a participative manner. It was one thing to set up participation groups and processes but quite another to see that they worked efficiently.

To address this problem, Weirton hired some organizational development professionals to help set up procedures to help people learn how to solve problems, make decisions, work in groups, share information, and support each other. A call for people to be trained as trainers/facilitators was sent throughout the company. More than three hundred people applied for the three jobs available. Of the three finalists, two were from the line and one was a nonmanagement employee from accounting. They were chosen by a management-labor steering committee. That was the beginning of the Employee Participation Group (EPG) program. The EPG charter gives as its objective "To establish an employee participation process throughout the corporation which will result in a better work environment and steel products of the highest quality by utilizing the experience and skills of all Weirton Steel employees in an atmosphere of mutual trust and respect."

There are now twelve trainers, and all but a couple formerly worked in the mill. The trainers also facilitate the groups that meet one hour a week to discuss issues and deal with problems in their work areas. The training sessions are part of the orientation process for new hires. All other employees are eligible and encouraged to take the training. Issues dealt with in the EPGs cannot intrude on the labor agreement (the collectively bargained contract between the union and the company).

Training sessions are held three days a week, Wednesday through Friday, every week. About fifteen people attend each session. The sessions begin with an overview of general ways of organizing work, followed by a talk about the roles of different group members, decision-making processes, and problems and techniques to deal with them. Many opportunities for interaction among the trainees are presented throughout the three days. There is a decision-making exercise and role playing in real-life situations. Information and exercises on communication are also included. Time on the last day of the training session is provided for the attendees to discuss, comment, suggest, and question. There is also a final group decision-making activity that brings home to the attendees that "participation is easy to say but hard to do." Wrap-up presentations are made, often by the company president and the union president. The trainees then go back and participate in groups in their function areas.

Weirton has turned a profit every year since the buyout and reports that this employee-involvement program has contributed immensely to the successful bottom line.

Information Sharing—From Bottom Up as Well as Top Down

When companies think of communicating, they often mean providing information to employees. That is valuable, of course, but by now it should be clear that what sets great companies apart is their ability to get information from employees. Communicating to people is relatively easy. Professionals can be hired to prepare the information. Getting important information from employees is much more difficult. Worzalla Publishing Company learned that—and dealt with it successfully.

Little progress was made for the better part of 1986 when Worzalla Publishing Company employees were negotiating to purchase the company from the two absentee owners in Chicago. It may not be far geographically from Stevens Point, Wisconsin, home to Worzalla, to Chicago, Illinois, home to the company owners. But it is a long, long way otherwise.

The company had been owned and operated for over ninety years by the Worzalla family before the family sold it to two Chicago investors in 1984. Some of the employees wanted to buy the company at that time but could not come up with the financing needed to make the purchase. Employees chafed while they watched their debt service go up and interest carriage double. The pension was terminated, and it looked as though all the money that could possibly be squeezed out was going to Chicago. Management talked the owners into an ESOP in 1985 to own one-third of the stock. In July 1986 a seemingly viable bid was made to the owners to buy out the rest of the company, but by October the deal had fallen through for financial reasons. By December, with the help of the city, which had an interest in Worzalla being locally owned, the company applied for a low-interest loan through a state economic development program. The review process for the loan was completed with admirable speed, and with some additional monies from banks and from the employees themselves, Worzalla became a 100 percent employee-owned Stevens Point company on the last day of 1986.

After the initial excitement ebbed, the work of actually running the company had to be dealt with. The management group who had negotiated the deal along with other employees set up a board of directors consisting of three management and three line people. These people had a personal interest in the company. Many had been employed there for their entire work lives; many were related; many were friends; they spent the money they earned at the local hardware store, the gas station, and the drugstore. They needed and wanted their jobs so much that they were willing to loan their company $300,000 to help complete the transaction and agreed to a raise freeze for five years. The work force of a little over two hundred people agreed to these conditions on a voluntary basis with no set amount required from any one person. Making a financial contribution is a big motivator toward making a project work.

Everyone knew that information had to be shared by all to return Worzalla to the strong and stable basis it had known for much of its history since 1892. After board meetings members meet with groups of employees to inform them of what took place. Employees are asked

for their ideas, which are presented to the board for consideration. In addition, there are many other mechanisms for employees
to receive and give information. The employees run education and
quality committees, for example, and tell management what they are
doing.

The company has been on a buying binge since the buyout, based
on suggestions and comments from the people who actually work
with the equipment. Over $6 million had been spent by the end of
1988, some of which went to purchase a four-color press and greatly
expand the building. The value of these expenditures is not lost on
the employees. They were willing to do whatever was necessary,
from working seven days a week to returning part of their paychecks
in the first year after the buyout, to help the company succeed. And
succeed it did. Sales were $14.4 million in 1986 and $25.5 million in
1988. About fifty additional people have been hired. The employees
shared $350,000 in bonuses in 1989, some of which they reinvested
in the company. This was a very different situation from the days
when the Chicago owners not only did not put money in but took
money out. John Butkus, one of the nonmanagement board members,
says, "There are always differences, and there's always going to be
complaints. But it's up to ourselves to work these things out."[13] One
of the biggest differences is that the employee-owners now have both
the opportunity and the responsibility to share what they know.

Participation Takes Longer
but Decisions Are Easier to Implement

Have you ever left a meeting and said to yourself or to anyone else
in earshot, "What a waste of time—I could have made that decision
myself in a few minutes." Indeed, you probably could have made
some decision. But would it really have been that one? Would you
have had all the information and all the ideas that were shared at the
meeting? And even if the decision were the same, or even better,
how easy would it have been to get people to carry out the decision
if they had no role in making it? How much time would be spent
policing, persuading, cajoling, and pleading with people to do what
they were told to do, compared to the time spent if they shared in
making the decision in the first place?

Learning that participative decision making takes more time but
produces better results is often one of the toughest tasks for any
employee ownership company. At Clay Equipment, the lessons have
been learned well.

Clay Equipment was ninety years old in 1990. For eighty-four of those years it was family- or family- and management-owned. The last six of those years the company has been employee-owned. The last six years have been more tumultuous than all the first eighty-four. The people at Clay sometimes wonder which has contributed more to the tumult, the economic uncertainty in their industry, farm and livestock equipment manufacturing, or the 100 percent employee stock ownership plan and all it entails. The plan was established to buy out the remaining family owner. That decision was made by a few managers and was a fait accompli within sixty days. It may have been the last quick decision that was made. Like many decisions made by a few that affect many, the ESOP was met with distrust at first.

But the company has changed, largely because Clay is willing to spend a great deal of time getting people involved in sharing information and making decisions participatively. The traditional tug-of-war with the union, the International Association of Machinists, has become more collegial since the ESOP was begun, but the nature of the negotiations has also changed. No longer is it "Give us higher wages and more benefits" from the union and "We can't afford it and you don't deserve it" from the company. The long-term health of the company is now considered in these meetings, which used to be disputes more than discussions.

The union realizes that what goes into one pot, such as higher pay, has to come from another pot, such as reinvestment in the company. The first may be immediately rewarding, but the second should be even more rewarding in the future. The company has to consider what is fair for the workers because everyone owns this company. Discussing company financial information at negotiations and trying to think of how the other side will view a negotiating position can be more time-consuming than the push-me, pull-you atmosphere in many company-union negotiations. But all parties end up more satisfied and more likely to accept the outcome than before.

Clay has also undergone changes in its performance evaluation process. Employees are asked to define key areas of their jobs and what is needed to perform well in them. The person conducting the review and the employee being reviewed discuss these features of the job and together establish a performance standard for the job and the person. Constant improvement is emphasized. This process takes more time than an evaluation that consists of meeting with an employee and simply saying he or she did all right, good, or excellent or poorly, unacceptably, or unredeemably bad. But again, everyone involved is much more satisfied with the decisions and more likely to accept them.

There are also meetings, that hallmark of participation. President Cal Schacht reports that he was never a believer in meetings; they took too much time. But now he favors them because there is less supervision. In fact, supervisors are not replaced when they leave because employees are included in initial decision making. Employees sit on the board; they bring up issues management would not have thought of. Dealing with these issues is time-consuming. Employees vote their allocated shares of stock, which is time-consuming. There is an all-employee meeting with the president once a month at which any questions may be asked. Again, this is time-consuming. All financial information and new developments in the business are shared; a weekly newsletter is published and sent to the workers' families; the president spends a lot of time on the floor talking to people; line employees (volunteers) were sent to a trade show.

The president is enthusiastic about this long-time talking, short-time doing approach. He says, "It's amazing how interested the employees are, and people working on a product have unbelievable ideas." But the best thing he heard was at a trade show when another builder approached him and asked who he was. He introduced himself. A line worker was with Schacht. When asked who he was, the worker replied, "I'm one of the owners." "That's really what we want," Schacht says.[14]

Keep Trying Different Approaches

The last lesson of Theory O is both comforting and distressing: there is no formula to make things work. What works for one company will not work for another. In fact, what works now for one company may not work for that same company later. Dividing employees into participation groups in their functional areas may solve many problems, but what happens when most of the problems are solved, or when problems that cut across functional lines come up, or when personnel or technology change? It may be time to try something different. This is disturbing, of course. But when companies keep trying, they eventually hit on workable solutions—and employees appreciate the effort.

Karl Reuther may think he has tried everything in the last two and one-half years, but chances are that two and one-half years from now he will look back and see that there was lots more to come. The ESOP at Reuther Mold and Manufacturing Company of Cuyahoga Falls, Ohio, was announced at the first Employee Ownership Week ever held, in October 1987. That seemed a very appropriate beginning for both events. Reuther single-handedly began the campaign to get the plan in order and to inform the employees.

Early in January 1987 he met with the company's managers and attended a national conference on the subject of employee ownership. He advised line employees about the impending change, read all the material he could find, then wrote up the first of what would become a series of handouts for employees. He responded to questions from the employees and did an interview that appeared in a full-page story in the business section of a local newspaper. All this occurred between January and October 1987, when the flag was put up at the 150-employee Reuther Mold declaring it an "ESOP Company." Reuther relentlessly continued to provide information to and instill enthusiasm in the new worker-owners at Reuther Mold. He wanted these people to feel like the new owners they were. This approach seemed right at the time. Doing everything by himself was also the only way to proceed at first.

In the middle of 1988, Reuther realized that he was no longer alone. A worker-owner now sat on the board; there was an ESOP committee; the shop committee had reviewed the policies handbook (for the first time); and small group meetings were going on all over the shop. He also noticed that many people were skeptical and tough questions were being asked. Reuther was not viewed as the "white knight" he had envisioned. He decided to listen more and talk less. He noticed an item on the agenda of a shop committee meeting entitled "Karl in the shop." He thought, "I'm awfully busy, but if they want me to spend more time in the shop, I'll just have to do it. I want these people to know that I am genuinely concerned about their needs." He went to the meeting. "Karl, stay out of the shop," he was told by the new worker-owners. "You are intruding where you do not have the expertise." Yes, listening more and talking less seemed to be the new order of business.

By the summer of 1988 a somewhat chastened but still determined Karl Reuther was saying that he had come to realize that his new role was that of educator and coach rather than cheerleader. He had expected applause, commitment, thanks, cooperation, elation, and new ideas. What he got was skepticism, withdrawal, interrogation, confrontation, apathy, and criticism. Nevertheless, he was undaunted because he had been educated in the workings of ESOPs and had heard stories of similar situations from other sellers. What he could not teach, he hired people to do—problem solving, group dynamics, and listening skills. He believed in what he was doing and was willing to give patience and repetition a try.

Reuther thought even more deeply than he had when he had considered whether he wanted to share ownership with 150 other people. He tried to understand his own and the workers' conflicts in roles such as stockholder, board member, committee member, and worker. He felt it was time to help workers understand and deal with these conflicts and to let them know he knew about and understood them and was trying to deal with them too. He resolved not to lose his enthusiasm and to be as open and available as needed. The negative feedback he had gotten made him appreciate that feedback was useful as one tries to change a negative situation into a positive one. And he realized he was talking about and trying to help bring about a major cultural change that could not happen overnight.

Reuther decided what was needed next was a "just do it" approach. All financial information had been shared; operators had the authority to stop production; a worker task force had been formed to make equipment purchases; and training had been conducted.

Worker-owners attended the first Employee Ownership Conference—Just for Employees during Employee Ownership Week in October 1988. They were there as students. One year later, at the same conference, the Reuther Mold attendees were there as teachers. They were enthusiastic, committed, and knowledgeable. As for the company, orders began to pour in, thanks to increased selling efforts and better-quality products. And profits were not one, not two, but five times greater in 1989 than the year before.

Conclusion

The case histories presented here are all positive. Experiences with Theory O have generally been positive as well, as the data indicate. This does not mean, however, that all has gone smoothly in the transition from using ESOPs purely as a tax planning device to using ESOPs as a springboard to organizational change.

As was noted in chapter 1, only about one-third of the companies with ESOPs are making efforts such as those described here. And even among this minority, most are using only a few of the ideas mentioned here or are involving only part of their operations. While this seems a much more impressive number than in non–employee ownership companies, there is clearly a long way to go.

Why don't more companies embrace Theory O? If it is such a good practice, shouldn't the market almost demand that they do? Part of the reason is that, although there are data to support the theory, the instincts of many corporate executives have been honed on very different practices. This group seems to be shrinking, however.

A tougher problem is inertia. Many people now intellectually agree that what Weirton, Avis, Stone, Reuther, and others are doing makes sense but are not ready to do it themselves. It is not hard to see why. Making these changes is not easy. It requires a great deal of staff time and often may require hiring more consultants at a time when the company has just faced heavy expenses for ESOP consultants to begin the plan. The results may appear quickly on the bottom line, but often they do not show up for years. Changing people's behavior takes time, and the implementation of new ideas may not show up on profit and loss statements for a while. Moreover, it is difficult to assess how effective these programs are in individual companies. How many ideas would have evolved anyway? How much cost saving would have come from greater effort? How much time is spent on participation that could have been spent working?

Once key executives have become committed to a program, more obstacles remain. If employees can do more on their own, will supervisors still be needed? Even if they still have a job, will their authority be diminished? Companies try to deal with this problem in a variety of ways, such as providing job security guarantees, urging managers to redefine their roles as trainers and teachers, or, as at Clay, reducing the number of supervisors through attrition. No one has come up with a perfect solution; everyone agrees the problem is difficult to solve.

Employees themselves can be a source of resistance. Participation adds more than an opportunity; it adds a responsibility. Many people just want to do their jobs and go home. Others are skeptical, feeling that these programs are disguised work speed-ups or a waste of time. Few employees have any experience in this approach in work or other settings such as schools or families. Our educational system, for instance, stresses individual competition, not learning collaborative skills. Companies have to learn to allow some employees just to do their jobs, while encouraging others to get involved. Even if only 20 percent of the work force becomes active, a lot more ideas and information could be generated. Many executives will understandably become frustrated, however, when they see 80 percent of the employees remaining skeptical. In short, Theory O demands a lifetime organizational and personal commitment. Therefore, it may be more surprising that so many companies, rather than so few, are undertaking participative employee ownership.

Change will continue to come in part because the companies that are combining ownership and participation are so visible at meetings and in the media, thus increasing the comfort level and the peer pressure for other companies to do the same. At ESOP meetings these days, the stars are clearly the Theory O companies, and everyone wants to be a star. Companies might agree to set up a few experimental structures and if they work, to expand further. If they work, attitudes will start to change. Attitudinal change almost always follows structural change, rather than the other way around.

In part, change will come as companies need to compete for employees. Especially because technology and demographics have combined to provide fewer opportunities for advancement in many companies, participation may be necessary to keep people interested, and ownership may be necessary to attract and retain people. Competition may also compel more firms to rethink their organizational philosophy.

All of these trends are reasons for cautious optimism. The combination of ownership and participation seems certain to continue to grow. This growth will probably always be constrained by the factors listed above, and perhaps only a minority of ESOP firms will embrace Theory O. For thousands of companies and millions of employee-owners, however, the path that has been lighted by the companies described here and many others will lead to more productive companies and fuller, richer lives.

5 Employee Ownership and Community Economic Development

Lauren Segarra

In the early 1970s, Roberts, Day, and Marshall counties were among the most depressed communities in South Dakota with unemployment hovering around 30 percent. One evening George Whyte was agonizing over the fall in the price of pork, which left his family, along with his neighbors, with a barnyard full of unprofitable swine. As Whyte fell into a gloom, he noticed his wife quietly crafting fabric, as she did most evenings. What began as an impulse turned into one of the finest examples of rural renewal ever witnessed. Because many of the local residents possessed the same impressive sewing skills, Whyte decided to organize a cooperative to produce and market local crafts.

An initial loan of $25,000 from the local community development corporation and $16,000 from church organizations was the only funding provided. Local civic clubs donated facilities and sewing machines. Meetings were held in surrounding communities. Samples of the residents' production were collected. The biggest job ahead for Whyte was to find buyers. Most contractors rejected the products, but one store placed a large order that got the company started. Workers volunteered day and night to meet the deadline, and the merchandise was well received. Workers sacrificed wages for eight months and then, living on minimum wage, put forty cents of each hour's pay back into the business. Initially, the business was structured as a worker cooperative, allowing each employee-owner to vote his or her share equally.

Today Dakotah, Inc., employs 320 people, and its sales for 1989 were $17.7 million. The business is a leading manufacturer of home furnishings, concentrating on bed coverings and decorative pillows. Dakotah's products are sold in department stores, through catalogs, and in design studios nationwide. A combination of handcrafted appliqué and computerized quilting machines helps the company maintain a competitive edge.

The growth has required several changes in structure over the years. Vice-President of Finance Terry Sampson feels that the cooperative structure was a good way to begin, but Dakotah, Inc., now offers employees ownership through an employee stock purchase plan. No single employee may own more than 5 percent of the company, and employees may purchase one share for every ten hours of service per year. The company has consolidated its seven facilities into four so as to oversee operations more effectively.

Workplace democracy is still an integral part of the company's operation, providing employee-owners with leadership skills and control over one of the most important aspects of their lives— their work.

In a free market economy, there are many opportunities for innovation, the best products and services will supposedly be produced to meet the needs, and individuals are given an opportunity to better themselves. Although this kind of economy works efficiently, there are obvious inequities resulting from fluctuations in the market and changes in industry, as well as race, class, gender, and other social issues. Private and public agencies are created to help alleviate these imbalances as well as to provide public services that a free market economy does not. In addition, state and municipal government agencies work to promote local economies that can provide jobs and opportunities for their citizens.

Every city, county, and region in America has one if not many economic development agencies. The goals of these agencies vary, based on differing views of what economic development is and what constitutes a successful program. Some seek to use real estate constructively; others are more interested in business development, regardless of how many jobs are created, who holds them, or who owns the businesses. Often the main function of such an entity is to create more jobs and maintain full employment. Some economic development agencies seek to retrain workers as the economy shifts and to train the disadvantaged, although this function is often administered by a separate agency such as the Department of Education. Others use downtown development to stimulate neighborhood economies.

Many of the policies endorsed at any given time reflect the political and economic realities of the nation as a whole. In the 1950s, government programs were adopted as a way to start over after World War II. A common development technique was slum clearance. Government grants were made available to develop public buildings, commercial centers, and better housing for the poor in place of deteriorated buildings. In the early 1960s, the era of community organizing and the civil rights movement, this technique was opposed because it destroyed neighborhoods and small businesses and evicted the poor. From that point on, clearance occurred more on commercial and industrial sites than in residential neighborhoods.[1]

In the late 1960s and early 1970s the model cities program was begun, resulting in a concentration of federal resources in target areas. By the 1970s, neighborhood rehabilitation became central to economic development policy. Although the intention was to assist declining urban areas, the result was often that block grant funds went to suburbs that needed the funding the least.[2]

In the early 1980s, public funds were commonly used to finance private enterprise development in the hope of creating more jobs. Oakland, California, for example, established such a public-private partnership by creating a consortium of thirty local corporations that became partners in a new hotel development. An Urban Development Action Grant covered 12.5 percent of the development costs. Oakland is considered to have been successful in realizing its goals of job creation for youth through this project, but there is little evidence that new jobs were created. Such ventures typically result in an expansion of office or retail space and an increase in space per employee but not an increase in the total number of jobs.[3] In addition, many academics and economists feel that there has been a lack of attention to job quality in the past few decades, resulting in many minimum-wage, dead-end jobs.

In the mid-1980s emphasis was placed on self-help and profit-making development agencies because aid to cities and nonmetropolitan communities had been cut as a result of the deficit and the probusiness Reagan administration as well as frustration with bureaucratic public programs that too often take benefits away or offer too few benefits.

Reaganomics also brought in the policy of government stepping aside to let business take its course. In this vein, during the 1980s the policy of offering incentives to job-creating companies began to replace the policy of offering direct subsidies to public programs. For example, although there has been no federal legislation passed for enterprise zones, many states have been actively promoting the policy. Enterprise zones remove government obstacles and other disincentives that affect private enterprise while providing tax incentives for companies to locate in target areas, thus creating new jobs for local residents, increasing tax revenue, and building neighborhood businesses.[4] Enterprise zones are popular with some liberals because they see the policy as a way of rewarding positive social action. One key problem with enterprise zones and with other tax incentives is that the more there are, the less effective they are. In addition, most companies hiring the disadvantaged have only low-skill jobs to offer and make little use of training programs. Companies can fit themselves into any given loophole without creating long-term social change.

One of the most common development methods over the last three decades has been to attempt to lure new, expanding, or relocating employers from other areas. This tactic generally does not create more businesses for the American economy but simply shifts jobs from one place to another.[5] This policy is now in disrepute as the focus has gone from attracting outside employers, to expanding and retaining existing businesses, to the now popular notion of enhancing the climate for entrepreneurship through business development.

Many economic development agencies have tinkered with existing policies, bringing about seemingly innovative policies and reforms. Some have diversified pension fund investments so as to help the state grow. Others have used tax reform to close unproductive loopholes or to revise the inheritance tax.[6] And, of course, welfare reform has been toyed with since its inception.

Aside from small changes in combining public assistance with job placement, career assessment, and on-the-job training with subsidies going to employers, little has changed except for the continual ballooning of the welfare rolls. Virtually all the incentives encourage recipients to remain dependent because they are cut off from those benefits as soon as their assets reach a minimal level and any jobs available are usually dead-end jobs. Some state welfare programs, such as the one in Massachusetts, maintain child care and health care when a parent takes a job, but programs such as this one are in the experimental stages. In this era of lessened support for public assistance, fewer and fewer benefits are combined with the requirement that recipients earn the benefits by participating in programs such as "workfare," and unfortunately, the work requirement is often not backed up by job training or placement.

Even the best economic development systems do not do a great deal for the poor. Although economic development can contribute to a local economy, it sometimes displaces residents in development areas or provides jobs not well suited to the skills of low-income people. The classic example of this is Atlantic City, where economic development brought in casinos and resorts but provided few jobs for the desperately poor people of the city. Tourism is a fickle industry that is extremely vulnerable to shifts in the economy and offers mostly part-time, low-quality jobs to residents. Even so, tourism continues to be a popular development strategy in every state in America. Even grants or subsidies designed to encourage businesses to locate in poor areas usually expose the weaknesses of simple job-creation programs by resulting in minimum wage jobs, with ownership outside the community. Furthermore, most of those on welfare are so far removed from the opportunities available in the mainstream economy that no matter how many jobs the economy creates, those on public assistance are not significantly affected.

Community development agencies, as opposed to other economic development organizations, are locally controlled and centered and have traditionally focused on providing social services and housing, establishing training programs to help the unskilled become desirable employees, and organizing members of the low-income community to help themselves. Typically, the social services provided are too piecemeal to have an effect.

The 1980s gave birth to a plethora of community development corporations (CDCs). CDCs concentrate on mobilizing investment capital from public and private sources as well as providing technical assistance to deteriorating communities. Members of CDCs are usually local residents who elect a board of directors. Members do not get direct financial gain from the CDC, but they benefit indirectly from the community's overall economic development. In some cities, CDCs have greatly affected housing rehabilitation and the economic stabilization of neighborhoods. They have had less impact on the formation of viable businesses, but this situation may be changing as these agencies are becoming more sophisticated in the field of business development.[7] For instance, the Northern Community Investment Corporation of Vermont developed more than $13.5 million worth of real estate and invested in more than 165 businesses.[8] Unfortunately, community development corporations do not change the patterns of private investment but merely substitute for that investment. For these organizations to succeed, government or philanthropists must invest in them heavily, and they must develop businesses and real estate tied into the mainstream economy. CDCs are primarily concerned with social services and view employee ownership as a long-term, theoretical goal far removed from the problems they encounter on a daily basis. CDCs are generally content to achieve a business presence, regardless of who owns those businesses, and continue to focus primarily on housing development.

Over the past few years, both economic and community development agencies have begun to reassess their tactics and priorities. The reasons for this reassessment are that development programs are vulnerable to shifts in the economy and public policy, funds have been seriously cut in the past decade, and none of the past policies have really worked to bring the disadvantaged into the mainstream economy. The value of antipoverty programs is in question; most of them are based on the trickle-down theory and transfer payments. A large percentage of the funds that trickle down are spent on administration and do not fundamentally change patterns of control and ownership. More important, these dollars too often fail to reach the poorest areas. Transfer payments have only marginally affected poverty in the United States. Billions of taxpayers' dollars are being spent on conventional antipoverty and development programs, which, even under the best of circumstances, leave core problems unsolved. Poverty and the skewed distribution of wealth and control remain relatively unchanged in one of the wealthiest and certainly most capable of countries.

Those working in community development are divided in their approach. Many have responded to fiscal uncertainty by focusing on short-term goals and objectives. Others have begun to focus on programs that offer more permanent value and a larger return on investment by attempting to develop home-grown, self-reliant communities.

Veterans in the field of economic development might see a theoretical model of progression as moving from transfer payments, to jobs with earned wages, to partial ownership of the company. One of the goals of community economic development should be to speed up this process. As the disadvantaged participate in the economy more fully as both workers and owners, they become less vulnerable and increase their control and contribution to the economy. Employee ownership fits in with the traditional goals of development agencies but is superior in that it is a permanent, long-term solution, not a band-aid.

Until the early 1980s, few states were responsive to employees' efforts to buy companies, even when such a buyout might have saved jobs. But by the mid-1980s, several state governments had developed proactive strategies of education and outreach to help employees respond to potential business closings. These state employee ownership programs will be discussed later in the chapter.

Some community economic development agencies are also beginning to focus on developing businesses in their local communities which will seek to employ citizens of varying income levels. These tactics are just starting to come of age, and in some cases, they have incorporated employee ownership. Although there are fewer than fifty employee ownership community development ventures, this figure is not small relative to the business start-ups that have been achieved through community economic development efforts as a whole. Furthermore, of the thirty cases studied by the NCEO, only three have failed and the remainder are either surviving or expanding.

Of course, there are serious obstacles to overcome when combining a business start-up with employee ownership, participation, and a disadvantaged work force. Although most of the employee ownership companies that started as community development efforts are still in business, many efforts to achieve an employee-owned company employing low-income people have failed. Though each element in the employee ownership process involves certain obstacles, those employed and the community as a whole can benefit when ownership, participation, and a disadvantaged work force are incorporated into the business venture. In addition, as more of these ventures are attempted, managers and developers are beginning to understand how to make such efforts succeed. In the 1980s there was a surge of innovation and experimentation, resulting in some of the first community development strategies that offer communities true self-reliance and a chance to bring the disadvantaged into the mainstream economy.

This chapter explores the use of employee ownership as a community economic development tool. It also explores ways in which successful employee ownership community ventures have been developed so as to reduce the risks and offset the obstacles. The successes have not come about without great struggle. Nevertheless, ownership must be promoted at the grass-roots level—ownership of labor, land, and capital—if citizens are to have more control over their communities and the poor are to have any chance of achieving self-reliance, economic development, and prosperity.

Employee Ownership as a Community Development Strategy

Studies have shown that as much as 75 to 90 percent of the income generated from chains such as MacDonald's or Safeway leaves the community in which the store is located.[9] A successful community development program would encourage companies to create jobs for low-income residents, pay livable wages, provide decent working conditions, and offer needed products or services. Outside capital would be sought, and local capital would be retained within the community.

Community development agencies face the added challenges of limited assets and organizational expertise, limited capital and start-up funding, the limited skills and low self-image of a low-income work force, and the need to create the maximum number of jobs per venture. And if a healthy commercial sector does not exist, the obstacles increase.

Employee ownership achieves many of the goals of a successful community development program. Employee ownership offers many benefits to the community at large, businesses, and individual employees. For the community, employee ownership anchors capital and retains jobs because employee ownership companies are unlikely to be sold. Companies that would be sold to outside investors can be sold to employees using pretax company earnings rather than after-tax employee earnings. Employee ownership, properly implemented, enhances corporate performance. Not only are more jobs and growth created than by conventional companies, but the community in which the company is located enjoys a broader tax base. Employee ownership promotes the distribution of wealth and decentralizes economic control, giving communities greater control of the direction of assets. Businesses attract and retain the best talent and enjoy low turnover, and managers can share some of the burdens of ownership while the company reaps tax benefits.

Government organizations can use employee ownership to create more growth and jobs, rather than shift jobs away from another community to their own. The broadened tax base from these companies can be used for other productive purposes. Employee ownership can also be used to save companies that would otherwise close. Some companies are apparently sold not because they are failing but because they are not providing as much return as stockholders would like. Employee-owners tend to be more patient stockholders. Employee ownership offers employees a reason to stay with a company, more chance to upgrade skills, and increased economic security. And, of course, individual employees have the opportunity to join the ranks of capitalists.

Employee ownership can even help break the cycles of poverty in migrant agricultural and reservation communities. With foundation assistance and the help of local volunteers, migrant workers in Indiantown, Florida, developed a cut-and-sew cooperative to create stable employment and a home base for their children. More than two hundred volunteers helped with marketing and transportation.

In Apopka, Florida, the Office of Farmworker Ministry (OFM) used cooperative programs to stabilize and increase employment and wages. Since the early 1970s, OFM has started a health care center, a housing program, and a workers' association composed of black, Hispanic, and Haitian farmworkers. By providing services to its members, the association helped them launch their own businesses. PEP Labor Crews, Inc., was the first cooperative started. By contracting with growers to buy their crops, harvest them, and sell to the juice plants in the area, members receive 20 percent more in wages than they did under the traditional contract system. PEP has formed several harvesting cooperatives around the country.

In short, employee ownership can help keep communities self-reliant, stable, and strong. Employee ownership provides local residents with something of permanent, local value, not quick-fix operations that ultimately make little difference.

Why Is Employee Ownership Uncommon among the Low-Income Population?

Employee ownership ventures are rare among the low-income population because of the nature of development programs, the characteristics of the population, and our society's present value system. Business development is just beginning to be accepted as a community development strategy. Many community development professionals believe it is philosophically wrong to develop businesses rather than social services. They see such activity as a sellout. In some instances, agencies have very strict agendas (e.g., they can only produce housing) that are dictated by financial support or law. In addition, business development requires a great deal of time, risk, and work. All businesses, employee-owned or not, low-income or not, take a long time to produce results. Education among community developers and increased flexibility for government programs are two ingredients necessary for increasing the number of employee ownership businesses.

Some development agencies are leery of employee ownership because they have been involved with an employee buyout of a troubled company that did not succeed. Many people think it is unrealistic to expect workers who lack skills to succeed as owners of a business that has been tagged as unprofitable by a professional manager. In some cases, however, the parent company may feel profits are too low, or a company with good products and markets may be temporarily weakened by poor management. Employee buyouts can save some troubled companies, provided the market essentials are in place and there is sound management to lead the company. Employee buyouts are not always a cure, however, and they will work in only a small minority of company closing situations.

The characteristics associated with a disadvantaged population also can create difficulty for a general business start-up, not to mention an employee ownership venture. For one, members of a low-income population often lack the skills and education required in a traditional industry environment. This severely limits the venture opportunities available, even if training programs are provided. Because many of our nation's poor are from other countries, they are likely to face language barriers. And for those whose entire lives have been spent in poverty, mental barriers such as low self-esteem and depression are to be expected. In addition, the transience that can accompany poverty causes obvious problems when considering the long-term aspects of ownership. Even if individuals are rooted in a community, it is difficult for someone struggling financially to sacrifice money now for money later or even to believe in the concept of investment.

Perhaps most important, the current values of American society are not conducive to encouraging people to work as managers and technical assistance providers for a community business. In obtaining information for this chapter, the National Center for Employee Ownership interviewed members of employee ownership community businesses. The one issue that continually arose was the extreme difficulty of finding qualified managers who are committed to the goals and needs of a low-income community.

To understand the tasks facing those who are creating a community-based employee ownership venture, it is helpful to consider some of the problems business developers face.

Every new business, regardless of available financial and human resources, must be able to operate competitively and pursue a viable business concept that has a demonstrated market. Many entrepreneurs conduct financial and market analyses. This may be as simple as looking in a phone book and talking to suppliers to determine the nature of the competition and whether the business will be able to capture a share of the market. Those involved in the business must be committed to facing the struggles ahead and must have or be able to develop the skills, knowledge, and characteristics required for the specific industry chosen. There must be a strong planning component with fiscal and operational systems that can maximize profits and ensure self-sufficiency. And if capital is not available, it must be possible to sell the idea to a private investor, a venture capitalist, or another source of initial funding.

An estimated 80 percent of all small businesses fail within three years of start-up. Although most of these are one- or two-person operations, often formed "on the side," this is still a dismal statistic, especially when one considers the additional problems associated with a disadvantaged work force with few skills, scarce capital, and few institutions willing to offer services. The capacity to build a community, the strengths found in existing community resources, and the inherent advantages of employee ownership and participation, however, can help offset these barriers.

Organizers, managers, and those providing support face tremendous obstacles in pursuing an employee ownership venture designed to assist the disadvantaged. What follows is an examination of how some organizations have met these challenges and some have not.

Issues for Developing Community Businesses

Building Community

Building a sense of community among the workers if one does not already exist can help people accept the greater risks and challenges of starting a business and give them the incentive to work hard. When people can identify with a larger purpose than their own immediate self-interest, this commitment is likely to increase. The extreme sense of individualism in American culture and the absence of identification with other members of the community, even among immediate family members in many cases, makes this difficult. One of the most powerful assets of the famous Mondragón cooperatives (see chapter 6) is the Basques' strong sense of identification with one another. In the United States, however, it is difficult to create businesses for just one ethnic group, even if doing so might have advantages. Legally, however, only a nonprofit organization could practice this form of discrimination. Still, many local communities are ethnically homogeneous, and though employers cannot hire only from certain groups, that may be the practical outcome. Even without this homogeneity, companies can still create a strong sense of common purpose, based primarily on the desire to succeed.

Manos Development Corporation, Inc., of Oakland, California, is a nonprofit umbrella organization for several community businesses, most of which are cooperatives. Although Manos is designed to serve the Hispanic community, Manos Home Health Care, a subsidiary, is open to any ethnic group. Currently, the home health care co-op is recruiting workers from an Ethiopian community center and the Greek Orthodox church of Oakland. Most immigrant populations are very tightly knit, and managers find that a networking effect develops once they have tapped into a community. The outcome is that a host of workers show an interest in the business.

Balancing Social and Business Goals

Community developers are much more concerned with the overall welfare of the community than are traditional businesses. In addition to providing as many good jobs as possible for a low-income constituency, community developers seek to provide high-quality, beneficial services while encouraging human development. There is an ever-present danger, however, that managers and organizers will be distracted from the goal of providing jobs and developing a successful business by other urgent needs. Kevin Rath, executive director of Manos, said, "Once we have satisfied the need for jobs I can go on to the next issue. So far we have not gotten to that point."[10]

Some managers have met the challenge of balancing business and social goals by offering socially useful products and services or by employing traditionally disadvantaged but employable workers. Trying to meet these nonfinancial goals can make success harder but not impossible.

Cooperative Home Health Care Associates (CHHC), a home health care cooperative located in the Bronx, New York, is an example of a community business that achieves social goals while providing a large number of jobs for a low-income population. Currently, two hundred workers, most of them black or Hispanic, provide high-quality, personalized service for the elderly and handicapped. Not only is the business flourishing, but it is actually driving up wages in New York City's health care industry.

The diocese's Employment Development Office of Pittsburgh, Pennsylvania, is working with the Order of Capuchins to establish local employee ownership businesses that employ the handicapped. The organization is focusing on bringing robotics into the work environment to assist such ventures. So far, a print shop has been established, employing nine people, one of whom is confined to a wheelchair.

A Viable Business Concept

One way to launch a viable business while reducing the risk is to start it within the context of a development agency. The agency can look at its own needs as a possible avenue for the venture or use existing ventures to subsidize new ones. For example, building management services can be started and then expanded to the outside market, or existing social service programs can be converted to self-sufficient and profitable ventures. Possibilities include home health care, day care, nutrition programs, housing rehabilitation, and weatherization services.

Cindy Coker, a former day care administrator, left her position at the Philadelphia Association for Cooperative Enterprise (PACE), an organization that provides technical assistance for employee buyouts and worker cooperatives, to set up a worker cooperative day care center in 1988. The Adrian Dominican Sisters' Loan Fund in Adrian, Michigan, provided a low-interest loan of $15,000, and the initial owners provided equity through cash and payroll deductions. By establishing a nonprofit affiliate to the cooperative, Coker was able to keep fees down and the quality of care high. The nonprofit affiliate also provides the leverage to raise scholarship funds for families unable to pay, thereby encouraging a mixed clientele. Today, one hundred children attend the day care center in Philadelphia, and all fifteen employees will be owners by the end of the year, when their probationary period is up.

Other venture opportunities exist outside the development agency. Markets can be developed by determining what businesses already exist and how they can be serviced. Existing businesses can be acquired with the assistance of local development organizations and foundations. Some economic development groups conduct studies of an area's economy and plans for revitalization. Although a community development venture normally is designed to keep capital within the local community, both national and local markets can be considered.

In this age of high demand for information and services, as well as direct mail marketing, several possibilities exist. The Watermark Association of Artisans, in Elizabeth City, North Carolina, is a worker cooperative that was established to combat the high unemployment in the area. The craft cooperative recruited women from hunger and battered women's shelters as well as other social service agencies. In the past few years, Watermark has sold most of its crafts by direct mail. The catalog, mailed to three thousand wholesalers, resulted in $150,000 in business in 1988 alone. Watermark sells its crafts in five hundred stores nationally, including J. C. Penney, Neiman Marcus, and Hallmark.

Employee ownership businesses can also use traditional, established companies as a marketing base. Workers Owned Sewing Company was the result of a buyout of a bankrupt sewing plant in Windsor, North Carolina. Twenty-five of the former workers and other members of the community bought the machinery for $15,000 and started a new company. Within three years the cooperative began manufacturing for K-Mart and Sears. The manager gradually sold shares to the workers at $100 each by withholding $2 to $5 from their weekly paychecks.

Keeping in mind that in most cases the customers are outside the low-income community, the possibilities expand further. Manos has established its businesses near communities where the residents can afford services such as home health care, landscaping, and housecleaning. Manos is one of the most successful community development organizations, and it carefully examines every aspect of any new venture. Its requisites include the largest number of jobs created for the least amount of start-up capital, a service industry, entry-level jobs with good pay and benefits to begin with, an easy business to learn, a job ladder, training in leadership skills, and promotion from within.

Rick Surpin, manager of CHHC, says that the home health care business was the Community Service Society's (CSS) only successful attempt at establishing an employee ownership business. Careful planning, a clear and slow transition to employee ownership, and the pure luck of hitting the market at the right time, are some of the elements that enabled CHHC to compete. The co-op has grown from ten to two hundred employees and is financially sound.

An example of a market study that failed is the O&O Market, which opened in the Strawberry Mansion section of Philadelphia. Several worker-owned O&O (for Owned and Operated) supermarkets had been established as a response to A&P store closings in the early 1980s. The Strawberry Mansion O&O was a new store built from the ground up in a low-income area. Projections were too optimistic, however, and even though an experienced store manager was hired from the outside, untrained employee-owners provided input into daily operations. The stores that had opened earlier had an established shopping pattern of former A&P shoppers, which not only resumed but increased after the first O&O stores reopened as employee ownership businesses. This was not the case in Strawberry Mansion.

Sometimes the best markets are not the most obvious ones. Suella Kobak, a lawyer and community organizer, noted that St. Charles, West Virginia, had an availability of hardwoods and carpentry and sewing skills. She suggested that employees pursue a casket factory. The workers had their minds set on a sewing factory, however, which is now in operation and wholly owned by St. Charles Enterprises Development Corporation. All profits go to increasing salaries and benefits as well as other development activities such as a laundromat business, which is currently in the development stages.

Managerial Commitment and Skills

Community businesses can fill many needs, but they require tremendous organizing, training, and managerial skills. Such enterprises offer low pay in a risky and often unprestigious environment. Finding managers who are qualified yet subscribe to the values and goals of the low-income constituency is perhaps the most difficult aspect of seeing a community business venture to fruition. An alternative to hiring qualified management from the outside is training and promoting individuals from within. Still, this avenue requires that community organizers or temporary managers identify and encourage potential leadership.

Manos is taking the time to try to promote leadership from within in its temporary services division. Because current managers of Manos are shifting their responsibilities to the new home health care business, Manos needs workers to step in and fill the management gap. In the past, Manos promoted a worker to take on the responsibilities of fund-raising. This did not work because she did not have the required skills. Now management is considering promoting two women members to handle job placement. Management has no qualms about firing workers or asking them to move on if they do not work out. Although some people think business ability may not be as rare in low-income communities as is popularly believed, management training, experience, and job-specific skills—let alone good contacts—are rare. Developing people in-house has been a difficult challenge. There is a double-edged sword in filling management positions: does the business take the chance of promoting people from within and take a risk on their abilities, or does the organization hire managers from outside the organization who will have to learn the business, may not identify with the workers, and may become discouraged with the salary offered?

A long history of poverty can cause people to lose heart if success does not come quickly, and success is rarely instant with any start-up. For this reason, it is helpful if a talented organizer or manager can step in and provide the framework, objectivity, long-sightedness, and faith in the other members. Most rare, yet most useful, are managers who are committed to the goals of the community and are able to work with people from a variety of income levels and ethnic groups. Asian Immigrant Women Advocates (AIWA) is a community development agency launching a potsticker cooperative in Oakland, California. (Potstickers are an Asian hors d'oeuvre.) Recognizing the importance of hiring a manager who is sympathetic to the needs and goals of the cooperative members, AIWA has been searching up and down the Pacific coast to find a talented manager who speaks both Korean and English.

Community businesses are often developed by activists who learn as they go. Many of those running community businesses are social workers, priests, and academics who do not have entrepreneurial experience or orientation. Commitment to the ideals and needs of the disadvantaged is important, but no business will succeed without competent management. These problems are heightened by the overall values of our society. We live in a world that commands top dollar for business talent that will be used to promote junk bonds, junk food, and junk mail, while the basic needs of many people go unmet. Given the social mores of today, nonmonetary rewards are usually not enough to encourage many individuals to run enterprises dedicated to assisting the disadvantaged.

One business that met this challenge is Watermark. The cooperative now grosses $250,000 per year, but it is not far removed from the days when the organization was $60,000 in debt and had 60 members who worked out of a former railroad station. Today, Watermark has 450 members, most of them low-income women. The organization is successful largely because Carolyn McKecuen, a self-taught entrepreneur, believed in the cooperative's members and the potential of the business. When she first took over, she joined her husband on his business trips to New York City. With boxes of goods in hand, she sought buyers. Impressed retailers placed $2,500 in orders, putting the cooperative on its feet. Today, the most active producers earn $10,000 to $15,000 per year in a region where the income averages between $7,000 and $8,500.

Lemoine Davis, a former high school psychologist and current manager of Blue Dot Energy Company, Inc., a construction cooperative in Junction City, Kansas, feels that the business can be truly successful with just three qualified managers overseeing office management, job management, and personnel, although it has not reached this stage yet. He is aware of the difficulty in finding managers who are sympathetic to the needs of members and believe in the value of a cooperative workplace. Although he and others have learned from mistakes, they recognize that they will still hire some management personnel who are unsuitable for their purpose. Some are sincere at first and later become more narrowly focused on making money. But, he asserts, the cooperative structure eliminates these people within two or three years, before they become too costly. He suggests that the better a cooperative is structured, the better chance there is of hiring the right managers. Blue Dot's method has been to advertise with other cooperatives, universities with construction science programs, and in magazines with a commitment to social issues.

Rick Surpin had to leave his job as a cooperative organizer with the Community Service Society because Cooperative Home Health Care Associates could not find qualified management. CSS was a large, private New York City social service agency. It started a project to develop a series of worker-owned businesses for low-income people in the early 1980s. Several were attempted, but only CHHC has succeeded in getting off the ground. Surpin observes how difficult it is to find someone who has talents in both the operations and marketing aspects of business. Most larger businesses solve the problem by hiring people for each specific area. Not only do the managers of a small community business have to wear many hats, but they must also bridge the class differences that usually exist between managers and workers. A former Fortune 500 executive who had been laid off was brought in to manage a construction cooperative the Community Service Society was assisting. Although he had excellent administrative skills, he had no respect for the workers. After years of experience in community development, Surpin has noticed that although individuals can learn a great many technical skills in a relatively short period of time, they cannot quickly learn community values or how to work with people effectively.

The Center for Community Self-Help (CCSH), a financing and development organization in Durham, North Carolina, has explored various ways of attracting sympathetic, qualified management over the years. In addition, CCSH has helped start a number of worker-, consumer-, and community-owned enterprises. Members from the organization are finding that social entrepreneurs, ranging from executives of Fortune 500 companies to individuals who have acquired experience in a variety of small businesses, are interested in fulfilling their activist ideals.

After eighteen months of searching, CCSH found several executives who were interested in the concepts of employee ownership and participation and eager to try something new or to escape the bureaucracy of their old firms. The key problem was placing them in both the industry of their expertise and their preferred geographical location.

To bridge the gap between general managers and workers resulting from class, race, or issues of participation, the CCSH relies on an extensive yet informal network of consultants to assist its efforts on a case-by-case basis. In contrast, PACE is more successful when it hires people with strong organizational development skills and trains future managers in substantive areas.

Developing Business Skills

The goals of employing disadvantaged people do not always coincide with the skills these people have to offer. One of the problems facing these companies, therefore, is to develop adequate training programs, often relying on public support to pay for them. St. Charles Enterprises has begun preemployment training for sixty women through a local college that offers twenty-five hours of training in the areas of motivation, teamwork, math, and sewing skills. Those who pass the course will become employees of the cut-and-sew cooperative. In addition, the business will try to develop child care and housing divisions.

Issues for Developing Employee Ownership Businesses

Ownership Structure

Employee ownership adds a barrage of issues to any business. It is usually a new concept for people and, for this reason, ownership principles and structures work best if they are designed to fit the prevailing culture and values.

In some instances, direct ownership may not be appropriate. For example, Dungannon Sewing Cooperative, located in Dungannon, Virginia, was undercapitalized, mismanaged, and losing money. The business closed after one year of operation. The board did not want to abandon the idea of worker ownership or the idea of the company being responsive to the needs of the community but felt that employee control led to mismanagement. The employee-owners lacked skills and understanding of the structure of cooperatives, people in leadership positions did not know how to use their power, and politics divided the membership. Education and training might have saved this cooperative, but Dungannon's board and employee-owners demanded a new structure. The community's priority was the creation of jobs because Dungannon, formerly a mining community, is one of the poorest communities in West Virginia, with 60 percent of its residents dependent on public assistance.

Dungannon was reopened as a community business in the literal sense. It is the subsidiary of a nonprofit company whose business activities are inspired by social objectives. Employees and other community residents are represented on the board, and the management structure is one of shared decision making. As a community-owned venture, profits are retained within the business but are not distributed to individual accounts, as in a cooperative. Although the workers do not own shares, they share in control of the direction of profits for the business as well as their other community interests. If the business proves stable and profitable, there is a strong possibility that it will be sold to the employees over time through conversion to an ESOP or will go back to being a worker cooperative. This strategy minimized the risk for individual residents, enabled the business to grow, and provided higher salaries for workers.

The reverse can also offer advantages. Employee ownership businesses can establish nonprofit development organizations to obtain grants for all facets of operation other than labor. This allows them to obtain the administration, consultation, and training they need to stay competitive while offering jobs to the disadvantaged. Blue Dot Energy Company, Inc., like other competitive cooperatives, established a nonprofit business to build shelters for the homeless and to provide other community services that would be in conflict with its for-profit activities. Kansas State University, through its departments of business and construction science, trains employees in leadership, the structure of cooperatives, and the specific skills required for the construction industry. The Job Employment Training Act pays half the workers' salaries while they are in training.

Similarly, Watermark's manager Carolyn McKecuen developed the Northeastern Education Development Foundation (NEED) to serve as a nonprofit training organization for the co-op. Classes are offered in craftmaking, and some members learn to make as many as fifty different products in order to increase their marketability. In addition to training in craftmaking, NEED offers classes in the principles of cooperatives, quality control, design, basic business and finance, taxes and record keeping, self-assertion, and other life skills.

It is possible to structure an ESOP democratically, allowing each employee-owner an equal vote. These ESOP companies are rare, but they do exist and can work well. In 1986, Levi Strauss closed its Tyler, Texas, manufacturing facility, leaving more than five hundred employees, most of them minority women, without jobs. The company closed as part of an effort to consolidate production and streamline manufacturing capacity. After the announcement, union leaders began raising money for a feasibility study for an employee buyout. The community, including Levi Strauss, pledged financial support.

A favorable feasibility study led to reopening the plant as Colt Enterprises, Inc., hiring plant management, and obtaining contracts. Union officials and employee leaders then began educating employees in the culture of employee ownership. Over the next few years, a democratic structure evolved. The board of directors consists of three employee-owners, three members of the professional and business community, and one international representative. Each worker has one vote on all issues. Employee-owners participate in decision making through informal quality circles and by attending meetings with management and union leaders to discuss the company's overall situation.

Despite the structure, productivity at Colt has been poor. Management blames workers for a lack of interest; workers say managers are not interested in their input. Because of these problems, Colt has had severe financial trouble, although it has managed to hang on. By contrast, the Center for Community Self-Help used a democratic ESOP to buy Ragan Thornton Mills in Thomasville, North Carolina, and that company has done well.

Democracy—More Than Just Participation

Although cooperatives are only slightly different in legal structure, they are run on an entirely different set of assumptions than other forms of employee ownership. Under traditional capitalism, profits are made by a select few. The cooperative model encourages individuals to work together to maximize the economic and social interests of everyone.

Some cooperatives have learned the hard way that it is difficult, if not impossible, for members to make every decision together. Many cooperatives progress from pure democracy to the delegation of powers and representative democracy. It is possible to delegate day-to-day management responsibilities while maintaining an overall democratic governance structure and a high level of employee involvement in job-level decision making. For example, at the O&O Market, every worker serves on standing and ad hoc committees. Members elect the board of directors on a one-member, one-vote basis and have a great deal of autonomy on the job, but management oversees and controls general operations.

One case in which a nonhierarchical structure was a key factor that led to the demise of a cooperative is International Poultry, which operated in Willamantic, Connecticut. Authority was so widely diffused throughout the membership and board of directors that the board was reluctant to act without consulting the entire work force. In addition, no single manager had authority over the others, making it difficult to coordinate decision making and leading to conflicts. The process proved too cumbersome, and the business closed within two years of starting.

In the short term it is difficult to weigh the benefits of democratic control against the benefits of more traditional management in employee ownership development efforts. The typical cooperative venture provides only ten to twenty jobs and can be relatively unstable. Decision making and training take a great deal of time. And though cooperatives offer their members a chance for control, skills development, and stable employment, limited return on investment may not suit all employee-owners. By contrast, companies that become employee-owned through the sale of an existing business to a more traditional ESOP structure can pose less risk and offer more jobs.

Alaska Commercial Company became 33 percent employee-owned when the nonprofit Community Enterprise Development Corporation of Alaska decided to set up an ESOP. The retail company employs 470 people and increased sales from $9 million to $55 million since the ESOP was begun. At least half the employees and 20 percent of the managers of the company are native Alaskans.

Similarly, Wyatt Cafeterias, an ESOP restaurant chain headquartered in Dallas, Texas, employs 6,500 people, most of whom would never have any other opportunity to acquire a significant stake in capital other than through the ESOP. Wyatt was not a result of any development agency's efforts. It was a successful business going through a normal ESOP sale. Its employees will not run the company, but they will have much more of a say in their work than before. What is notable about Wyatt is that through the more traditional ESOP method, it provides ownership opportunities to more low-income people than all the employee ownership economic development companies described here combined. It is, of course, not the only ESOP company to do so.

Access to Capital

It is always very difficult to convince banks or any other private lending source to lend to start-up enterprises. That difficulty is compounded if the initiators are low-income and further compounded if they want to use a cooperative business structure. Lending institutions are not skeptical of employee ownership per se, but some are wary of lending to any democratically managed employee ownership business because of a perception that management controls will not be adequate. In addition, most loan funds for community development activities are authorized to extend credit only to established ventures, not start-ups. There are, however, several ways to secure financing for low-income business ventures. Some grants are tagged specifically for employee ownership ventures. A variety of foundations and churches offer high-risk capital at favorable or no-interest rates. The National Campaign for Human Development in Washington, D.C., and the Irvine Foundation in New York frequently fund low-income ventures that seek to make their workers owners.

One of the more dramatic success stories in developing funding for employee ownership businesses targeted to low-income people is the Center for Community Self-Help. When CCSH was trying to help 450 workers buy a family-owned furniture manufacturing company, conventional lenders were willing to put up 75 percent of the money needed to buy out the firm. The center could not raise equity money for the bid, however, so the firm was sold to another bidder. The center realized it had to create its own capital pool to avoid such situations in the future. A combination of low-interest loans and grants from churches and private foundations was earmarked for employee buyouts in 1984 to help meet such needs. The Englewood Investment Corporation and the Self-Help Ventures Fund have equity capital totaling $3 million. Together they provide secured loans to employee ownership businesses, moderate and low-income housing efforts, and democratic nonprofit organizations. These special sources of financing greatly increased CCSH's success rate with community ventures.

Other special credit sources for employee ownership enterprises exist as well, such as the Industrial Cooperative Association Revolving Loan Fund in Somerville, Massachusetts, and the National Cooperative Bank in Washington, D.C. In addition, legal agencies, credit unions, and suppliers can extend credit and socially responsible investment groups can be encouraged to invest in employee ownership businesses. Often, once a community business is established with support from such an agency, it is easier to obtain funding from conventional sources.

In some cases, the workers can raise the capital themselves. In Emporia, Virginia, when a local sewing plant closed, thirty workers raised $30,000 from their own resources, obtained free technical assistance from a local community college, and started Lucky 13, retaining all the old contracts from the closed plant. The employee-owners paid themselves back in their first year of operation.

Sympathetic private businesses can also provide development support. Much of CCSH's support comes from political conservatives who are attuned to the idea of individuals becoming capitalists and therefore interested in seeing the companies become successful and profitable. This avenue is discussed further later in the chapter.

Several public programs exist to help small businesses acquire capital. Some offer loan guarantees to businesses unable to obtain financing through private sources. In addition, many state programs provide funding for employee ownership ventures, especially in the case of employee buyouts of companies that would otherwise be sold to outside interests. Federal funds might be made more readily available if a particular venture were tied to employee ownership. The concept has long had bipartisan support in Congress. Urban Development action grants, Economic Development Administration loans, private industry councils, small business investment companies, minority enterprises small business investment companies, and community development block grants are among the sources of public assistance. Government agencies can also subsidize the cost of establishing employee ownership plans or contract with consultants to help educate employee-owners about business basics.

The Freedom Quilting Bee, a worker cooperative in Epes, Alabama, employs twenty workers who produce ceramics and sewing items. Dry bedroom goods are sold to boutiques and department stores, including Sears. Now self-sufficient, the cooperative initially received a federal community development block grant to rehabilitate an old building within a housing project to serve as a central office, plant, and day care center.

Credit unions can be invaluable community resources and are more likely than other lending institutions to loan to low-income individuals. The CCSH/Self-Help Credit Union is a state-chartered lender that operates like a traditional bank but with a limited range of services. Individuals and nonprofit organizations open insured savings accounts at interest rates competitive with those offered by local traditional banks, and the deposit funds are used to make loans to low-risk ventures. Traditional banks put up loan loss reserves because the credit union complements the efforts of banks rather than competing with them. Over the past eight years, the credit union has approved more than $20 million worth of loans to low-income groups, 15 to 20 percent of which are employee ownership businesses.

Learning from Failures

Much of the discussion so far has focused on successful efforts to use employee ownership for economic development. But there have been failures, and the lessons they offer are important. Rainbow Cooperative is one example. Ironically, Rainbow had an abundance of technical assistance and capital and was intended to be the showcase of economic development experiments. Instead, it turned into one of the most widely publicized failures in the field of community development.

The painful lessons started in 1984, when rumors began circulating that Sierra Designs' Oakland, California, plant was about to close. With encouragement from the Oakland Plant Closures Project, the parent company, an outdoor equipment manufacturer, agreed to hold a sale to help start a worker cooperative and agreed to become a major customer. Rainbow began with myriad loans, including $200,000 in soft loans, $100,000 in training grants, and $30,000 from the Sierra Designs sale. After a year of operation, however, Rainbow closed.

It is difficult to determine the main reason for the cooperative's demise, but among the problems were a lack of capable management, competition from low-wage sweatshops, and productivity problems. A financial crisis arose when the co-op entered a new market and expanded the work force but could not get high enough prices to support the payroll. An emphasis on cooperation and job creation made it difficult to fire people who did not meet productivity standards. The women in the cooperative represented a variety of ethnic backgrounds, making communication and identification with the company and with each other difficult. Furthermore, the abundance of soft financing and the lack of careful bookkeeping made the financial situation seem better than it was. Any single factor could have led to bankruptcy—the combination ensured it.

One key lesson to be learned from such an experience is repeated in many such development efforts: democratically managed businesses can succeed in the market only if as much emphasis is placed on business as on governance. Jan Gilbrecht, a member of Rainbow's board of directors, wrote in a letter to the editor of *Image*, "For those who had the privilege to know this amazing group of worker-owners, the Rainbow Co-op will live on as a symbol of the courage and hope that can be found when workers come together to fight for control over their lives."[11] Though the spirit of the workers and the community is inspiring, this failure might have been prevented if the business had received as much emphasis as the social goals did.

The Center for Community Self-Help has made a positive impact on North Carolina's economy, but it has had its share of mistakes and failures. In the late 1970s, the founders thought that all that low-income communities needed was capital and opportunity. Reality proved that the riddle of community development was a bit more complex.

When a New Berne, North Carolina, yarn factory closed, putting five hundred people out of work, CCSH stepped in. An initial plan to run the factory as an employee-owned business was replaced with an effort to launch an employee-owned wholesale and retail bakery, employing mostly black women. Although the employee-owners learned a host of new skills and worked for three years, the business eventually failed. Not only was management lacking in supervisory, financial, and marketing experience, but those involved in the business were not willing to market their products aggressively. To do so they would have had to penetrate a white market in the face of racial tension.

In the early years of its existence, the center suffered many such failures by working with buyouts of troubled companies and then assisting ventures with no sure sources of financing. It was not until an internal credit pool was established that the success ratio turned around. CCSH became more selective about the ventures it supported in part because it became a partner. CCSH found it was much easier to support a variety of ventures with technical assistance, and to convince lenders to accept the deal, when the risks were placed outside the organization.

CCSH has also appealed directly to minority entrepreneurs to convert their businesses to partial employee ownership because minorities so desperately need opportunities for ownership. Interestingly, however, minority business owners are not so sympathetic, most likely because they feel they have struggled more than whites and deserve the entirety of the fruits of their labor.

Another example comes from a different part of the country. In 1987, the Concerned Citizen's Coalition in Great Falls, Montana, began developing a plan in conjunction with the Industrial Cooperative Association to build a senior services cooperative with twenty general assistance recipients. The effort failed because the manager did not have sufficient experience and the group as a whole was not businesslike. Jill Storey, the consultant who assisted in the feasibility planning, hesitated to work with the project for these reasons.

Reducing the Risks

Several development agencies that have been involved with employee ownership ventures have learned from their experiences. Staff members at PACE have learned that they are best at converting larger family businesses to employee ownership companies. CCSH has also followed this route in some instances. The organizations most experienced with employee ownership and community development tend to use the elements that form a sound base, focus on opportunities that provide a low-income population with a chance at success, and make it a showcase. Following the guidelines below can take the edge off the struggle.

Because most employee ownership ventures need extra time and assistance to develop, having a nurturing community base can be helpful as the business moves forward. This base can include institutions that have the potential to supply business opportunities and ongoing financial and technical assistance, as well as city officials and community organizers who could offer local resources, come to meetings, and help with fund-raising.

Call on Our People is a housecleaning cooperative in Youngstown, Ohio. The co-op was established when a group of unemployed women learned about cooperatives through the YWCA. A group of ten people began to explore business possibilities. In addition to obtaining grants from local churches and private foundations, they received technical assistance from Youngstown State and Kent State universities, and a local attorney volunteered to write incorporation papers.

Community businesses can use a disadvantaged work force as a marketing tool to obtain free or low-cost assistance from lawyers, bankers, and business consultants. Many people realize the inconsistencies in our political economy and are glad to do what they can to bring a balance to their communities. In other cases, potential customers may be legally required to do a portion of their contracting with businesses owned by disadvantaged people. Blue Dot Energy Company makes bids and negotiates projects on the basis of providing a high-quality service at a competitive price, as well as employing disadvantaged, minority citizens who own part of the business. Recently, the company won a bid to build a $1.6 million flight simulator. Manos and AIWA both received feasibility, work, and planning assistance at below-market rates from a San Francisco consulting company.

Many cooperatives help each other by marketing jointly. Dungannon and St. Charles are currently forming a marketing network that will include other sewing plants in the area.

Assistance can also be given in the form of free services that do not require a significant amount of time but are skills or positions of influence that workers do not possess. For example, Indios Cooperative is assisted by the president of a local bank, who seeks out contracts, and by a local pilot, who maintains the sewing machines. The Service Corps of Retired Executives, a program of the U.S. Small Business Administration, offers the expertise of retired lawyers and business people who can serve as free or low-cost consultants.

Cooperatives and other community businesses can use their membership to obtain group services. Blue Dot uses its membership to barter for food, shelter, clothing, advertising, and other needs workers may have. For instance, when the cooperative needed a truck, Blue Dot did a job for a trucking company and decreased the bill for the construction services. Bartering also helps to keep dollars flowing within the community, rather than going to operations where the majority of the profits will leak out.

Churches have been central to the success of many community businesses and, on the whole, have been strong promoters of such ventures. Because some churches support collective community action, many have shifted from promoting traditional social and recreational activities to developing economic survival strategies for low-income residents.

In the early 1980s, plants were closing and the unemployment and poverty rates were growing. In response, the Southern Tier Office of Social Ministry in Elmira, New York, decided to link the unemployed with community groups. The Social Ministry staff proposed the establishment of employee-owned businesses to help improve the local economy. Cornell University initiated a program to assist workers starting cooperatives. Ministry staff and Cornell students attended the course and assembled a group of unemployed workers that met weekly and eventually began the Southern Tier Wood Products Cooperative.

In Milwaukee, a coalition of churches, worker cooperatives, and nonprofit businesses developed a technical arm to assist existing and start-up cooperatives. The organization, Select Staff, makes agreements with local companies to hire workers on a permanent basis. Quad/Graphics, one of the nation's largest printers and a "five-star" employee ownership company, agreed to build a plant in the inner city and hire through the cooperative.

In some cases, cooperatives are established for the sole purpose of assisting and promoting other cooperatives. Jobs for People (JFP) in Cincinnati, Ohio, serves as this type of economic development organization and also supports JFP Enterprises, a cooperative labor company. The organization consists of a coalition of forty churches and synagogues. The organization is the initial owner of all businesses created, but once each worker has paid a $100 ownership share, the venture is spun off as an independent employee ownership business.

Southwest Detroit Construction Cooperative (SWDCC) was sponsored by Weatherization and Retrofit Maintenance (WARM), a nonprofit training program designed to assist the unemployed by creating jobs through worker cooperatives. WARM sponsors workshops in construction and provides technical assistance and fund-raising support. In addition, the organization teaches cooperative members management skills and helps them develop business plans and land contracts. Today SWDCC grosses more than $200,000, and in 1987, WARM started two other cooperatives, Renovation Cooperatives Services and SPARCCO Maintenance. Since WARM's inception, the organization has supported itself with grants from religious orders, foundations, and corporations.

Many community ventures are started with the assistance of a variety of sponsors. In the early 1980s three activists started Worker Owned Network in Athens, Ohio, to combat the high rate of unemployment in the region. With help from an administrator in the county's department of human services, the Industrial Cooperative Association, and funding from the state, churches, and private foundations, the network was able to start several businesses, including converting a family business to a cooperative bakery and beginning a Mexican restaurant, a cleaning business, a home and family care business, and a crafts cooperative. Several of these ventures, including a business to provide services to the elderly and handicapped, employed recipients of Aid to Families with Dependent Children.

Fifteen states have developed programs to promote employee ownership and involvement. Typically, such programs are administered by the Department of Labor, Department of Commerce, or Department of Community Development. Most state and federal programs that aid business can be used to finance employee ownership. Methods of financing can include commercial loans, government-backed loans, bond issues, the sale of public stock, and private investors.

The legislation for state involvement in promoting employee ownership runs from simple policy declarations to extensive, full-time programs. The latter are achieving such impressive results on small budgets that the Employee Ownership Act of 1990 has been introduced. The bill would authorize the Department of Labor to allocate up to $10 million to state programs promoting employee ownership and participation.

State programs offer one or a combination of the following activities: public outreach and education, financial assistance, technical assistance, research and policy reporting, and general policy support. Outreach can involve publishing and distributing brochures and manuals, referring individuals to qualified practitioners, actively seeking out retiring individuals, organizing workshops and conferences, and acting as an information clearinghouse. Several states have committed themselves to financing technical assistance or matching employee contributions. Technical assistance is usually in the form of legal work, technical training, and feasibility studies. Statements of policy support serve several purposes. Passing policy declarations concerning employee ownership can be a first step toward creating awareness of the idea in agencies that might occasionally deal with the issue. States can also help by simplifying the process of starting an employee ownership company. Legislation can reduce legal problems or ambiguity, increase the time required for companies to notify employees of pending closings, provide tax incentives, or exempt employee ownership companies from state securities regulations.

In addition to providing special provisions for ESOPs, some states have created a legal framework under which cooperatives can organize. State business statutes are inadequate as a basis for incorporating worker cooperatives, leaving cooperative members, lenders, and lawyers uncertain about the legal authority of the enterprise. This ambiguity makes borrowing and incorporating difficult. Furthermore, some state labor codes do not permit mandatory stock purchase, making it difficult for employees to invest in the company they work for. In addition, by providing a legal structure for internal capital accounts, a special internal accounting system designed to value each member's equity separate from the value of the cooperative as a whole, new members are able to buy into a cooperative for a reasonable fee.

In the early 1980s, most state programs were reactive, focusing on employee ownership as a response to plant closings. An employee-owner at Mansfield Ferrous Casting, located in one of the most depressed cities of Ohio, was asked what he thought the foundry's chance of success was. He replied, "I don't know. But I do know that it's all up to us now."[12] Although the employees saved the firm, which offered the only jobs they knew how to do, they sold it in 1989 and continue to work at Mansfield but not as employee-owners.

By the late 1980s, state programs were increasingly using employee ownership in start-up situations or to buy out owners of successful, closely held firms, rather than taking a role in distressed situations. These organizations are still providing information on employee ownership to distressed companies, but they realize that preventive strategies are usually more successful.

The new proactive and much more successful model of a state employee ownership program focuses on providing information as an economic development strategy. The goals of these programs are to create and retain jobs through education concerning employee ownership regardless of the scenario (plant closing, buyout of a retiring owner, corporate divestment of a subsidiary, start-up). These programs also strive to anchor capital, improve the productivity of the work force, enhance labor relations, enable employees to accumulate substantial equity in their companies, improve economic stability, and offer buyout assistance so that communities can avoid the costs of liquidation or the risks of absentee ownership. Some state programs offer preference to buyouts or start-ups that intend to structure the employee ownership program democratically. Several state programs have done studies supporting NCEO's research linking employee ownership and participation to improved corporate performance. They realize that participative management contributes not only to an improved quality of work life but to the economic health of the state as well.

New York, Ohio, and Michigan have the most developed state employee ownership programs as well as the largest operating capacity. Although they are organized differently, they achieve the same goals—promoting employee ownership through information and outreach.

Members of Kent State University's political science department and the Labor Management Cooperation Center at Ohio University submitted a grant proposal to the Ohio Department of Development. The grant money was split between the two universities, which manage the Ohio Employee Ownership Education Project. Legislation supporting an employee ownership center was passed after the program was established in 1988, and legislation for a cooperative statute is currently under review. The Ohio program provides a complete list of local practitioners in the fields of employee ownership, information on employee ownership, prefeasibility studies, and presentations and workshops. The Ohio program is very active in bringing representatives of employee ownership companies together to discuss common problems and devise solutions. The result of these outreach efforts is a monthly forum.

In 1979, the Employee Corporations Act was signed by the governor of Michigan, giving the Office for Industrial Training (OIT) a role in encouraging employee ownership. OIT was later consolidated into the Governor's Office for Job Training (GOJT). Today, Michigan's employee ownership program is jointly funded, managed, and staffed on a part-time basis by GOJT and the Department of Commerce. These entities also administer a $1 million revolving loan fund that makes money available to establish ESOPs.

In addition, the Michigan Center for Employee Ownership and Gainsharing, which was founded in 1988, assisted sixty-two companies during its first seven months of operation. The state program provides information on employee ownership, technical assistance, training, and identification of financial sources for employee ownership ventures.

The GOJT works with the Bureau of Employment Relations in the Department of Labor as a mediator between Michigan employers and their unions. The GOJT also provides technical expertise when gainsharing and employee ownership become a part of collective bargaining agreements.

As early as 1983, New York became committed to promoting employee ownership through the Employee Ownership Assistance Act, with the focus of the legislation on buyouts of troubled companies. The act provided for the state's Job Development Authority to make loans available and required agency staff to make routine visits to businesses in the state and identify those in danger of closing or relocating. New York also enacted a Worker Cooperative Corporations Act in the early 1980s.

The New York State Industrial Council (ICC) was established by the governor in 1986 to identify changes in state law or policy that could improve the state's business climate. In the late 1980s, the ICC began to inform the public of the potential of employee ownership.

Today, New York has the largest operating capability of any state program. The New York Center for Employee Ownership and Participation (NYCEOP) works with the Department of Commerce to offer educational assistance, training to managers and employee-owners, feasibility studies and buyout assistance, financial and marketing analysis, start-ups of new employee ownership companies, and research. The program has three full-time staff members and contracts with an attorney for legal services. NYCEOP also trained all staff in the Regional Economic Development Division through the Program on Employment and Workplace Systems at Cornell University's School of Industrial and Labor Relations.

The new state employee ownership programs not only create a more favorable legal environment and educate the public and internal staff, they also offer a preventive, proactive economic development strategy. To reach the poorest of the poor, the state programs might offer financial assistance in cases in which a large percentage of low-income people would become employee-owners. This policy also creates an economic climate in which the ripple effect of a collapsed economy—decaying homes, empty schools, collapsing infrastructure—is avoided.

Conclusion

Employee ownership and community development face problems of poor management, power struggles, lack of skills, and lack of capital. The prototype firms need much more professional assistance and time to experiment and make self-corrections.

There is no question that community economic development is a challenging field. Building a community, organizing and empowering people, and developing businesses with little financial or technical assistance are difficult tasks. The breadth of examples demonstrates, however, that developing community employee ownership businesses is not limited to particular locales, races, or cultures. These examples also show that the poor can become self-sufficient if those offering assistance are committed and competent.

When communities are losing their capacity for self-reliance, employee-owned, employee-operated firms offer the hope of moving toward a decentralized, humanized economy. Given the general lack of government and corporate responsibility, this is not merely a grand goal, it is a necessity.

6 Stock Ownership Plans Abroad

Gianna Durso and Raul Rothblatt

The growth of employee ownership in the United States has been impressive. But of the 5 billion people in the world, only 245 million are in this country, and they are, relatively speaking, a prosperous lot. Arguably, then, employee ownership could make a more important contribution abroad. During the late 1980s and early 1990s, employee ownership did gain considerable support internationally. This chapter will discuss why and how this happened. Of course, the ideological and practical appeal of employee ownership varies greatly from country to country. In one place, it is a way to make privatization of state-owned enterprises acceptable; in another, it provides a way to share the wealth with peasants without breaking up large farm units; in still another, it is a way to ease upward pressure on wages while being fair to employees. Models for the use of employee ownership vary as well. Some countries have trust laws through which ESOP-like laws can operate, but most do not. As a result, employee associations, direct stock purchase incentives, internal trusts created under corporate by-laws, and a variety of other arrangements exist. Government incentives vary greatly as well.

The result of this patchwork of approaches has been the establishment of employee ownership laws or administrative procedures in England, Australia, Egypt, Poland, Canada, Argentina, and the Philippines. More laws are being considered. Eastern European nations seem especially interested. Though in none of these countries does employee ownership account for more than a handful of firms, precedents have been set, and the future is encouraging.

The International Ideology of Ownership

To its supporters, capitalism is the greatest engine of economic growth the world has ever known. To its opponents, it is a heartless system that condemns large portions of the population to poverty, enriching only a few. To its supporters, socialism is a rational, planned approach to managing an economy so that everyone benefits. To its opponents, it is a guarantor of, at best, an equality of mediocrity.

Since the industrial revolution, virtually every country has chosen some variation of capitalism or socialism. Some capitalist countries have tried harder than others to ameliorate the inequality the system creates through social welfare systems or even by introducing some socialized ownership of key economic sectors. Some socialist countries have sought economic stimulation by providing for at least some private ownership. The dilemmas of both systems, however, have never been resolved. Capitalism is almost universally recognized as highly productive but not very equitable; socialism is more equitable but rarely very economically productive.

This dilemma came into particularly sharp focus during 1989–90 as Eastern Europe and the Soviet Union struggled to find ways to make their lagging economies more productive. But though our imagination has been captured by the dramatic events in these countries, the capitalist nations should not be too quick to declare victory. The changes in Eastern Europe are far from over, and it is yet to be seen whether pure capitalism will benefit the average citizen. In South Africa the government must find ways to make its capitalist economy more fair to the majority of its population. The United States must find ways to deal with a large and growing underclass, as well as a generation of people whose standard of living is projected to fall below that of their parents. At the same time, developing nations, which have often practiced a mix of capitalism and socialism, are struggling to find ways to reform patterns of landownership that can help prevent revolution, while privatizing sluggish state-owned companies in a way that prevents exploitation.

The conventional view remains that countries must choose one approach or the other, perhaps with some compromises, and then try to deal with the consequences as well as possible. Inequality must be accepted in capitalism and less than optimal economic performance in socialism. But employee ownership challenges this conventional wisdom. With employee ownership, there is still the opportunity to become very wealthy, and there continue to be free markets within which entrepreneurial companies flourish so there is sufficient motivation for growth. Yet the fruits of capitalism can be widely shared, not hoarded by a few. This compelling logic is attracting more and more converts around the world.

Overview of International Application

Employee ownership can be found in countries as diverse as Ireland, Egypt, the Philippines, South Africa, Costa Rica, Sweden, Japan, and Australia. Employee ownership is being considered as a major alternative in Eastern Europe, and leaders in many countries, including Sri Lanka, Uruguay, Morocco, Belize, and Indonesia, to name just a few, have shown interest in the idea.

Employee ownership has also been implemented in Western Europe, although it is still much more the exception than the rule. French law states that companies with more than a hundred employees must have some sort of gainsharing plan, which can include stock ownership. Ireland offers tax incentives to both employee ownership companies and their employees. Britain has passed legislation promoting employee ownership, or employee share ownership plans, as they are called there. The West German government provides incentives for employees to buy stock and requires that employees be represented on the boards of corporations.

Employee ownership exists in other developed countries, although in relatively few companies does a broad cross section of employees have substantial ownership. Japanese workers can own stock through employee stock ownership associations, and Canadian workers are given incentives to buy stock both individually and through labor-sponsored venture capital corporations. Australia has had a long tradition of employee ownership, and some major companies there, including Cadbury Schweppes, have substantial plans. Multinational corporations, including Barclays Bank PLC and Wellcome PLC, which has employees in twenty-two countries, have started employee share-owning schemes.

Employee ownership is also well suited to less developed countries. The Solidarista movement throughout Central America allows employees to gain ownership in their companies by pooling their investments and getting matching contributions from their company. Costa Rica appears likely to pass ESOP legislation, and Mexico and Argentina require employee ownership of newly privatized firms. President Corazon Aquino of the Philippines has signed legislation allowing employee ownership. Employee ownership is found there in both industrial corporations such as the Manila Electric Company

(Meralco) and as a means of land reform, as in Hacienda Luisita. Although employee ownership through stock mechanisms is not widespread in any of these countries, the idea does seem to have taken root.

In Eastern Europe, Poland has passed legislation that would allow workers to buy up to 20 percent of the shares of their companies when they are privatized. Shares would be offered at half price. Employees could also start their own worker-owned businesses. In the Soviet Union, draft proposals being circulated in the summer of 1990 would privatize much of the economy either through leasing businesses to entrepreneurs, managers, or employee groups or selling them to employees.

Cooperatives

This book mostly focuses on employee stock ownership plans and similar approaches, but in several countries, cooperatives are the major form of employee ownership. In 1977, there were nearly 2,700 worker cooperatives in Italy, employing almost 150,000 people. That number appears not to have changed much in recent years. Cooperatives are strong in India and Indonesia, and there are 100,000 "cooperatives" in the Soviet Union, although there any private business is called a cooperative, even if just a few of its workers are owners. France also has a substantial cooperative sector, employing about 33,000 people. The Mondragón cooperatives in Spain, with almost 20,000 worker-members, are among the most successful employee ownership firms in the world. Cooperative ownership tends to stress economic democracy and joint decision making. These goals are often a factor in a company's decision to implement a cooperative structure.

In Italy, there are three umbrella organizations comprising the community of cooperatives: the Lega, the Associazione, and the Confederazione. These support organizations enable the member cooperatives to function better in the economy through their combined influence.[1] Each umbrella group has its own political constituency. The groups represent all co-ops in Italy—consumer co-ops, credit unions, agricultural marketing co-ops, worker co-ops, and so on. The worker cooperative sector is concentrated in the construction industries, thanks to local laws favoring contracts to these firms. Many of these firms employ hundreds of people.

Another community of cooperatives that has attained worldwide recognition is the Mondragón group in the Basque region of Spain.

A Basque priest started this cooperative network with one firm in 1956 in hopes of finding an answer to the poverty and unemployment in the region. Today, there are more than one hundred cooperatives employing almost twenty thousand members in manufacturing, service, technology, and other businesses. Consumer cooperatives for housing, food, education, and other services have been established as well. Perhaps the most important contribution of the Mondragón system, however, is the innovative way in which the society deals with the problems that traditionally plague cooperatives.[2]

Mondragón pioneered three main structures to encourage and sustain cooperative ownership. It has its own bank, the Caja Laboral Popular, which exists for the express purpose of lending to cooperative enterprises. A section of the Caja Laboral acts as an entrepreneurial incubator, developing new cooperative enterprises. When people want to start a new business, they go to experts at the bank, who identify potential enterprises. Mondragón also pioneered the system of internal capital accounts to keep track of cooperative members' rights and to keep the cost of buying into the cooperatives as low as possible. Under this system, new members make an investment of up to several thousand dollars to join a co-op. The investment can be funded through loans from the bank and forms the basis for an account in the company. Each year, the member's pro-rata share of the firm's profits is added to the account. Ten percent goes to the community, however, and 20 percent or more stays in the cooperative for reinvestment. The account earns modest interest and is paid out when workers leave. In the meantime, it serves as working capital for the cooperative.

In addition, the Mondragón group funds schools that teach the staff, parents, and children of cooperative members, strengthening the sense of community. Mondragón has its own advanced technical institute for conducting research and development projects for its member firms and funds its own social security system. Only one of its worker cooperative firms has ever failed, and studies have found the firms to be exceptionally productive.[3]

By World War I, there were 120 worker cooperatives in France; by 1980 there were 1,500. The growth was largely attributable to the "spirit of May 1968" student movement in France, which awakened broad interest in alternative ways of doing business. Approximately 35,000 people work for French co-ops; about 1 percent of these firms employ more than 500 people, and three-quarters of them employ fewer than 30. As in Italy, French cooperatives are concentrated in building, engineering, and printing, with the remainder in a variety of service and industrial fields.

French law provides a clear legal framework for worker cooperatives, and local governments are technically required to give cooperatives preference in bidding for certain contracts (hence the concentration in building and engineering firms), although this preference is often ignored. Local governments can also subsidize co-ops with direct loans and grants, although they have seldom done so. French cooperatives benefit from a very strong umbrella organization, the Société Coopérative Ouvriére de Production (SCOP), which has been helpful in providing both training and, through the cooperative bank, financing. Nonetheless, total employment in French worker cooperatives fell almost 20 percent from its peak in 1984 to the end of the decade.[4]

Mondragón and the cooperative associations in Italy, France, and elsewhere have survived by creating umbrella organizations to deal with the problems facing cooperatively owned businesses. Although the cooperative structure has been very successful in Spain and Italy, other forms of employee ownership are probably more widely applicable.

Stock Plans

Although there is a strong cooperative tradition in some countries, many people think that cooperatives are unlikely to serve as a model for systemwide change in most countries. Cooperatives have been around since the mid-1800s but have yet to account for more than 1 percent of the work force in any country. Rules governing cooperatives—one person, one vote, with only worker-owners voting—are too restrictive for established companies to consider and too unconventional for banks and other sources of capital to be willing to fund on a large scale. Investors are reluctant to put up capital because they are not allowed any control in the company. Cooperatives thus often need special financing institutions created specifically to meet their needs, such as the Caja Popular Laboral in the Mondragón cooperatives. Such a major change seems unlikely, especially in countries that see employee ownership as one way to privatize state firms. These companies must often attract major outside investment, which a cooperative governance structure would preclude.

By contrast, noncooperative stock ownership models are much more flexible. Employees can own any percentage of stock and have any degree of control over the business acceptable to them, and stock can be allocated to employees, managers, and investors on any basis that is acceptable to the parties involved. Stock ownership can be accomplished in two principal ways: through individual purchases or grants or through a pooling mechanism such as a trust. Pooled ownership can be structured to assure that shares are allocated in an equitable manner, that employees will continue to be owners as long as they work for the firm, and that the "pool" can be used to borrow money to buy shares. In the United States and Britain, this pooling is done through a trust.

Countries that do not have trust law can pool interests in employee-owned businesses in other ways. Employee associations can be formed, as in Guatemala and Egypt, or internal trusts (trusts established within a company under company rules, not national laws) can be established, as U.S. economist David Ellerman has proposed. These variations show how flexible stock plans can be, which is why they are likely to be the agent of most employee ownership abroad.

Opportunities and Obstacles to Implementing Employee Ownership Abroad

Employee ownership is appealing in foreign countries for many of the same reasons it is in the United States. It can improve productivity, create a more equitable distribution of wealth, help anchor capital in communities, and make work more satisfying. It may have a particular appeal, however, in countries that are experiencing the rush toward market economies.

There appears to be little doubt that advocates of market-based, rather than planned, economies have prevailed. Market economies are more successful than planned economies in producing goods and services. For Eastern Europe, the Soviet Union, and many developing nations, the question becomes how to make the transition to a market economy without giving up basic social values or causing unacceptable political turmoil. Employee ownership is an obvious answer. When countries start to privatize state-owned businesses, for instance, employees can be one logical buyer, if not for the entire equity, then for part of it. This approach has been used successfully in England and discussed in the United States, but neither country approaches the vast public holdings of socialist nations.[5]

Employee ownership also offers a way to maintain the values of equity for all citizens that many of these nations still hold. This can extend to issues of democratic control as well. Workers who for years have been told the country's resources are theirs may not be ready to accept the sale of their companies to outside interests that may see employees only as tools of production, providing them little or no say in what was "their" company, if only in rhetoric.

As appealing as the idea may sound, there are several difficulties with broad implementation of employee ownership. First, almost invariably, national laws must be created to provide adequate legal structures and economic incentives. For many Eastern European countries, this step must be preceded by the creation of corporate law in general. Second, employee ownership does not usually yield significant corporate capital, except possibly through employee wage concessions. Outside investors are usually needed, and they may want more ownership and control than employees think is desirable. Third, employees and investors must remember that employee ownership alone will not turn around troubled companies. If used too often for that purpose, the idea will attain a reputation for failure. Fourth, employees may have no experience with, and no interest in, being stock owners. Companies must be willing to make substantial investments of time and money to educate workers. Finally, the relationship between ownership and performance described here is based on U.S. experience. This may or may not be the case in other countries and cultures.

Regional Issues in International Employee Ownership

The following sections detail the reality of and potential for employee ownership throughout the world. This issue is put in context by addressing regional political and economic issues and the rationale for employee ownership in each region before exploring models for employee share ownership.

Commonwealth Countries

In Britain, the growth in employee ownership is largely a result of Margaret Thatcher's privatization programs. Thatcher's political agenda is very similar to Ronald Reagan's efforts to cut government programs. Britain, however, started out with more state-owned operations, and, unlike the United States, which ended the Reagan era with huge deficits, Britain achieved a nearly balanced budget partly by selling off its state enterprises. Many sales involved employee share purchase. One company in which employees entered into widespread financial participation is National Freight. In 1982, the 10,233 workers, pensioners, and their families bought 82.5 percent of the company and, within a year and a half, saw the value of their stock rise from 1 pound per share to 3.20 pounds per share. The typical privatization, however, involved only a minority of employees buying a small minority of the shares. In the National Freight case, most of the shares were made available only to the employees.[6]

Another model that has been applied is the "case law" British ESOP, which was developed by the law firm of Clifford Chance. The model requires case-by-case approval from the British tax department, the Inland Revenue. The first such ESOP was implemented at Roadchef in 1987, and there are now seventy-five plans in Britain and more under discussion there and in Ireland. Most provide 10 to 20 percent of a company's shares, but some are more substantial. Clifford Chance designed the U.K. ESOP to resemble the American version, but there are important differences in structure, tax treatment, and the results for employees. The U.K. ESOP is composed of a leveraged employee benefit trust and an Inland Revenue–approved employee benefit trust. The former purchases the shares for the employee, and the latter oversees distribution. There is nothing inherently better about using two trusts; it was simply the easiest way to approximate the advantages of U.S. tax law within the U.K. legal structure. Because this structure is based on case law, it could face challenges from Inland Revenue on the tax deductions claimed.

One example of a case law ESOP is the Provincial Bus Company, a national transport company that was forced to privatize by the 1985 Transport Act. Provincial Bus had two main potential buyers, a management team and Devon & General, a rival bus company. The employees were not happy with either contender so under the leadership of manager James Freeman, they put together a competing bid. The bid was successful, and Provincial Bus became the 100 percent employee-owned People's Provincial.

The ESOP at People's Provincial seems to have been remarkably successful. Absenteeism has dropped significantly, and internal theft has disappeared altogether. Despite a drop in passengers of 7 percent per year, revenues have remained fairly steady. This has been achieved through major cost trimming and some employment attrition. Most important, according to Freeman, the attitude at People's has changed dramatically. Drivers are now very concerned about the business. They take an interest in delivery schedules and marketing and have expanded service into several new areas.[7]

There is also a statutory ESOP in British law that is very similar to the Clifford Chance ESOP but requires that stock be divided more evenly among employees and that employees have equal representation on the trust committee that governs the plan. This statute has never actually been used because most companies want to give management a significantly higher proportion of the stock. Although the companies could just have two plans in operation, one for management alone and one for all employees, most companies have chosen other methods. The 1990 budget contains a provision much like the American rollover provision, wherein a private seller who sells at least 10 percent of the company to an ESOP can defer the capital gains taxes by reinvesting the proceeds from the sale. This provision should make the statutory ESOP more appealing. This is the first major tax incentive for ESOPs in Britain, and proponents of employee ownership there expect the new law to create hundreds of new plans.[8]

The benefits for employees of the U.K. ESOP differ somewhat from those of the American ESOP. The main difference is that the U.K. version is designed to put the shares into the hands of the employees before they retire or leave the company, whereas the American version distributes shares upon termination of employment. For many countries, the U.K. style may be more appealing because ownership may seem more real to employees if they see the advantages quickly.

Ireland. Until 1982, there was no particular financial incentive in Ireland for a company to allocate shares to employees or for employees to hold them. With the 1982 Finance Act government entered the arena, altering the situation dramatically. The relevant clauses of that act, together with amendments in 1983 and 1984, provide for generous tax concessions for both individuals and companies setting up approved schemes for employee shareholding. This move has stimulated interest and activity, and it is estimated that by the end of 1985 twenty to thirty schemes, the most famous of which probably is Waterford Crystal, may have been formally approved by the revenue commissioners.

The Irish Productivity Centre believes that significant growth in employee shareholding through profit sharing will take place in the next few years. It is equally likely that other complementary systems will come into being, such as share option schemes and collective shareholding arrangements. There have been no privatizations to date, but there have been rumors, and if they come to fruition, this may increase the number of employee shareholders.

Canada. In both public and private companies employee ownership is seen primarily as a way to increase productivity and provide for retirement. Only secondarily is it considered a source of capital because employee investment is typically small. The Canadian provincial governments, however, see employee ownership as a way to keep industries in the region, so though the Canadian federal government has few employee ownership programs, the provincial governments have been creating local incentive programs.

Quebec has established a labor-sponsored venture capital corporation (LSVCC). Any investor can buy shares in the provincewide Solidarity Fund, which is controlled by the Quebec Federation of Labor. The plan offers tax deductions or credits according to the value of the shares purchased in companies based in the province. Alberta is considering modeling a stock savings plan on the Quebec program.

British Columbia passed the Employee Investment Act in 1989. This law was designed to promote employee ownership as a means of increasing equity financing, as an incentive for improved employer-employee relations, and as a means to create and maintain jobs. The Ontario Ministry of Revenue will pay a grant of one-third of eligible set-up costs incurred by a corporation to a maximum of Can$10,000. Employee groups may also qualify for grants equal to one-half of eligible costs of negotiating, evaluating, and implementing a plan to a maximum of Can$5,000. There are also considerable provisions for stock purchase and stock option plans nationwide.

Canadian companies are having a difficult time convincing their employees that buying their employers' securities is a good use of their money. Progress has been slow. At MacMillan Bloedel, a forestry company, very few employees had any personal experience with equity ownership and therefore were slow to buy company stock. According to company vice-president Gary Johncox, the employees "were not and are not financial buccaneers. They are conservative investors," but the "company's initial 20% contribution, and later 30% contribution provided downside risk protection, and lunchroom discussion built confidence in the plan over time."[9]

Australia. In 1910, Australia had a Labor government in power and was one of the world's most advanced countries in providing political and social welfare. A system of centralized wage fixing developed to set uniform wages throughout many industries. Anthony Jensen, founder of the Association for Employee Ownership in Australia (AEOA), notes that the country enjoyed one of the world's highest standards of living. Yet by the 1980s, Australia had one of the lowest levels of social welfare of any advanced country and had slipped to sixteenth in the standard of living. Australia is now searching for a way to recreate its earlier economic success.

The 1970s brought stagflation and employee rescues of factories, including the Whyalla Glove Factory and the New Venture Corporation, both of which were later sold to private interests. In 1978, after two years in power, the New South Wales provincial Labor government established a Worker Cooperative Development Program. The first phase of the program consisted of an unsuccessful attempt to form worker cooperatives with unemployed young people. The second phase began in 1983. In only eight months, twelve firms converted via employee buyouts to what was termed a "common ownership company." The firms were generally very successful and small, with ten to seventy employees.[10] Unfortunately, the provision that allowed the first Aust$1,500 of dividend income to be tax-free to shareholders was rescinded in 1983 under criticism that the tax incentives were a scam.[11]

Australian regulatory procedures allow for plans similar to the U.S. ESOP, although with many fewer tax benefits. Australian firms can make tax-deductible contributions to a trust that holds shares for employees. Companies must apply for authority to set up a plan on a case-by-case basis because there are only regulatory interpretations, not specific laws. The tax disadvantages for employee share ownership were removed in 1988, and employee ownership is now tax-neutral or eligible for tax credits through the reformed Tax Imputation Regulations. Further, companies can sell employees up to Aust$2,000 of stock per year at a 10 percent discount and employees do not have to pay taxes on the benefits.[12]

At Siddons, a hand tool manufacturer, an employee stock plan has been very popular. When 1 million shares were issued in 1982, employees applied for over 2 million shares. The company had to restrict the issue to 50 percent of what each eligible employee had applied for.

Employee ownership in Australia is now supported by both major political parties, but for different reasons. The federal government's Department of Industrial Relations has taken a cautious lead in employee ownership and sees it as part of a range of economic reforms to enhance productivity and eliminate restrictive work practices through employee participation. A macroeconomic reform agenda is being conducted through the centralized wage-fixing system and has brought wage stability and restraint, as has an accord with the Australian trade union movement. Employee ownership could help provide support for what workers may see as a sacrifice of wages. The Liberal party (Labor is the other) and commercial sector see it as a means to deregulate the economy further and reduce the centralized role of the trade unions and the Arbitration Commission in national wage negotiations. Although both parties support the idea, neither has yet endorsed a specific proposal.

Western Europe

The economic unification of Western Europe in 1992 could provide a major new impetus for employee ownership. Economic unification will make it very easy to make a product in Spain, where labor is cheaper, and ship it to West Germany for sale. All of the European Community (EC) countries will be under pressure to keep local plants from relocating, and encouraging employee ownership is an excellent way to anchor capital. If employees own a plant, they are not likely to relocate to another country. The EC is considering laws favoring employee-owned firms, but the final form of these laws is still undetermined.

American and European approaches to employee participation differ in that Americans are less likely than Europeans to legislate such things as management style. For example, in France profit sharing is compulsory for companies with more than one hundred employees. Legislation is being considered in France to extend that requirement to employee ownership. American lawmakers would be very reluctant to pass such a law.

Some firms offer employees the option of placing their profit-sharing money in share purchase plans. In these deferred profit-sharing plans, in which profits are set aside for employees each year, income taxes are also deferred. Employees cannot draw out those shares or funds until retirement or departure from the company. Such plans have not resulted in employees investing much in their own companies because the employees often choose to receive their profit-sharing distribution in cash rather than place it in the share purchase plan.

One major impediment to widespread employee ownership in France and in several other countries is highlighted in a 1986 article in the *Wall Street Journal* that points out how difficult it is to convince French consumers to buy stock.[13] Television and print advertisements stressing the value of owning stock, both to the individual and to the national economy, were a government priority. Plans were designed to encourage share purchases both of employer companies and in the stock market at large but had little success. In other cases, employees considered buying entire companies, but employees feared that they would be sold failing concerns and would lose everything if the company closed. Floor-price put options, in which the employees always have the right to sell the stock back to the company for at least the original purchase price, and buyback agreements, in which the company agrees to provide a market for employees' shares, may assuage some of these concerns.

In Germany, the impediment to employee ownership is that employees already have significant benefits and see no reason to change the system. Germany passed the Works Constitution Act of 1972 and the Codetermination Act of 1976 to balance the interests of labor and capital. Both laws are designed to give workers a say in company management; neither provides incentives for employee ownership, which German unions believe is both too risky and too likely to blur the division between labor and capital. The model of separation and cooperation between labor and capital has helped Germany transform itself from large-scale destruction after World War II to its present economic strength.

Under the Fifth Asset Formation Law, employees with an annual taxable income of no more than DM 22,000 if unmarried or DM 54,000 if married may receive an investment premium of 20 percent toward the purchase price of shares or other securities in the company, up to a maximum of DM 936 a year. The premium by which the government adds a percentage investment to any qualifying employee investment is unique to German law. The employee must invest his or her money in the company for a minimum of six years. The majority of these employee investments are loan stock (similar to bonds), nonvoting shares, and other securities that fall short of full ordinary or common share status. The reason for the maximum figure of DM 936 is that it is divisible by both 12 and 52 so that it makes no difference whether an employee is paid on a monthly or weekly basis.

Approximately 1.5 percent of all West German workers, or 1.3 million employees, own shares in their companies. Approximately 1,500 companies representing 2 percent of those eligible have employee ownership programs. About 27 percent of these 1,500 companies allow their employees to participate only by way of debt capital. In such cases, employees usually make a loan to the employing company, which is often repaid with a share of company profits rather than interest. This type of financial participation can be a way to ease employees into equity capital participation. Large companies with employee ownership include BMW, Siemens, Bertelsmann, and Hoechst.[14]

Africa

There is not a great deal of employee ownership activity in Africa except in Egypt and South Africa, two countries that are not typical of the continent. There is potential for employee ownership in other countries, however, because governments are under financial pressure and may need to raise money through privatization. These pressures are increasing because international financial aid is being redirected toward Eastern Europe. In Morocco, for instance, legislation has been passed for the privatization of four banks, thirty-seven hotels, and seventy-two other state concerns in the course of the next six years. Strategic enterprises not listed include the phosphate monopoly, the national airline, the railways, water, and the electricity utility. Foreigners will be allowed minority ownership, and special provisions will be made for employee shares.

Some African nations are attracted to employee ownership because of the self-reliance and economic justice it offers. It can reduce the dependence on developed countries that colonialism forced onto Africa. A small worker cooperative movement has developed in some countries, including Zimbabwe. Libya has begun to encourage private business so long as the workers will be "partners and not wage slaves," according to the *Financial Times* of London.[15] The article reports that Libya, which has had a heavily state-dominated economy, intends to "expand gradually the role of individuals and cooperatives in the economy." Part of the new program, begun in 1988, transfers ownership of state-owned factories to employees, and the results are encouraging.

Egypt. The Egyptian approach to employee ownership is probably the one that is most applicable to other nations. Many of the countries considering major employee ownership legislation, including those in Eastern Europe and many developing countries, do not have trust laws that would make the ESOP approach of the United States and Britain practical. The trust mechanism may not be appropriate in every country, and it may even involve a drastic change in the legal structure. The solution in Egypt is to have employees own stock through an employee stockholder association (ESA), which is legally established as a nonprofit organization. Not only is the ESA an effective means for employee ownership, but it is more understandable and streamlined.

ESA stockholders vote their shares directly, thus avoiding the problem in U.S. ESOPs of having shares voted by a trustee who may face a conflict between following employees' directions and the dictates of trust law. In addition, ownership through a trust is not intuitively obvious to those who do not have experience in finance, which includes most employees. Those unfamiliar with the concept may find it odd that employees are allocated stock as the loan is repaid. Some critics think that the average employee cannot understand the mysterious words and numbers of finance. But it seems likely that employees will begin to learn about finance when *their* money is on the line. Nonetheless, trusts may seem suspicious when initially introduced to employees. The ESA makes ownership easier to understand. It also gives control more clearly to the employees rather than to some distant third party.

Establishing employee ownership seems to fit with the sixth definition of human rights in Islam, the right to private ownership of productive property, *Haq Al Mal*. Islamic law presents problems, however. For instance, it prohibits charging more than 7 percent interest, which can make banking difficult when the inflation rate is 20 to 25 percent.

In the case of Alexandria Tire Company, the first (and at this point only) ESOP in Egypt, the banking laws caused some consternation and structuring the ESOP loan required a good deal of innovation. A loan contract was proposed that took into account the interests of all parties and was compatible with the idea of employee ownership. Instead of charging an interest rate on the loan, the ministry and the ESA will be equity partners in the new company. Based on the project feasibility study, the lender will get back the purchasing power of the loan plus a 16 percent risk premium, regardless of the rate of inflation. The recovery of the loan will hinge on the performance of the employees and the company. Only if the company is profitable will they be able to acquire ownership and pay back the loan.[16]

This loan structure works in the case of Alexandria Tire partly because of the heavy investment by other successful companies, Pirelli and TRENCO. The financial stability and reputation of these firms reassure lenders that the company will eventually become profitable enough to repay the loan. Such substantial backing may not be available for other employee ownership ventures, and conservative lenders will not want to take the risk of being an equity partner. If the bank prefers a more conventional loan repayment schedule, the high rate of inflation will cause problems. Thus this loan structure may not work when the lender has a low risk tolerance.

Nonetheless, the prospects for employee ownership in Egypt are good. Eight other companies have applied for special funding from the ministry, and the U.S. Agency for International Development (AID) is working with companies ranging from a cement firm to a bank to implement some form of employee ownership. An Egyptian Center for Employee Ownership called ADALA (meaning justice in Egyptian) has been established with an extremely powerful founding board of directors. Plans are moving forward for a second chapter of the organization to be based in Alexandria.

South Africa. Since the late 1970s and early 1980s, groups around the world have called for companies to pull out of South Africa in protest of apartheid, a process called divestiture. Some companies left early on. Others sold their assets to businesses owned by whites, which, as predicted, did little to eliminate apartheid. Still other companies looked for enlightened and creative ways to manage the withdrawal so that blacks benefited. Often this involved selling part of the company to an employee trust and implementing an employee stock plan.

South Africa has no laws mandating or defining employee stock ownership plans. Most of the trusts are established in other countries. There is, however, growing support for a fund to establish these plans and make worker buyouts more practical. This fund is a private venture organized by business leaders who wish to ensure a place for market capitalism in the event of majority rule.[17] These business leaders fear black rule will bring socialism without broad ownership opportunities.

Not all employee stock plans involve divestitures. Anglo American Corporation, by far the country's largest mining concern, is starting an employee stock plan and is not planning to leave the country. Anglo American had four main objectives when beginning its stock plan: fairer distribution of wealth, increasing employee identification with the company, promoting an understanding of the financial machinations of a free market economy, and encouraging employee loyalty.[18]

Eastern Europe and the Soviet Union

Even though employee ownership can work in countries with various trust and pension laws, until recently all Eastern European countries had such radically different laws or such loosely defined economic policies that direct translation of ESOPs would have been impossible. The Soviet Union and Yugoslavia, for instance, not only have no trust law and dissimilar corporate law but also have no clear definition of the basic concept of ownership. They must reconcile or replace socialist laws with a privatization program designed to revive their failing economies. The extent of reform varies from country to country, from Albania, which has shown next to no desire to reform, to Hungary and Poland, which are well on their way toward free market economies.

The recent literature has emphasized the positive changes taking place in Eastern Europe but has minimized the difficulties involved in economic restructuring. The largest of these is that transition to an economy with more private ownership brings surges of inflation and other problems for which the current governments do not want to be blamed.

A second factor working against reform is the entrenched bureaucracy that has a vested interest in the old system. Although the people as a whole may benefit from reforms, the numerous and powerful bureaucrats stand to lose their jobs. There is a fair amount of popular resentment against the communist bureaucrats, especially those associated with men like Nicolei Ceaucescu, the former leader of Romania. The nemesis of the communist era was the robber baron, and if reform means that powerful bureaucrats become powerful capitalists, the nemesis of the next age may be the robber bureaucrat. Unfortunately, these bureaucrats have some much needed management experience, and they are a large and important sector of the population. Any successful reforms will need their input and at least partial approval.

Yet another factor working against reform is inertia. Most Eastern Europeans have no experience with profit motivation, and companies have no desire to be faced with bankruptcy and unemployment. Czechoslovakia and Hungary did have market economies before Soviet hegemony, but other countries had almost no experience with capitalism even before the Soviet Union gained control.

On top of all of these forces working against change, there is yet another working against employee ownership specifically. Yugoslavia is often seen as a model for employee ownership in the region, and it is seen as a failure. Yugoslavia's system is actually "social ownership" in which enterprises are owned by everyone in the society, yet no one has any equity stake in a company. If it closed, its assets were transferred to other companies. A company could not be sold. Individual companies are partially controlled by employees but not owned by them. The state controlled many of the decisions of corporate planning. But when many Eastern Europeans think of employee ownership, they think of the Yugoslav system.

Even if none of these impediments existed, and everyone was willing and motivated to change to a capitalistic system, this transition would still be difficult because there are no capital markets. How can a house or a tractor be sold when the price and amount of these products have been predetermined without considering demand? Foreign investors have already faced this difficulty in Hungary and Poland, where transactions have hit snags because it was impossible to set a price that all parties could agree upon. Not only are capital markets lacking, but so is capital. Sources of outside capital may or may not be willing to support substantial employee ownership.

Nevertheless, great changes have taken place in Eastern Europe, and more change seems inevitable. Employee ownership may be the most comfortable way to transform to a more market-oriented economy because it fits into the Marxist ideal of worker control of the means of production. As government budgetary constraints grow, the pressure toward privatization of public agencies will increase. Selling part or all of a company to the employees may be the most politically safe way to get these agencies out of the government budget without arousing an antigovernment reaction.

The Soviet Union. The Soviet Union is considering implementing market reforms as well. The government has only recently recognized private property as a legitimate form of ownership, but it has not defined how a transition to private ownership will occur. Employee ownership is one of several options being discussed. Individual republics may end up setting their own policies as well.

In addition to the need to reconcile economics and politics, the Soviet system must overcome some tremendous hurdles that have developed in the last fifty years, not the least of which is the centrally planned economy. In the Soviet Union, it is not uncommon for a decision to go through fifteen to twenty levels of administration before reaching the person who will implement it. The financial reformers see new, more independent enterprises as a means to streamline this system.

Progress has been predictably rocky. Some attempts to make prices responsive to the market have been thwarted because of poor planning. In one case, for example, a company that supplied the raw materials to a manufacturing plant was allowed to raise its prices, but the manufacturing company was not. With no way to pass the increase in the price of materials on to the consumer, the manufacturer saw profit margins shrink to nothing. In other cases, the new company may become a victim of its own success. People who make too much money are viewed with suspicion and jealousy. In one experiment, cab drivers who were allowed to rent their own taxis and charge competitive rates increased their monthly earnings to two or three times the national average, yet the experiment was discontinued. It illustrates how much difficulty the Soviet Union is having accepting the inequality that is integral to private enterprise. One recent poll reported that 55 percent of the Soviet people prefer a small salary as long as they do not have to work hard. Just 37 percent said they would like to be rewarded for hard work, and only 7.3 percent favor full legalization of private enterprise.[19]

Despite these problems, there is reason to think that employee ownership could make more progress in the Soviet Union than in any other communist or formerly communist states. As of September 1990, for instance, the principal proposal to privatize Soviet-owned enterprises would involve either outright sales of companies to employees or leasing businesses to employees, managers, or investors.

Thousands of cooperatives are operating in the Soviet Union. Various observers put the total number of employees in these private businesses at between one hundred thousand and 4 million, a commentary on the lack of adequate data or even clear definitions. There appears to be no consistent definition of the term *cooperative*. Clearly, many of the cooperatives are simply part-time businesses run by a few people; others are small full-time businesses actually owned (within the ambiguous definition of that term now in effect) by employees; still others are more like conventional businesses. But how many there are in each category, no one knows. What is clear, however, is that Soviet citizens have already demonstrated their commitment to worker ownership on a substantial scale.

Leasing programs already under way in the Soviet Union could help pave the way toward employee ownership. In twelve hundred to two thousand Soviet enterprises, an experimental program in which workers lease plants and equipment from the state and run them as independent operations has been implemented. According to John Logue of the Northeast Ohio Employee Ownership Center, who recently visited the Soviet Union, "The leasing stage is temporary. Either these businesses will be collectively owned by workers or they will return to state ownership."[20]

Taxi Fleet Moscow is one of three employee-leased taxicab operations in the Soviet Union. The independence of the Soviet taxi system—companies have neither radios nor dispatchers—lends itself to a decentralized system. The 1,650 workers in Taxi Fleet Moscow run the company through work groups. Members of each work group, composed of a number of cab drivers, two in each cab, and several mechanics, work together to bring in enough cab fares to cover a basic operating fee. Any excess fares brought in go to the drivers, and bonuses are distributed among the work group members depending on each one's individual contribution. During 1989, the leasing system increased the average employee's income by 25 percent. Since becoming employee-leased, the enterprise has accumulated enough rubles to purchase 250 new cabs. Unfortunately, only 175 cabs were available for purchase.[21]

One model for Soviet employee ownership has been suggested by David Ellerman of Employee Ownership Services, an international consulting group. Companies would create an "ESOP" entity that was virtually self-contained. Ellerman calls it an "Internal ESOP." Its structure does not rely on specific laws but is a creature of the company's by-laws. A government would have to allow it, but any special treatment for it would be a policy decision outside the company's control.

Ellerman suggests modifying or drafting corporate law in these countries to allow the ESOP to be *inside the corporation itself*, rather than an external trust. This approach is different from that used in Egypt, where a new type of shareholders' association was created. The internal trust, by contrast, keeps the workers' part of the equity inside the company, held in one or more of several types of accounts. An individual account would hold all the shares the worker had earned, and an additional account would track the stock that had been set aside but not yet earned by the employee.

The first two internal ESOP worker buyouts were arranged in a Moscow firm manufacturing food processing equipment and a building materials firm outside of Moscow. Both had operated for over a year as lease firms. The buyouts were designed by Valery Rutgaizer, an economist and deputy director of the All-Union Center for Public Opinion Research. The firms go beyond the lease model by transferring the ownership of the means of production (the capital goods used) to the workers' firm. The ministry running the plan supplied the credit for employees to buy the firm. These first two "ESOPs" also have a local institution as the minority partner, which later may be bought out.

The company manufacturing food processing equipment is called Moscow Experimental Plant (Catering), a name it acquired in 1965 when it was a part of other experiments. It has about seven hundred workers. The company was originally set up in 1929 so a good part of the plant is sixty years old. The company was in a crisis several years ago, when Mikhail Gorbachev's anti-alcohol campaign sent orders for bottling equipment plummeting. After the firm was merged and divided, employees decided to become a lease firm.

Ellerman suggests using the internal ESOP to break up the large, unwieldy socialist firms that are dragging down socialist economies. This is a radical change for workers in a country with guaranteed employment. The new employee-owned firms would have to improve their efficiency, which would almost certainly mean layoffs.

Poland. There is also considerable interest in employee ownership in Poland. Under a 1990 law governing the privatization of state-owned enterprises, coupons will be given out to citizens, who can exchange them for shares in the emerging companies.[22] Employees of the companies would be able to buy up to 20 percent of the stock at a 50 percent discount. Because no details on how this would work are available, it is unknown how the companies will be valued, whether citizens or employees must hold shares for a minimum period before they can sell, and whether, after the initial buyout, employees could band together to buy more of the company at a nondiscounted price. Several Polish companies have shown an interest in employee ownership, and one hundred of them have banded together to form a Polish ESOP Association. Poland has sent delegations to the United States to investigate employee ownership, and Solidarity has endorsed the idea.

Prospects for Employee Ownership in Eastern Europe. Anchoring capital is not a major motivation for the development of employee ownership in Eastern Europe. The problem is not losing industries to other regions but starting or expanding industries or selling existing ones to foreigners who can bring in new capital. Losing control, however, is an issue. Foreign investors and firms may be very attracted to the skilled, low-cost labor in Eastern Europe and want to move operations there, but they probably will want to control the companies in which they invest. Employee ownership may be an answer. When employee ownership is used, the financially strapped Eastern European countries will most likely sell majority interests to outsiders but reserve a minority of stock for employees and perhaps for the government, thus retaining at least some local influence.

Deciding whether to give up control of state-owned firms is one of the more vexing issues facing Eastern Europe. It seems unlikely that every country and company will come up with the same solutions to the new economic problems. There will probably be a variety of ownership forms, including ESOPs, cooperatives, West German–style cross ownership (in which companies are owned by other companies, which are owned by yet other companies), and state ownership.

Several countries are already planning different forms of employee ownership. One of the three bills designed to promote free markets in Czechoslovakia allows state enterprises to sell shares to their employees. According to the *Wall Street Journal*,[23] the Yugoslavian government intends to sell an undetermined portion of state-owned assets through direct sales, employee share arrangements, and competitive bidding. According to the same article, the government of East Germany intends to sell stakes in some of its giant industrial enterprises, *kombinat*, to workers and other investors, although there are still barriers to its doing so. An employee ownership association is also getting started in the Soviet Union. Despite the drawbacks, the prospects for employee ownership in Eastern Europe are good.

Latin America

Economic justice is a major concern in the development of employee ownership in Latin America, but conceptions of what that term means vary widely. In the United States and Europe, employee ownership is seen as a way to temper the extremes of capitalism and socialism while realizing the ideals of each by developing both entrepreneurship and worker empowerment. In Latin America, the focus may be more on breaking up the holdings of the very wealthy. One Peruvian leftist government appropriated a number of large corporations. Instead of nationalizing them, it converted them to employee-owned enterprises. The government unfortunately failed to bring in capable management, and the companies folded.

Employee ownership is usually associated with centrist and right-wing agendas in other parts of Latin America. In Central America, the Solidarista movement, which has taken the lead in developing employee ownership, is thought by some to have the additional goal of undermining labor unions. Nevertheless, employee ownership is getting a broader base of support in the 1990s. With the support of both political parties, Costa Rica will likely pass employee ownership legislation in mid-1990 that is aimed at meeting concerns of labor and management.

Pressures from the World Bank, huge deficits, and other economic problems are forcing Latin American governments to reduce expenditures and leave government services to the private sector. But privatization is seen by many workers as a way to enrich the already rich at the expense of government services to the poor. Governments have begun using employee ownership to soften the effects of privatization. For example, both the Mexican and Argentine governments are using employee ownership as a way to spread the benefits of privatization. These countries are relying on individual-choice models of employee ownership. Just how much of a broadening of equity that will produce is unclear.

The principal hindrance to setting up U.S.-style ESOPs in Central America is the trust structure. A trust is not considered a legal person as it is in the United States. In most of these countries, trusts are treated as mercantile entities and are subject to taxation. Currently, companies receive no special tax incentives for contributing to employee stock plans, though company contributions as an advance on severance pay obligations are pretax corporate deductions.

Instead of a U.S.-style ESOP, an association is formed for the benefit of the employees of one or several companies. These Solidarista associations are unique to Central America. They are external to the company, although companies may help set them up. They are civil associations of workers and provide employee members with benefits ranging from savings programs to loans for education and business investments. Companies and employees make contributions to the association, and the tax benefits vary by country. To use a Solidarista association for employee ownership, which has been done only once, the associations could borrow money, which they could then use to buy stock in the company. The company could agree to repay the loan by making contributions to the association for this purpose. Legal changes could allow this on a tax-deductible basis. Employee contributions could also be used for this purpose. The contributions on both sides would be outside of normal company retirement or severance pay obligations. The association would hold the stock in accounts for employees, where it would be subject to much the same treatment as in an ESOP.

One example of employee ownership in Central America is La Perla (the Pearl), a coffee and cardamom plantation on approximately ten thousand acres in the northern Guatemalan province of Quiche. It has more than five hundred full-time employees and a farm population of five thousand people. In 1984, the estate's owners began a ten-year program to give its employees 40 percent ownership in the estate's common stock, capital appreciation, and earnings. Full voting rights at the signing of the legal documents were immediately passed through a trust to the employees.[24]

Employees purchased the stock for an estimated (1985) market value of $1.6 million (book value plus an evaluation based on present and future dividends) with a combination of past corporate severance pay obligations (approximately $150,000, which under Guatemalan law is obligatory only if an employee is dismissed), future dividends on employee-held stock, and monthly contributions to an employee Solidarista association (averaging 3 percent of total payroll for the employees and the company). The two employee associations at La Perla (for the two geographical divisions of the estate), as legal beneficiaries of the stock, have two seats, elected by employees, on La Perla's board of directors. The Arenas family, holding 60 percent of the common shares, has three seats on the five-person board. All income received by the Arenas family for the sale of its stock will be donated to or invested in rural development programs.[25]

The Arenas family decided to build a political constituency among employees and transfer an ownership stake to them primarily to protect the estate against present and future insurgent attacks and possible government-backed agrarian reform. This objective was tested in March 1985, when 120 insurgents attacked the estate, occupying the main farm installations. Two hundred armed workers (organized with the help of the Guatemalan military) subsequently forced the insurgents to retreat, leaving several insurgents and workers wounded and dead. After the attack, the estate's three hundred unarmed worker-owners petitioned the Arenas family for additional rifles to defend against future attack, volunteering to help pay for the guns through a payroll deduction plan.[26]

The Solidarista movement today encompasses more than two thousand companies, 24 percent of the labor force in Costa Rica, and hundreds of companies covering fifty thousand employees in Guatemala, Honduras, and Panama. Combined assets as of May 1989 were over $100 million. The movement is expanding in many areas to include large agricultural estates, manufacturing facilities, multinational corporations, and public institutions. The movement has as its principal goals better employee-employer relations, the promotion of social and economic justice for the working class, the education of workers on how a market economy functions, an increase in savings and investments, and the promotion of the formation and ownership of capital. Although employee ownership has not been a major goal, the associations could be adapted to this end.

Asia

Asia is extremely diverse politically and economically. The political concerns of the new economic superpower Japan are very different from those of the lumbering giant Indonesia, which are very different from those of strife-ridden Cambodia.

A widespread perception about Asia is that tremendous economic growth is not only possible but expected. Japan is seen as only the first of the Asian giants, to be followed by such other "Asian dragons" as Singapore and South Korea. Just a few steps behind the dragons of the 1980s are the potential dragons of the 1990s, including Malaysia, Thailand, and Indonesia. One of the keys to the success of Asian countries in the past was the availability of cheap labor, but as the price of labor in Japan and other countries increases, these countries will in turn fill their labor needs from other parts of Asia.

Asia is one of the least active areas of the world in the employee ownership arena. The government of China showed interest in the idea, but after the upheaval there in 1989, it is not clear what will happen. Both India and Indonesia have shown strong interest in a cooperative approach. Employee ownership also fits into Sri Lanka's national privatization strategy.

The Philippines. The one country in Asia that is enthusiastic about employee ownership is the Philippines, where it is valued not only as a means toward higher productivity but as an excellent solution for the unequal distribution of wealth and land. Traditional land reform is now seen as impractical because it makes no sense to break up a large plantation into unworkably small plots run by peasants. Under a model for land reform based on employee ownership, the farm workers get shares in the whole plantation rather than small plots of land. Under this plan, peasants not only get control of the assets of the plantation, but they are also able to pool their resources. Moreover, employee ownership allows for outside investors to bring in capital, connections to markets, new technology, and a plethora of other benefits. Employee ownership has also been associated with privatization, and employees of Manila Electric (Meralco) will get to buy stock at a discounted price.

Land reform is a major black eye for the Aquino administration. Despite the slow pace, there are laws to support land reform. On June 10, 1988, President Corazon Aquino signed into law Republic Act No. 6657, commonly known as CARL. It is "an act instituting a comprehensive agrarian reform program to promote social justice and industrialization, providing the mechanism for its implementation, and for other purposes." CARL provides for "corporate farming" as a method of land reform. Instead of distributing land, plantations issue stock to employees.

Probably the most remarkable example of employee ownership in the Philippines is Hacienda Luisita. Hacienda Luisita was spun off from the Tarlac Development Corporation (TDC) in 1988 into a separate corporation, starting with five thousand hectares of agricultural land and other related assets and liabilities. TDC was founded in 1957 and is owned by the Cojuangcos, President Aquino's family. The Cojuangco complex is the largest employer and taxpayer in the province of Tarlac.

Hacienda Luisita operates under the land reform law CARL, but its features are more liberal.[27] Philippine law normally provides that beneficiaries must pay for stocks. In contrast, shares of stock in Hacienda Luisita worth 33.3 percent of the company are distributed free to farm workers/beneficiaries (FBs) on the basis of number of days worked. Hacienda Luisita provides each FB a small home lot, also free. Every year, FBs receive 3 percent of the gross sales of the corporation in cash or incentive bonuses on top of their regular compensation. In fiscal year 1987–88, this amounted to 5.5 million pesos; in fiscal year 1988–89, 7.3 million pesos (21 pesos = U.S. $1). CARL provides that 3 percent of gross sales be given to FBs until the distribution of shares actually begins but does not require it thereafter. FBs are given proxies to vote for four members out of an eleven-member board. The FBs also continue to enjoy benefits under the collective bargaining agreement.

The employees of Hacienda Luisita are daily witnesses to the persistent desire of their neighbors who live in the periphery of the hacienda to be hired as Hacienda Luisita employees because of the better standard of living at Hacienda. These neighbors, living in the barrios of Dumarais, Sierra, and Comillas, were the original beneficiaries of land reform when some eighteen hundred hectares of rice land that formed part of Hacienda Luisita were parceled off to workers in the 1950s. They were forced to sell off the land over the years because it could not sustain them. The reasons for the failure were myriad—lack of support services, low organizational skills, no financing, and poor marketing, among others. About twenty people, who were not even beneficiaries, own these lands now; there were some three hundred beneficiaries originally.

Conclusion

Recent visitors to Eastern Europe reported that so many people had been promoting the idea of employee ownership abroad that foreign leaders thought it was the bedrock of the American economy. In this chapter an effort has been made to discuss the most recent developments, but it is not meant to give the impression that employee ownership is sweeping the world. There is activity, to be sure, but it is preliminary and embryonic. This information should not be interpreted as the tip of the iceberg, with a vast array of developments occurring beneath the surface. Rather, the information here should be seen as the foundation of a building. It shows the first steps that countries are taking, but there are many more bricks to be laid before the structure will be inhabitable.

7 Conclusion: What Next?

Karen M. Young and Corey Rosen

In 1981, when we started the National Center for Employee Ownership in a small room in our basement (we are married as well as colleagues), it seemed more than unlikely that ten years later the center would have grown to seventeen hundred members and, more important, that employees would own three of the ten largest steel companies, two of the five largest shipbuilders, three of the ten largest hospital management firms, two of the ten largest engineering firms, and many other leading companies in the United States. It would have seemed even more farfetched that as communism collapsed, employee ownership would be discussed as at least a partial economic alternative, or that visitors from dozens of other countries would regularly make pilgrimages to the United States to learn about how employees were becoming owners here.

In 1980, employee ownership was not exactly a household word. Although a few thousand companies had plans, only a few firms with more than a few hundred employees were employee-owned. The largest ESOP-leveraged transaction to that point had been for just $25 million. Only a few lawyers and other professionals were familiar with the idea; only one state had an employee ownership program (Michigan); only a handful of bankers were interested in making ESOP loans. By the summer of 1990, over $50 billion had been borrowed through ESOPs, more than ten thousand U.S. companies had plans, and almost 12 million employees were owners. An infrastructure had grown up to support employee ownership, including nine active state organizations covering about one-third of the U.S. population. Employee ownership organizations had sprouted in England, Australia, Canada, Poland, the Soviet Union, Egypt, and Guatemala, among others. We even had a growing staff and a large office of our own.

The future of employee ownership, though, is not certain. If it is to continue to grow, it must demonstrate that it can add to corporate competitiveness and economic equity. This is as true in the United States as in the Soviet Union. Although employee ownership has broad ideological appeal, its success will be measured by concrete results. This book has raised several questions, the answers to which will determine that success. Will employee-owned companies be managed in a way that translates the financial rewards of ownership into the practice of the sharing of ideas and information between employees and management? Will employee ownership plans be managed to promote the financial interests of employees or the narrow interests of management and investors? Will governments continue to provide sufficient tax subsidies to employee-owned companies to motivate people who are skeptical about the virtues of sharing equity? How will unions react to employee ownership? Will employee ownership be able to survive severe recessions or political turmoil? Will changes in technology and organization make employee ownership more or less needed, or will new forms of compensation be developed to cope with radically different notions of employment? These issues are not comprehensive, but they seem to be key ones and worth elaboration.

We believe the most important issue will be how employee-owned companies are managed. It has been stressed throughout the book that employees like being owners and that companies perform best when ownership is tied to involvement in decisions affecting work. This is much more than the occasional quality circle or putting up a suggestion box. It is instead a set of attitudes and procedures based on the idea that every employee has the potential and responsibility to contribute significantly to the success of an organization.

Companies that adopt these attitudes help promote employee ownership beyond their corporate walls in three important ways. First, when governments look at tax incentives of employee ownership, they will inevitably ask whether these incentives increase economic efficiency. This may be an unfair question. Is it not enough that employee ownership makes the distribution of wealth more equitable? A good argument can be made that it is, but the experience in the United States and the expectation in other countries is that the taxpayers' representatives want a return on investment. This view is reinforced by the business press. When a conventionally owned company fails, reporters do not write that traditional corporate ownership is at fault; when an employee-owned company closes or performs poorly, they often write that employee ownership is the culprit.

Second, if participation is part of a company's structure, employees will like being owners more. Eventually, people may choose employers because they offer ownership plans. Demographics could intensify the importance of this consideration. In the United States and several other developed nations, slower population growth could mean greater competition for qualified employees. At the same time, employees will have increasingly higher levels of education. They will look for work to provide fulfillment in addition to a good income; companies that offer a combination of ownership and involvement may gain a competitive edge.

Third, and most important, what succeeds in market economies is imitated. If employee-owned companies are better competitors, more companies will make their employees owners. There are some signs that this is happening already. Printing companies, for instance, say they want to be like Quad/Graphics; technology companies want to be like W. L. Gore Associates. So far, these are exceptions, but it is very early in the employee ownership game. In Japan, the practice of quality circles grew almost entirely by this process over a two-decade period starting in the early 1950s.

Another major issue is whether employee-owned companies are managed for the interests of the employees or the plans' initiators. First American Bank and Trust of Florida set up its ESOP primarily to give its president an opportunity to use contributions to the plan to invest in other banks, most of which he eventually came to control. The ESOP was able to invest almost half its assets, which came from tax-deductible corporate contributions, to make these investments. Because the president controlled the ESOP, he could use these tax-payer-supported investments to further his own empire-building goals. Unfortunately, First American went bankrupt, and many of the investments soured. Employees, whose only retirement plan was the ESOP, ended up with nothing. Other examples of cases in which the ESOP was not used to further employee interests were noted earlier in the book.

Overall evidence, however, suggests that ESOPs have worked very well for employees, and for every discouraging story like that of First American, there are dozens like that of Lincoln Electric, a small Nebraska firm that makes batteries for golf carts. In 1988, a woman who cleaned the offices left with an ESOP distribution of over $120,000. Lincoln Electric's ESOP benefited the management and owners of the company, but it also benefited the employees.

It is too early to tell whether employee-owned companies in other countries will be managed responsibly. It is not too early to say, however, that every bad case will count in the public eye for many good ones. There seems to be an innate skepticism, whether in the United States, the Soviet Union, or Guatemala, that any business structure can benefit both employees and owners of capital. This skepticism will have to be overcome before employees will be eager to work for employee-owned companies, unions will negotiate for it, or governments will support it.

The government's perception of how well employee ownership works for companies and employees will be critical in determining whether it supports the practice, and its support is vital. But there are other issues as well. In Eastern Europe and the Soviet Union, support may hinge on the government's willingness to foster private enterprise, which would lead to some employees becoming relatively wealthy. Outside capital investments will also be crucial. On the plus side, employee ownership might be seen as the only way to make privatization of state-owned companies politically acceptable. In these as well as in developing countries, the availability of government money to provide direct subsidies or tax incentives will be an important concern. In all countries, an adequate legal and financial framework will be important. Finally, there is the element of chance. If Louis Kelso had not existed, would ESOPs? If Russell Long had been governor of Louisiana, not the chairman of the Senate's tax-writing committee, would ESOPs have made their way into federal law?

Organized labor presents more complex issues. Unions, which represent about 15 percent of the U.S. private sector work force, have almost always been officially neutral about employee ownership. Though the limited unionization of the work force will always constrain labor's role in ESOPs, active union involvement is likely to make employee ownership work favorably for employees. Where unions have initiated ESOPs in the United States, they have usually, if not always, helped set up effective employee-involvement programs. A positive union role, therefore, could be an important force in making employee ownership work. In other countries, this role is much more critical. Unions cover a large percentage of the work force in many nations and often have considerable political clout as well.

In these countries, the success of employee ownership may depend on its acceptance by unions.

Employee ownership could be a new avenue for unions to build their strength. As strikes have declined in potency in the United States, unions need other ways to represent the interests of their members. The formation of a union-controlled leveraged buyout fund in 1990, the almost successful effort of three unions to buy United Airlines, and the continued success of the United Steelworkers with employee ownership are all signs of the beginning of a substantial union role in this arena.

The role of unions abroad is murkier. In England, a union-financed bank has taken the lead in lending to ESOPs, but unions themselves have mostly ignored the idea. In Eastern Europe, unions are still feeling their way as independent entities. In developing countries, unions have been Marxist in orientation, more inclined to support government ownership than employee ownership.

Two remaining concerns are more speculative. One is the course of political and economic events. Another depression, for instance, could discredit employee ownership, especially if ownership is an employee's main savings plan. That was the lesson of employee ownership in the 1920s. Today's employee-owners, however, seem more likely to have additional investment and retirement plans, and the idea may be rooted deeply enough, at least in the United States, to withstand such a shock. A second concern is political turmoil in Eastern Europe, where employee ownership might be associated with current regimes. If those regimes are discredited or replaced, employee ownership could collapse. Eastern European countries could turn to fascism, become enmeshed in political chaos, or take other courses that would make employee ownership impossible.

Finally, there is the issue of technology. Today, we think of work as something done for eight hours a day at a business site. This could change. People might work more at home. Technology could reduce the need for work or for permanent workers. More people may be specialists in certain areas, contracting with companies as they need to work. Our notions of what it means to be an employee, or an employee-owner, could change along with these developments. Or, as Louis Kelso predicted, technology could advance to the point that almost all value added to a product comes from capital. Companies might be able to get by with many fewer workers, and there might not be new opportunities for work. Wages could be forced down both by the decreased need for workers and the decreased level of skill needed or by the steady shift of employment to service jobs. All of this would exacerbate the concentration of wealth in market economies. Employee ownership could be the only way to deal with the inequity.

Whatever the future brings, however, it is worth reflecting on how far we have come. No one would have predicted in 1980 that employee ownership would be as important as it is in the 1990s. Although some critics may complain that ESOPs are not democratic enough, no critic would have guessed in 1980 that there would be as many democratic ESOPs as there are today. Other critics fear that employee ownership may be too risky or replace other important benefits, but none of these critics would have predicted in 1980 that so many employees would be sharing so much wealth by 1990. While still other critics say employee ownership is too often used to protect management interests, none of these critics would have envisioned in 1980 the revolution in management style that characterizes a large and growing number of ESOP companies. And certainly the critics who said in 1980 that employee ownership would never amount to anything would never have expected the strides it took in the United States and the world by 1990.

As satisfying as these developments have been to believers in this concept, there is still much to be done. For every private sector employee in the United States who is an owner, there are eight who are not; for every employee in the rest of the world who is an owner, there are thousands who are not. For every company that treats its employees as owners, there are two or three employee-owned companies that do not and hundreds of nonemployee-owned companies that do not. There is still a long way to go. Fortunately, as a poster in our office points out, "Getting there is half the fun."

A Primer on Business

Corey Rosen

A story in a newspaper business section might read as follows:

International Multiproducts Responds to Raider

In a tersely worded statement, International Multiproducts (IMP) has responded to hostile raider John Buck by saying it will oppose any effort to lure shareholders into tendering their shares to Buck. "We plan to fight this all the way," said an IMP spokeswoman. "We are currently investigating a number of options, such as going private, doing a leveraged recapitalization, establishing an ESOP, or doing a self-tender through a Dutch auction. Meanwhile, we plan a thorough review of operations with the goal of maximizing our return on equity and earnings per share. Through asset redeployment, changes in our debt to equity structure, and redeeming common stock and replacing it with convertible preferred, we think we can accomplish these objectives."

Most well-educated people would not have a clue about what this means. It seems inordinately complicated and maybe even boring.

Actually, it is not so complicated; it is just that the language is unfamiliar. It does not even have to be boring. What follows is a basic introduction to business, which we hope will help readers understand this book and maybe the newspaper business section as well.

Organizing a Business

Just about any establishment that sells something and is not part of the government is a business. Farms are businesses, the Avon lady is a business, the corner deli is a business, doctors and lawyers are businesses. But businesses are organized in many different ways. They can be sole proprietorships (one person owns everything) or partnerships, for instance. In these simple organizational forms, the owners are taxed for any profit the business makes. Let us say that Jones and Smith start a bookstore. They decide to be partners. In the first year, they sell $100,000 worth of books. Typically, it will cost $50,000 to buy the books and about $12,000 for a small storefront. Utilities, insurance, and other costs come to another $10,000. The partners agree to pay themselves modest salaries of $10,000 a year. The business pays about another $2,000 in taxes on these salaries for its contribution to Social Security and unemployment. They end up with $6,000 in profits. They can keep this princely sum, in which case they have to pay taxes on it personally to the government as if they made the money as individuals. If they keep the money in the business, perhaps to provide a cushion against downturns or to use for later investments, they still have to pay tax on the profits, even though they never actually saw the money. The partners, not the company, pay the taxes, and any profits of the company must be allocated to each owner.

This system can work very well for a while. The profits are taxed to the partners at their personal income tax rates, which are low because they do not make much money. They might pay 15 percent of the profits in taxes to the federal government, plus some to the state. If, however, the business expands, hiring employees and making more money, problems will emerge. For instance, say they want to expand by borrowing money from a bank. They and the bank believe the expansion will generate enough new business to pay for the loan. But what if they are wrong and instead lose money? The bank will come after their personal assets. Builders or book suppliers to whom they owe money could sue. Other people who might invest in the business would probably not put up their money if they knew the bank could come after them too if a loan was not repaid.

The corporation was invented to prevent this unpleasant possibility. A corporation has two unique characteristics: limited liability and the ability to act as a legal person. Limited liability means that the assets of the people who own the corporation cannot be taken to repay the obligations of the company. If you own stock in Chrysler, and Chrysler goes bankrupt, your stock is worthless, but creditors cannot get personal assets to repay Chrysler's loans. Similarly, if the corporation is sued, you are not a party to the suit.

As a legal person, the corporation pays tax on the profits it makes. This has advantages and disadvantages. Let's say Jones and Smith's bookstore attracts a few investors, and the partners still own some of the company. If they make a profit, the bookstore pays taxes, up to a 34 percent rate if they make enough money. They can choose to pay part of the profits directly to themselves and other owners, but they must pay tax on that amount too, which means the profits are taxed twice. Or they can keep the profits in the business, perhaps using them to expand further or to build a cash reserve. This will make the company worth more. Because the owners are not yet getting any of this money, however, they do not have to pay tax. In fact, they do not pay tax on any of these reinvested profits until they sell their ownership share. If they do not need the money now, this is a good deal. It is always better to pay later.

For these tax, liability, and other reasons, most businesses of any size—more than ten or twenty employees—are almost always corporations. People with businesses that large do not want to take the risks inherent to partnerships and sole proprietorships. Even though corporations can be taxed double on profits, their ability to retain earnings untaxed to the owners can be more important, especially in businesses that have tangible assets such as property and machinery, rather than just personal services (such as a small accounting firm would have). Some people believe that the nineteenth-century invention of the limited liability corporation was a key to industrial development.

Dividing Up Ownership

A corporation will most likely have stock (there are nonstock corporations, but they are not relevant for employee ownership). Stock is a way to represent on paper the different ownership interests of a firm's owners. There are two kinds of corporations, public and private, and both can have stock. Public companies are the ones whose stock anyone can buy and whose prices are set by buying and selling on stock exchanges. There are about ten thousand public companies in the United States. Private companies are those whose stock is not openly traded. In many of them all the shares are owned by a family, an individual, or a few people. There are at least 250,000 private corporations in the United States employing ten people or more.

Where does this stock come from? Quite simply, it is printed. When a corporation is formed, its directors decide how many shares they would like to issue. The value of each share is the value of the business divided by the number of shares. Some or all of these shares may be given to the founders of the company. Let's say that when Jones and Smith started their bookstore, they printed one thousand shares. Each partner put up $10,000 and they shared duties at the store. In addition, Jones's brother-in-law and Smith's old college roommate each put up $10,000. How much stock would each get? Most likely, they would agree that Jones and Smith would get more than 25 percent each because they were putting up "sweat equity," working for low pay to get the business going. Just how much more would be a matter of negotiation.

Now let's move up a few years. The business has expanded, and more money is needed. In business, this is called capital. There are two kinds of capital: debt and equity. Debt means the money is borrowed; equity means someone invests money in the business. Either way, the people supplying the money have to be repaid.

With a loan, it is clear exactly how much has to be repaid, and repayment starts immediately. Equity is less certain. The investor buys shares in the company. To raise new capital, more shares are issued and sold. The owners now own a smaller percentage of the business, but the business is worth more.

Unlike the lender, the equity investor is patient and does not demand that repayment start right away. Instead, the investor hopes the value of the business will grow and the shares will be sold for a good return. The owner might agree to repurchase the shares sometime, or the investor can try to find another buyer. The owner might also agree to start paying the investor some interim returns in the form of a dividend. Dividends are profits paid to investors. Usually, dividends are equal to between 1 and 5 percent of the value of the shares, figured on an annual basis. Because the equity investor is not sure how much, if any, return there will be on the investment, the investor will demand a higher rate of return than the lender. A lender might be happy with 10 percent a year; an investor might expect twice that.

There are advantages and disadvantages to either source of capital. Debt is cheaper but requires faster repayment; equity is more patient but demands more money back in the long run.

Finally, let's imagine that the business keeps growing. Jones and Smith need a lot of money to go directly into book publishing. They have several bookstores and are doing well, but they need megadollars to get into the publishing business. Even under the best scenarios, however, it will take a few years for the publishing division to start generating revenues to pay for itself. At the same time, some of the investors are demanding that the company buy their shares. One solution would be to "go public," issue new shares, and hope that the public will pay for them, bringing new money into the business. This is an expensive process, requiring legal and financial filings, among other things, but it would make the stock available to anyone. It would also provide a market for the company's investors to sell their shares to other buyers, rather than to the company, which would be a saving to the company. It would also mean having many new shareholders, new legal responsibilities, and other headaches. But no solution is perfect.

There are many forms of stock. The most common, logically, is called "common." Shares of common stock usually have one vote each (when, for example, voting for the board of directors). They may or may not receive a dividend. The next most common kind of stock is "preferred." Preferred shareholders get paid first if the company goes bankrupt; common shareholders usually end up with nothing in that case. Preferred shareholders also get a dividend, and it is higher than the dividend, if any, paid on common. People who buy preferred pay more for the privilege. Both kinds of stock go up and down depending on the performance of the company.

What Is a Business Worth?

If the company goes public, it will be easy to determine how much each share of stock is worth. It will be worth what people are willing to pay for it. But what if instead the decision is made to borrow the capital and not go public? Some of the investors still want to sell. How much is their stock worth?

To find out, a business valuation is necessary. A valuation expert tries to figure out how much someone would be willing to pay for the shares. The first task is to decide how much the business is worth. The process is complicated, but the theory is simple. The value of businesses depends on the value of their assets on the market and the earnings they can generate. The assets are the easy part. Buildings, real estate, machinery, bills owed to the firm (called receivables), trade names, and patents can all be sold, and there is often an active market for them. Earning capacity is different. The bookstore may be making $1 million a year, after payment of taxes, salaries, and all other expenses. That profit is a result of the quality of the inventory, the locations of the stores, the physical attributes of the stores, the company's reputation, the savvy of the managers in buying good books, the public's interest in buying books, the state of the economy, and other factors. Someone buying the company wants to know whether the business will continue to earn $1 million a year or whether it will make more or less. The valuation expert makes some judgment on that, then figures out how much people are paying to buy similar businesses earning the same amount of money. These figures are blended with the calculations for asset value to figure out what the business is worth.

It is still not clear what the shares are worth. An individual investor, for instance, might own 10 percent of the shares. If the business is worth $10 million, the shares are worth $1 million, right? Wrong. The investor has two problems. First, Jones and Smith are not a public company so it is not easy to sell the shares whenever desired. This makes the shares worth less than shares of, say, IBM. Liquidity—the ability to sell at any time—is worth something. Second, 10 percent of the company is not enough to exert any control. Imagine that the bookstore has some properties in hot new development areas that the owners bought years ago for a song. Selling books in the stores is profitable, but if the stores were torn down, the land could be sold for a fortune to a developer who wants to build condos. As the controlling partners in the company, Jones and Smith can make this decision at any time and rake in the dollars. But a 10 percent investor cannot. This makes the investors' shares worth less than the owners' because the latter have an extra desirable feature—control. This is why shares that were selling for $50 may go up to $75 or $100 when raiders mount a hostile bid to buy a company. The raider is willing to pay a premium for control.

So the valuation expert will discount the value of the shares for these considerations and come up with a price. If an employee stock ownership plan is inaugurated, much the same process will be used, with some variations for the special features of an ESOP.

Profits, Taxes, Deductions, and Credits

Taxes are a fact of corporate life. For every dollar earned, income tax is owed to the federal and (in most states) state government. The firm also pays sales taxes on purchases, payroll taxes (Social Security and unemployment) on wages, property taxes, and a variety of others. For the purposes of this book, an understanding of income taxes will suffice.

Corporate tax rates vary depending on the amount of profits made, but most companies large enough to have an employee ownership plan pay at a 34 percent federal rate, plus several percent more for the state. That means that for every dollar earned, the company pays about forty cents in income taxes.

Profits are, of course, what is left from revenues after expenses are paid. It sounds simple, but it isn't. Some expenses are obvious—rent, payroll, utilities. Others are not so clear. Say a building is bought. Is it an expense in the year it is purchased? It will be used for many years so the government says it cannot be counted as an expense for just one year. It must be depreciated over a period of years, meaning that only a part of the expense counts each year. In theory, this is meant to spread the cost over the useful life of the asset, although the schedules for depreciation do not always reflect that. Then there are items that seem like expenses but are not. For instance, interest paid on loans is an expense, but the principal portion is not (the theory is that the interest does not buy anything but the principal does). Profits paid to shareholders as dividends are also not expenses.

The tax term for what can be counted as an expense is a deduction. A deduction is any cost that can be counted against total income, thereby reducing the total amount of profit on which tax is owed. People will say, "Oh, it doesn't cost them anything; they can deduct it." This is not true. A dollar in deduction is worth the dollar times the total tax rate, or about 40 percent. A tax credit gives a dollar back for every dollar spent. Credits for business are rare these days, however.

As this book explains, ESOPs provide added value for many companies because they let companies deduct certain expenses, such as the principal paid on a loan, that could not be deducted otherwise. ESOPs provide another tax benefit as well: tax deferrals. This simply means tax is not due until later. Employees, for instance, accumulate stock in an ESOP but do not pay any tax on it until they actually get the shares when they leave the company. This means they have the use of more money now, and everyone would rather have a dollar today than a dollar tomorrow.

Beyond Basics: Techniques of Corporate Finance

This discussion of the most basic of business issues would not help much in understanding the newspaper article at the outset. That article is concerned mostly with issues of corporate finance. The simplest forms of finance are borrowing and selling shares. When companies borrow money, they are said to "leverage," which is the source of the term *leveraged ESOP*. In a leveraged buyout, or LBO, an entire company is bought, mostly with debt. The assets of the company serve as collateral for the loan (collateral is the assets the bank can get if the loan is not repaid). Rarely can a leveraged buyout be done entirely with debt, however. It would be the same as asking a bank to loan an amount equal to the entire worth of the company. There is no room for error; if the company loses money in the first year, there is none left to pay the bills. So banks ask for some equity, money that can be used now and repaid later when revenues are better.

When more than one investor is involved in an LBO, it is called a multi-investor LBO. These investors have to figure out a fair equity allocation. Different investors may bring different assets to the transaction. In ESOPs, the employees may be acquiring the stock by having their ownership plan borrow money, then having the company repay the loan out of future earnings. This does not add much to the company's initial pool of money. Just about all it adds are the tax breaks ESOPs get. In other cases, employees may make concessions in wages or benefits. These are worth more but not as much as cash that is invested up front. The investors need to negotiate between them just how much each kind of investment is worth.

The investors can get different kinds of stock (preferred or common) for their investment, or they can get other securities. Securities are different ways of paying people back for their investment, of which stock is one way. Corporate bonds are another common kind of security. Companies sell bonds, often through those fabled specialists known as investment bankers, to raise debt capital. Books International, the now large firm created by Jones and Smith, could go to the investment banking firm of Nicholls and Dymes, for instance, and say it needs $10 million. Nicholls and Dymes would have bonds printed that would promise to pay the buyer a certain rate of interest for a certain number of years. At the end of that time, the bonds would be redeemed; that is, the company would pay the face value of the bond. A $1,000 bond might pay 10 percent for ten years, for instance. Nicholls and Dymes gets a percentage of the total amount of capital they raise by finding people to buy the bonds.

The more risky the company, the more interest it is necessary to pay to get people to buy the bonds. A utility, for instance, can pay a low rate because everyone knows it will be in business for a long time. If the book company had shaky earnings in the past or was not very well known, Jones and Smith would have to pay a higher rate of interest. Bonds that have to pay a high rate of interest are called junk bonds.

Warrants are another kind of security. A warrant is like stock, except that it becomes valuable only if the common stock goes above a certain price. For instance, Books International might sell warrants at $10 per "unit" (as they are called) when the common stock is at $5. Each unit of the warrant could be converted into common shares for a defined period of time, say ten years. Of course, one would not want to do this if the stock were less than $10, but if it does well an investor could get a windfall.

Both bonds and warrants can be sold at any time, assuming that someone wants to buy them. How much they are worth depends on how well the company is doing, the state of the economy, what the firm's prospects are, and, in the case of bonds, what the current competing interest rates are. If you have a $1,000 bond paying 10 percent, for instance, and interest rates drop to 8 percent, someone will pay you much more than $1,000 for your bond.

There are a number of other securities as well. Most are a way of combining debt and equity investments. The point is to provide whatever is needed to get investors on the best terms possible.

Corporate finance is not limited to leveraged buyouts, even though these get most of the publicity. Corporations need money to expand, for instance. They also need to buy stocks, bonds, and other securities back from their holders from time to time. They may need to borrow money to do this. Public companies sometimes buy back some of their own shares and retire them because they think their own stock is a good investment or because they want to increase the price of the shares. Their offer to buy stock should make the price go up because demand has gone up. Increasing the share price can make a public company less vulnerable to a raider because the raid will be more costly. In an extreme case, a company can do a leveraged recapitalization, in which it borrows money to pay a substantial percentage of the company's worth to the shareholders. The company ends up heavily in debt and may no longer be attractive to a buyer.

How Companies Are Governed

Corporations have boards of directors elected by the shareholders. In almost every case, each share has one vote, although there are exceptions. The boards usually meet every few months to review operations. They also appoint the officers of the company. In most small and medium-sized companies, the board serves more as a source of advice than a policy maker. In public companies, boards take a more active role, although the recommendations of management are almost always approved.

The approval of the board or the shareholders is needed to sell a company. In private companies, these often are the same people. In public companies, board members almost always own only tiny percentages of the company's stock. If someone wants to take over a company that does not want to sell, there are two alternatives. One is a proxy fight, in which stockholders are solicited to vote for a slate of directors preferred by the raider. This is a long and difficult route. The second is a tender offer in which the raider offers to buy shares for a price above the current market price and hopes enough people will sell so the raider can take control. The board may decide to agree to the tender beforehand, making life easier for the raider.

As much as we hear about takeovers, it is wise to remember that most companies are private and are not subject to such tactics.

The Structure of American Business

When we think of business, we often think of big business. Big business is important, but about half the nation's employees work for companies with fewer than five hundred workers. There are more than 4 million business establishments in the United States, but only about 1 million of these employ more than twenty people. About 175,000 businesses are in manufacturing. Many smaller firms are in industries with very transient employment such as fast-food restaurants (7 percent of the population has its first job at McDonald's, for instance). Many others are themselves transient, with a short life expectancy. Still others have erratic or no profits. Only firms with stable work forces, reasonable profits, and, generally, more than twenty employees are good candidates for most employee ownership plans.

The ownership of business is highly concentrated. Total equity in America's corporations is about $2.5 trillion. According to the Federal Reserve Board, about 20 percent is owned by pension plans, 5 percent by foreigners, 8 percent by institutions (mutual funds, insurance companies, and the like), and the remaining 66 percent by households. Half the stock owned by households is owned by the wealthiest 1 percent.

Some have argued that pension funds are owned by workers, but that is generally not true. Most pension assets are in defined benefit plans, which provide a guaranteed annual income after retirement. A company or government is obligated to ensure that there is adequate funding to accomplish this. To do that, it invests in stocks, bonds, certificates of deposit, real estate, and so on. If these perform well, the company needs to contribute less money to the pension fund; if they do not, the company must contribute more. Workers do not benefit from an increase or suffer from a decline in the value of "their" investments; they get the same amount no matter what. Nor do they have any say in where "their" money is invested or when it is sold. In fact, the real owners of the pension plans are the people who own the companies, most of whom are already rich. Similarly, the primary owners of mutual funds and insurance policies are very rich.

Resource Guide

Legal and Technical Information

Ellerman, David. *What Is a Workers' Cooperative?* Somerville, Mass.: Industrial Cooperative Association, 1979.

A good brief discussion laying out the ICA's innovative model for structuring cooperatives.

ERISA: The Law and the Code. Washington, D.C.: Bureau of National Affairs, 1987.

A compilation of laws relating to ESOPs and other qualified employee benefit plans.

Industrial Cooperative Association. *ICA Model By-Laws for Worker Cooperatives.* Somerville, Mass.: Industrial Cooperative Association, 1978.

A detailed guide for setting up a worker cooperative.

Journal of Employee Ownership Law and Finance. Published quarterly by the NCEO since December 1989.

Each issue discusses a different aspect of ESOP law and finance in detail. The first issue dealt with public companies; vol. 2, no. 1, with leveraged ESOPs; vol. 2, no. 2, with banks as ESOP sponsors; vol. 2, no. 3, with plan administration; and vol. 2, no. 4, with employee rights. Articles are written by experts in the field.

Kalish, Gerald, ed. *ESOPs: The Handbook of Employee Stock Ownership Plans.* Chicago: Probus, 1989.

A general overview of how ESOPs work.

Kaplan, Jared, Gregory K. Brown, and Ronald L. Ludwig. *ESOPs*. Washington, D.C.: Tax Management, 1987.

A detailed explanation of ESOPs, containing technical explanations of legal issues, required legal forms, and a list of ESOP regulations and statutes.

National Center for Employee Ownership. *An Employee Buyout Handbook*. Oakland, Calif.: NCEO, 1988.

A detailed, step-by-step explanation of the process of evaluating whether an employee buyout is worth pursuing, including a variety of financial questions and guidelines.

———. *Employee Ownership: Alternatives to ESOPs*. Oakland, Calif.: NCEO, 1990.

An examination of non-ESOP methods to achieve employee ownership. Includes chapters on stock bonus/stock purchase, 401(k), profit-sharing, and stock option plans, as well as cooperatives and new ideas.

———. *Gainsharing and Employee Ownership*. Oakland, Calif.: NCEO, 1988.

A discussion of profit sharing, bonus plans, Scanlon plans, and other productivity-related incentive plans.

———. *A Model Employee Stock Ownership Plan*. Oakland, Calif.: NCEO, 1989.

A 100-page compilation of the legal language for an ESOP, a plain English explanation of each provision, a suggested model for an employee handbook, a list of consultants, and other material. Contains several different options for tailoring plans to specific needs.

Pratt, Shannon. *Valuing a Business*. 2d ed. Homewood, Ill.: Dow Jones–Irwin, 1989.

A standard reference work that includes extensive material on ESOPs.

Smiley, Robert W., and Ronald J. Gilbert, eds. *Employee Stock Ownership Plans*. New York: Prentice-Hall, 1989.

A compilation of detailed articles on most key aspects of ESOPs, including leveraging, valuation, communications and participation, research, and ESOP regulations. Authors include leading ESOP consultants.

Case Studies

Barnes, Peter. "Confessions of a Socialist Entrepreneur." Unpublished paper. Available from the NCEO.

The best article on what it actually is like to organize and run an employee-owned business from the founder of the Solar Center.

Berman, Katrina. *Worker Owned Plywood Companies*. Pullman: Washington State University Press, 1967.

A pioneering study of worker plywood cooperatives.

Davis, Grant, Norman Weintraub, and William Holley. "Employee Stock Ownership Programs and Their Use in Trucking." *Logistics and Transportation Review* 23 (Fall 1987): 243–63.

ESOPs were popular in return for wage concessions in the trucking industry in the early 1980s, but few succeeded. This article explores how these plans were set up.

"ESOP at the Barricades: Polaroid Uses a Novel Anti-Takeover Defense." *Barron's* 69 (February 6, 1989): 38–40.

Polaroid was the first company to use an ESOP successfully as a takeover defense.

Gibney, Alex. "Paradise Tossed: How a Chance to Save American Capitalism Was Sabotaged at Eastern." *Washington Monthly*, June 1986, 24–34.

Best short discussion of how employee ownership at Eastern at first succeeded, then faltered.

Hansen, Gary, and Frank Adams. "Saving Jobs and Putting Democracy to Work: Labor Management Cooperation at Seymour Specialty Wire." Labor-Management Cooperation Brief No. 11. U.S. Department of Labor, Bureau of Labor Management Relations, 1987.

Seymour was bought by its unionized employees and implemented a very democratic structure. This analysis looks at some of the problems that developed in implementing it.

Hartzell, Hal. *Birth of a Cooperative*. Eugene, Ore.: Yew Books, Hulgosi Cooperative, 1987.

An interesting and well-written account of the start of a tree-planting cooperative in the Northwest.

Hester, Steven. "The White Pine ESOP." *Michigan Bar Journal* 66 (May 1987): 398–400.

White Pine was a failing company bought by its unionized employees and eventually sold at a considerable profit.

Hochner, Arthur, Cherlyn Granrose, Judith Goode, Elaine Simon, and Eileen Appelbaum. *Job-Saving Strategies: Worker Buyouts and QWL.* Indianapolis: W. E. Upjohn, 1988.

Discusses the first two years of an employee buyout of the O&O supermarkets in Philadelphia, comparing them to other markets bought by another company and emphasizing quality of work life programs instead of ownership.

Kirkpatrick, David. "How Employees Run Avis Better." *Fortune* 118 (December 5, 1988): 103ff.

Describes how employee ownership and participation have succeeded at Avis.

National Center for Employee Ownership. *Employee Ownership Casebook.* Updated annually.

One- to two-page case studies of approximately seventy employee ownership companies.

Perry, Stewart. *The San Francisco Scavengers.* Berkeley: University of California Press, 1978.

Describes large, successful worker cooperative garbage collection firms in the Bay Area.

Quarrey, Michael, Joseph Blasi, and Corey Rosen. *Taking Stock: Employee Ownership at Work.* Cambridge, Mass.: Ballinger, 1986.

Collection of fourteen case studies of employee ownership companies studied by the NCEO.

Rhodes, Lucien, and Patricia Amend. "Turnaround." *Inc.*, August 1986, 31ff.

Describes Springfield Remanufacturing, one of the most successful and participative ESOP companies.

Rowe, Jonathan. "Weirton Steel: Buying Out the Bosses." *Washington Monthly* 15 (January 1984): 34–46.

Best discussion of how employees were able to buy Weirton Steel, one of the largest employee-owned companies.

Severin, Werner. "The Milwaukee Journal: Employee-Owned Prizewinner." *Journalism Quarterly* 56 (Winter 1979): 783–87.

Overview of what is now Journal Communications, a major media firm owned directly by employees.

U.S. Department of Labor, Bureau of Labor Management Relations. *Labor Management Cooperation at Eastern Airlines*. Washington D.C.: Department of Labor, 1988.

A detailed monograph describing employee ownership and participation programs at Eastern in the mid-1980s.

General Studies

Blasi, Joseph. *Employee Ownership: Revolution or Ripoff?* Cambridge, Mass.: Ballinger, 1988.

A critical look at ESOPs, including a detailed political and economic history.

Bloom, Steven. "Employee Ownership and Firm Performance." Ph.D. dissertation, Harvard University, 1986.

Shows that little relationship exists between tax credit ESOPs and corporate performance in large companies.

Bradley, Keith, and Alan Gelb. *Worker Capitalism: The New Industrial Relations*. Cambridge, Mass.: MIT Press, 1983.

A study of selected worker buyouts of troubled firms in the United States and Europe and of the Mondragón cooperatives in Spain.

Bureau of National Affairs. *Employee Ownership Plans*. Washington, D.C.: BNA Books, 1987.

Contains general introduction, legal and technical articles, case studies, and other material. Prepared with the NCEO.

Center for Economic Stabilization and Community Development. *Survey of Organizations Assisting Employee-Owned Companies*. Portland, Ore.: Center for Economic Stabilization and Community Development, 1989.

Provides a description of state and nonprofit programs that provide technical assistance, education, and outreach for employee ownership.

Chang, Saeyoung. "Employee Stock Ownership Plans and Shareholder Wealth: An Empirical Investigation." *Financial Management* 19 (Spring 1990): 48–58.

ESOPs increase short-term share prices in public companies unless the ESOP is used as a takeover defense, in which case they decrease it.

Chaplinsky, Susan, and Greg Niehaus. "The Tax and Distributional Effects of Leveraged ESOPs." *Financial Management* 19 (Spring 1990): 29–38.

Empirical analysis finds that employees in public companies generally do not give up compensation for participation in plans and, largely as a result, shareholders do not benefit from ESOPs.

Conte, Michael, and Arnold Tannenbaum. *Employee Ownership*. Ann Arbor: Survey Research Center, University of Michigan, 1980.

A comprehensive study of the effects of employee ownership on profitability which finds that employee ownership firms are 1.5 times as profitable as conventional firms.

Durso, Gianna. "Usage of ESOPs in Public Companies." "*Journal of Employee Ownership Law and Finance*" 1 (Fall 1989): 75–88.

Describes how public companies are using their employee-ownership plans, based on a study of ESOPs set up in 1989.

"ESOPs: Special Section." *Pensions and Investment Age* 17 (September 18, 1989): 35–38.

Good summary of current uses of ESOPs and ESOP issues, particularly in large companies.

Farrell, Christopher, and John Hoerr. "ESOPs: Are They Good for You?" *Business Week* 116 (May 15, 1989): 19ff.

Balanced cover story focusing on ESOPs in public companies.

Hammer, Tove, and Robert Stern. "Employee Ownership: Implications for the Organizational Distribution of Power." *Academy of Management Journal* 23 (March 1980): 78–100.

Looks at how workers and managers see their roles in a company bought by employees.

Hoerr, John. "ESOPs: Revolution or Ripoff?" *Business Week* 112 (April 15, 1985): 94ff.

Generally skeptical cover story article on ESOPs.

Jackall, Robert, and Henry Levin, eds. *Worker Cooperatives in America*. Berkeley: University of California Press, 1985.

A reader on worker cooperatives that brings together most of the best writings on the subject.

Jones, Derek, and Jan Svenjar. *Participatory and Self-Managed Firms*. Lexington, Mass.: Lexington Books, 1982.

Collection of essays, including several empirical studies, on worker-managed firms throughout the world.

Kelso, Louis, and Mortimer Adler. *The Capitalist Manifesto*. New York: Random House, 1958.

The basic book explaining Kelso's philosophy of broadened ownership.

Kelso, Louis, and Patricia Hetter. *Two-Factor Theory: The Economics of Reality*. New York: Random House, 1967.

A brief explanation of Kelso's theory.

Klein, Katherine, and R. J. Hall. "Correlates of Employee Satisfaction with Stock Ownership: Who Likes an ESOP Most?" *Journal of Applied Psychology* 73 (November 1988): 630–38.

Based on extensive surveys, researchers find that satisfaction with employee ownership is not a function of socioeconomic characteristics.

Kruse, Douglas. *Employee Ownership and Attitudes: Two Case Studies*. Norwood, Pa.: Norwood Editions, 1984.

Discusses two detailed case studies and the general philosophy of employee ownership.

Logue, John, and Cassandra Rogers. *Employee Stock Ownership Plans in Ohio: Impact on Company Performance and Employment.* Kent: Northeast Ohio Employee Ownership Center, 1989.

Careful survey of experience with employee ownership in Ohio.

Long, Richard. "Job Attitudes and Organizational Performance under Employee Ownership." *Academy of Management Journal* 23 (December 1980): 726–37.

Examines effects of employee ownership in three firms and finds that positive impact is greatest when amount owned is highest and degree of employee participation strongest.

Marsh, Thomas, and Dale McAllister. "ESOP Tables: A Survey of Companies with Employee Stock Ownership Plans." *Journal of Corporation Law* 6 (Spring 1981): 551–623.

Based on a survey of 229 companies with ten or more employees, this study covers the structure, performance, and characteristics of ESOP firms. It concludes that these companies are much more productive than their conventional counterparts.

Nasar, Sylvia. "The Foolish Rush to ESOPs." *Fortune* 120 (September 25, 1989): 141–46.

Critical article on the use of ESOPs in public companies.

Nassau, M. J. "ESOPs after Polaroid—Opportunities and Pitfalls." *Employee Relations Law Journal* 15 (Winter 1989): 347–65.

Discussion of how ESOPs can be used, particularly as a takeover defense.

National Center for Employee Ownership. *An Employee Ownership Reader.* Oakland, Calif.: NCEO, 1989.

A comprehensive introduction to employee ownership, containing practical articles on ESOPs and cooperatives, case studies, and suggestions on organizational development and legal structure.

Olson, Deborah Groban. "Some Union Experiences with Issues Raised by Worker Ownership in the U.S.: ESOPs, TRASOPs, Co-ops, Stock Plans and Board Representation." *Wisconsin Law Review* 5 (December 1982): 729–823.

An excellent review of union concerns and possibilities on these issues.

Park, Chong. "The Record of ESOP Leveraged Buyouts." *Journal of Employee Ownership Law and Finance* 2 (Winter 1990): 29–50.

An empirical analysis of large ESOP leveraged buyouts finds they perform as well as or better than their industries.

Patard, Richard. *Employee Stock Ownership Plans in the 1920's*. Oakland, Calif.: NCEO, 1990.

Historical review of the "new capitalism" movement of the 1920s.

Presidential Task Force on Project Economic Justice. *High Road to Economic Justice*. Arlington, Va.: Center for Economic and Social Justice, 1986.

A report on how employee ownership can be used as part of a development strategy in Central America.

Quarrey, Michael. *Employee Ownership and Corporate Performance*. Oakland, Calif.: NCEO, 1986.

A before-and-after study of the effect of employee ownership on corporate performance.

Rosen, Corey, Katherine Klein, and Karen Young. *Employee Ownership in America: The Equity Solution*. Lexington, Mass.: Lexington Books, 1986.

Reports on the four-year study by the National Center of Employee Ownership of what makes employee ownership work better in some companies than others. The book also includes a general introduction to employee ownership. Intended for general audiences.

Rosen, Corey, and Michael Quarrey. "How Well Is Employee Ownership Working?" *Harvard Business Review* 65 (September–October 1987): 126–30.

Reviews NCEO study on the relationship between employee ownership and corporate performance.

Russell, Raymond. *Sharing Ownership in the Workplace*. Albany, N.Y.: SUNY Press, 1985.

Reviews the theoretical underpinnings of employee ownership, provides case studies of taxicab co-ops, garbage collection co-ops, and employee ownership in professional group practices.

Scholes, Myron, and Mark Wolfson. "Employee Stock Ownership Plans and Corporate Restructuring: Myths and Realities." *Financial Management* 19 (Spring 1990): 12–28.

Argues that ESOP tax benefits are more useful for private than public companies and that ESOPs are mostly useful for companies as part of a takeover defense or corporate restructuring.

U.S. Senate Committee on Banking, Housing, and Urban Affairs. *Hearings on Employee Ownership and Hostile Takeovers*. Washington, D.C.: U.S. Government Printing Office, 1987.

Testimony of various experts on the subject.

Washington Department of Community Development. *A Study of Employee Ownership in Washington State*. Olympia: Department of Community Development, 1989.

Detailed survey of employee ownership experience in Washington State.

Workers as Owners. Labor Research Review 6 (Spring 1965).

A collection of essays on worker ownership from a labor union perspective.

Young, Karen, ed. *The Expanding Role of Employee Ownership in Public Companies*. Westport, Conn.: Greenwood Press, 1990.

The most detailed publication available on the structure and use of ESOPs in public firms.

Employee Participation and Communication

Freund, William, and Eugene Epstein. *People and Productivity*. Homewood, Ill.: Dow Jones–Irwin, 1984.

A study by the New York Stock Exchange on the relationship between employee participation and corporate performance in large U.S. companies.

National Center for Employee Ownership. *Beyond Taxes: Managing an Employee Ownership Company*. Oakland, Calif.: NCEO, 1988.

Case histories and specific examples of how companies get their employees more involved.

————. *Employee Participation Programs in Employee Ownership Companies*. Oakland, Calif.: NCEO, 1989.

A practical guide based on experiences of employee-owned companies, discussing formal and informal programs.

Simmons, John, and William Mares. *Working Together*. New York: Knopf, 1983.

Excellent account of over fifty companies using employee ownership or quality of work life programs.

International Aspects of Employee Ownership

Blum, Fred. *Work and Community: The Scott Bader Commonwealth and the Quest for a New Social Order*. London: Routledge & Kegan Paul, 1968.

Describes a pioneering English worker-owned firm.

Bradley, Keith, and Alan Gelb. *Cooperation at Work: The Mondragón Experience*. Brookfield, Vt.: Gower, 1983.

An economic analysis of the Mondragón cooperatives.

Holstrom, Mark. *Industrial Democracy in Italy: Worker Co-ops and the Self-Management Debate*. Brookfield, Vt.: Gower, 1989.

Italy has one of the largest worker cooperative sectors in the world. This book presents an overview.

International Labor Organization. *Labor Cooperatives*. Geneva: International Labor Office, 1989.

Examines labor cooperatives in Italy, India, Poland, New Zealand, and Israel.

Jones, Derek. "Producer Cooperatives in Industrialized Western Economies: An Overview." *Annals of Public and Cooperative Economy* 49 (Spring 1978): 149–61.

History of worker cooperatives and summary of information about their performance.

National Center for Employee Ownership. *International Developments in Employee Ownership*. Oakland, Calif.: NCEO, 1990.

A guide to employee ownership worldwide, including models, a discussion of regional economic and political issues, country and company case studies, and international contacts.

Paton, Rob. *Reluctant Entrepreneurs: The Extent, Achievements, and Significance of Worker Takeovers in Europe.* Philadelphia: Open University Press, 1989.

The only general survey of worker buyouts in Europe.

Toronto Stock Exchange. *A Survey of Employee Equity and Profit-Sharing Plans of Toronto Stock Exchange Companies.* Toronto: Toronto Stock Exchange, 1984.

Finds that many companies offer share purchase plans for employees and that these companies generally perform better than companies that do not.

Whyte, William Foote, and Kathleen King Whyte. *Making Mondragón: The Growth and Dynamics of the Worker Cooperative Complex.* Ithaca, N.Y.: ILR Press, 1988.

Examines the history and development of the Mondragón cooperatives.

Notes

Chapter 1

1. Data on capital accumulation from U.S. General Accounting Office, *Employee Stock Ownership Plans: Interim Report and a Survey on Economic Trends* (Washington, D.C.: U.S. General Accounting Office, 1986), p. 37. Data on ESOP wealth accumulation from National Center for Employee Ownership (NCEO) estimates. Estimates are based on tracking from published sources leveraged ESOPs borrowing over $10 million. These account for the large majority of dollars borrowed through ESOPs; the remainder are conservative estimates.

2. Tax cost estimates from the Office of Management and Budget and the Congressional Joint Tax Committee, as reported by the ESOP Association of America, a trade group, in conversations with the author.

3. Quoted in Franz Foerster, *Employee Stock Ownership Plans in the U.S.* (Princeton: Princeton University Press, 1926), p. 62.

4. Derek Jones, "American Producer Cooperatives and Employee Owned Firms: A Historical Perspective," in Robert Jackall and Henry Levin, eds., *Worker Cooperatives in America* (Berkeley: University of California Press, 1985).

5. Arthur Hochner, Cherlyn Granrose, et al., *Job-Saving Strategies: Worker Buyouts and QWL* (Indianapolis: W. E. Upjohn, 1988), pp. 16–17.

6. Robert Brookings, *Economic Democracy: America's Answer to Socialism and Communism* (New York: Macmillan, 1929), p. xxiii.

7. Arundell Cotter, "Social Consequences of Employee Ownership," *Proceedings of the Academy of Political Science* 11 (April 1925): 13.

8. Richard Patard, "ESOP Deja Vu: The Employee Stock Ownership Movement of the 1920's," unpublished paper (1982), pp. 11–12.

9. Louis Kelso and Mortimer Adler, *The Capitalist Manifesto* (New York: Random House, 1958), p. 68.

10. U.S. General Accounting Office, *Employee Stock Ownership Plans*, p. 37.

11. U.S. General Accounting Office, *Benefits and Costs of ESOP Tax Incentives* (Washington, D.C.: U.S. General Accounting Office, 1986), p. 20.

12. Ibid.; see also Washington Department of Community Development, *A Study of Employee Ownership in Washington State* (Olympia: Department of Community Development, 1990), p. 7.

13. U.S. General Accounting Office, *401(k) Plans* (Washington, D.C.: U.S. General Accounting Office, 1988), pp. 36–37.

14. Unpublished data from an ongoing research project by Douglas Kruse and Joseph Blasi at Rutgers University, New Brunswick, N.J.

15. Thomas Marsh and Dale McAllister, "ESOP Tables: A Survey of Companies with Stock Ownership Plans," *Journal of Corporation Law* 6 (Spring 1981): 596; *ESOP Association Annual Survey* (Washington, D.C.: ESOP Association of America, 1990).

16. U.S. General Accounting Office, *Employee Stock Ownership Plans*, p. 13.

17. Marsh and McAllister, "ESOP Tables," p. 596; *ESOP Association Annual Survey*; Corey Rosen, Katherine Klein, and Karen Young, *Employee Ownership in America: The Equity Solution* (Lexington, Mass.: Lexington Books, 1986); National Center for Employee Ownership, *Employee Stock Ownership Plans: How the Average Worker Fares* (Oakland, Calif.: NCEO, 1990).

18. "The Foibles of ESOPs," *Newsweek*, October 19, 1987, pp. 58–59.

19. Sylvia Nasar, "The Foolish Rush to ESOPs," *Fortune*, September 25, 1989, pp. 141–46.

20. "Chancy Capitalism," *National Journal*, September 17, 1988, pp. 2313–16.

21. Results from a Gallup poll commissioned by the Employee Benefits Research Institute, Washington, D.C., reported in *Employee Ownership Report*, November–December 1989, p. 2.

22. U.S. General Accounting Office, *Benefits and Costs of ESOP Tax Incentives*, p. 35.

23. NCEO, *Employee Stock Ownership Plans*.

24. U.S. General Accounting Office, *Employee Stock Ownership Plans*, p. 23.

25. NCEO, *Employee Stock Ownership Plans*.

26. "Survey of Consumer Finances, 1983," *Federal Reserve Bulletin*, September 1984.

27. "ESOP Survey, 1990," reported in *Employee Ownership Report*, November–December 1989, p. 6.

28. Michael Conte, "ESOPs in Public Companies," *Journal of Employee Ownership Law and Finance* 1 (Fall 1989): 96–97.

29. Gianna Durso, "Usage of ESOPs in Public Companies," *Journal of Employee Ownership Law and Finance* 1 (Fall 1989): 86–87.

30. Susan Chaplinsky and Greg Niehaus, "The Tax and Distributional Effects of Leveraged ESOPs," *Financial Management* 19 (Spring 1990): 37–38.

31. Blasi, *Employee Ownership: Revolution or Ripoff?* (Cambridge, Mass.: Ballinger, 1988), p. 119.

32. U.S. General Accounting Office, *Employee Stock Ownership Plans*, p. 33.

33. Blasi, *Employee Ownership*, p. 44.

34. See, for instance, Thomas Marsh and Dale McAllister, "ESOP Tables," in Michael Conte and Arnold Tannenbaum, *Employee Ownership* (Ann Arbor: University of Michigan Survey Research Center, 1980), p. 30; and Corey Rosen and Katherine Klein, "Job Generating Performance of Employee Owned Companies," *Monthly Labor Review*, August 1983, pp. 15–19.

35. Rosen, Klein, and Young, *Employee Ownership in America*, chap. 5.

36. Corey Rosen and Michael Quarrey, "How Well Is Employee Ownership Working?" *Harvard Business Review* 65 (September–October 1987): 126–30.

37. For an example of the research on participation, see John Cotton, David Vollrath, et al., "Employee Participation: Diverse Forms and Different Outcomes," *Academy of Management Review* 13 (January 1988): 8–23.

38. U.S. General Accounting Office, *Employee Stock Ownership Plans: Little Evidence of Effects on Corporate Performance* (Washington, D.C.: U.S. General Accounting Office, 1987), p. 30.

39. Patrick Rooney, "Employee Ownership and Worker Participation," paper presented at the University of Notre Dame Economic Workshop, April 20, 1990.

40. U.S. General Accounting Office, *Benefits and Costs of ESOP Tax Incentives*, p. 41.

41. Washington Department of Community Development, *A Study of Employee Ownership in Washington State*, p. 12.

42. John Logue and Cassandra Rogers, *Employee Stock Ownership Plans in Ohio: Impact on Company Performance and Employment* (Kent: Northeast Ohio Employee Ownership Center, 1989), pp. 16–18.

43. Chong Park, "The Record of ESOP Leveraged Buyouts," *Journal of Employee Ownership Law and Finance* 2 (Winter 1990): 29–50.

44. Conte, "ESOPs in Public Companies," pp. 96–97.

45. "ESOP Survey, 1990."

46. Rosen, Klein, and Young, *Employee Ownership in America*, p. 110.

47. NCEO, *Voting and Participation in Employee Ownership Firms* (Oakland, Calif.: NCEO, 1986).

48. U.S. General Accounting Office, *Benefits and Costs of ESOP Tax Incentives*, p. 40.

49. Park, "The Record of ESOP Leveraged Buyouts," p. 45.

Chapter 2

1. Robert Schatz, "Lending to ESOPs," in Gerald Kalish, ed., *ESOPs: The Handbook of Employee Stock Ownership Plans* (Chicago: Probus, 1989), chap. 4; Sections 133 and 4975 of the Internal Revenue Code; Section 408 of ERISA.

2. Thomas Marsh and Dale McAllister, "ESOP Tables: A Survey of Companies with Employee Stock Ownership Plans," *Journal of Corporation Law* 6

(Spring 1981): 593; Corey Rosen and Jonathan Feldman, "How Well Do ESOPs Reward Employees?" *Pension World*, February 1986, p. 35.

3. John Logue and Cassandra Rogers, *Employee Stock Ownership Plans in Ohio: Impact on Company Performance and Employment* (Kent: Northeast Ohio Employee Ownership Center, 1989), p. 12.

4. For an overview of the basic legal requirements, see Gregory Brown and Jared Kaplan, "Tax, ERISA and Securities Issues," in Robert W. Smiley and Ronald J. Gilbert, eds., *Employee Stock Ownership Plans* (New York: Prentice-Hall, 1989), chap. 13; Gregory Brown, "Overview of ESOP Legal Requirements," in Kalish, ed., *ESOPs*, chap. 1; Sections 401, 404, 409–11, and 414 of the Internal Revenue Code.

5. Sections 404 and 415 of the Internal Revenue Code.

6. Section 411 of the Internal Revenue Code.

7. Sections 409 and 1042 of the Internal Revenue Code (as amended by the Tax Reform Act of 1989).

8. U.S. General Accounting Office, *Benefits and Costs of ESOP Tax Incentives* (Washington D.C.: U.S. General Accounting Office, 1986), p. 20.

9. NCEO, *Voting and Participation in Employee Ownership Firms* (Oakland, Calif.: NCEO, 1986).

10. Corey Rosen, Katherine Klein, and Karen Young, *Employee Ownership in America: The Equity Solution* (Lexington, Mass.: Lexington Books, 1986), chaps. 1, 5.

11. Ronald Gilbert, "Above the Limit," in *The Employee Ownership Reader* (Oakland, Calif.: NCEO, 1989), pp. 59–60; Section 404 of the Internal Revenue Code.

12. Gianna Durso, "Usage of ESOPs in Public Companies," *Journal of Employee Ownership Law and Finance* 1 (Fall 1989): 75–88.

13. Chester A. Gougis, "The Role of Convertible Preferred Stock in Public Company ESOP Transactions," *Journal of Employee Ownership Law and Finance* 1 (Fall 1989): 9–22; Robert Bumgarner, "Using Convertible Preferred Shares to Increase Dividend Deductions," *Employee Ownership Reader*, p. 54.

14. Section 401(a) (28) (B) of the Internal Revenue Code.

15. Section 409(h) of the Internal Revenue Code.

16. Raul Rothblatt and Corey Rosen, *How ESOP Companies Are Handling Repurchase Liability* (Oakland, Calif.: NCEO, 1988); Robert Smiley, "Repurchase Liability," in Smiley and Gilbert, eds., *Employee Stock Ownership Plans*, chap. 17; Robert Bumgarner and R. Alan Prosswimmer, "ESOP Repurchase Liability," *Journal of Employee Ownership Law and Finance* 2 (Fall 1990): pp. 35–68; Ronald Gilbert, "How to Plan to Repurchase Stock from Departing Employees," *Employee Ownership Reader*, pp. 50–51.

17. Converting from one pension plan to another can be very complicated, particularly if funds are moved from one to the other. See Brown and Kaplan, "Tax, ERISA, and Securities Issues," in Smiley and Gilbert, eds., *Employee Stock Ownership Plans*, pp. 13-59–13-64; Gregory Brown and Alan Hawksley, "Converting Other Employee Benefit Plans to ESOPs," *Employee Ownership Reader*, pp. 47–48.

18. Stephen Hartman, "The ESOP Trustees' Duties to Vote and Tender Stock," *Journal of Employee Ownership Law and Finance* 2 (Summer 1990): 3–24; Brown and Kaplan, "Tax, ERISA, and Securities Issues," pp. 13-19–13-29; William Wade, "Employee Benefit Plans in Control Contests: An Analysis of Participant 'Pass Through' Arrangements," *BNA Pension Reporter* 17 (July 23, 1990): 1290–1306; Sections 404 through 409 of ERISA.

19. David West, "ESOP Reporting and Disclosure Obligations," *Journal of Employee Ownership Law and Finance* 2 (Fall 1990): 3–20; Shela Turpin-Forster, "The ESOP as Elephant," *Journal of Employee Ownership Law and Finance* 2 (Fall 1990): 21–36.

20. James Willis, "The ESOP Rollover and the Investment Decision," *Journal of Employee Ownership Law and Finance* 2 (Spring 1990): 63–82.

21. Malon Wilkus, "Divesting a Subsidiary through an ESOP," in Karen Young, ed., *The Expanding Role of ESOPs in Public Companies* (Westport, Conn.: Quorum Books, 1990), chap. 6.

22. David Kirkpatrick, "How Employees Run Avis Better," *Fortune* 118 (December 5, 1988): 103ff; "Is Avis Moving into the Passing Lane?" *Business Week*, May 9, 1988, pp. 100–101.

23. Alan Hyde and Craig Livingston, "Employee Takeovers," *Rutgers Law Review* 41 (Summer 1989): 1131–95.

24. Jack Curtis, "ESOPs as a Takeover Defense Strategy," *Journal of Employee Ownership Law and Finance* 1 (Fall 1989): 49–62; "Lockheed Dons New Armor to Keep the Raider at Bay: The Defense Contractor Is Selling More Assets and Creating an ESOP," *Business Week*, April 17, 1989, 20ff; "ESOP at the Barricades: Polaroid Uses a Novel Anti-Takeover Defense," *Barrons* 69 (February 6, 1989): 38ff.

25. *Shamrock Holdings, Inc.* v. *Polaroid Corp.*, Fed. Sec. L. Rep. (CCH) Sec. 94,176 (Del. Ch. Jan. 6, 1989).

26. Corey Rosen and Michael Quarrey, "How Well Is Employee Ownership Working?" *Harvard Business Review* 65 (September–October 1987): 126–30.

27. Eugene Epstein, "Reluctant Capitalists," *National Review* 37 (February 22, 1985): 38–39; "Has Weirton's ESOP Worked Too Well?" *Business Week*, January 23, 1989, 66ff.

28. Alex Gibney, "Paradise Tossed: How a Chance to Save American Capitalism Was Sabotaged at Eastern," *Washington Monthly* 18 (June 1986): 24–34; Robert Kuttner, "Sharing Power at Eastern Air Lines," *Harvard Business Review* 63 (November–December 1985): 91–101.

29. Michael Quarrey, Joseph Blasi, and Corey Rosen, *Taking Stock: Employee Ownership at Work* (Cambridge, Mass.: Ballinger, 1986), chap. 11; James Wilson and Corey Rosen, *Trading Stock for Wages: Employee Ownership in the Airline Industry* (Oakland, Calif.: NCEO, 1987).

30. Kenneth Lindberg, "Combining ESOPs with 401(k) Plans," *Journal of Employee Ownership Law and Finance* 1 (Fall 1989): 23–48.

31. "Why Does It Cost So Much?" *Employee Ownership Reader*, pp. 57–58.

32. Gerald Kalish, "Planning for an ESOP," in Kalish, ed., *ESOPs*, chap.

2; Robert Smiley and Ronald Gilbert, "The Preliminary Assessment" and "Making the Decision to Implement an ESOP: The Full Feasibility Study," in Smiley and Gilbert, eds., *Employee Stock Ownership Plans*, chaps. 5, 6.

33. Richard Braun, "Valuation Issues in Public Companies," in Young, ed., *Expanding Role of ESOPs in Public Companies*, chap. 5; Richard May, Robert MacDonald, and Bradley Van Horn, "Valuation Issues in Leveraged ESOPs," *Journal of Employee Ownership Law and Finance* 2 (Winter 1990): 99–122; Mary McCarter and Shannon Pratt, "A Primer to the Appraisal Process," *Employee Ownership Reader*, p. 44; Paul Much, "ESOP Valuation Considerations," in Kalish, ed., *ESOPs*, chap. 3; Christopher Bower and Jay Abrams, "Valuation of Companies for ESOP Purposes," Shannon Pratt, "ESOP Valuation Controversies and Court Cases," and Gregory Range, "Advanced Valuation Issues in ESOP Leveraged Buyouts," in Smiley and Gilbert, eds., *Employee Stock Ownership Plans*, chaps. 8, 9, 10.

34. For a general introduction to ESOP financing issues, see Robert Smiley, "Financial Aspects of ESOPs" and R. W. Pricer, "The Use of an ESOP for Corporate Finance," in Kalish, ed., *ESOPs*, chaps. 5, 8; Robert Smiley, "ESOP Financing," in Smiley and Gilbert, eds., *Employee Stock Ownership Plans*, chap. 11; Robert Smiley, "ESOP Financing," *Journal of Employee Ownership Law and Finance* 2 (Winter 1990): 51–84.

35. Rebecca Miller, "Accounting for ESOP Transactions," *Journal of Employee Ownership Law and Finance* 2 (Summer 1990): 61–94; Rebecca Miller, "Accounting for ESOP Transactions by the Plan Sponsor," in Kalish, ed., *ESOPs*, chap. 6; Kevin Reilly, "Accounting Aspects of ESOPs," in Smiley and Gilbert, eds., *Employee Stock Ownership Plans*, chap. 12.

36. Karen Bonn, "The Post Transaction ESOP," *Journal of Employee Ownership Law and Finance* 2 (Summer 1990): 25–44; Donald Israel, Donald Weinstock, and Timothy Fisher, "ESOP Plan Administration," *Journal of Employee Ownership Law and Finance* 2 (Summer 1990): 45–60; Anthony Mathews, "ESOP Administration," in Smiley and Gilbert, eds., *Employee Stock Ownership Plans*, chap. 16.

Chapter 3

1. Quoted in "Saluting 50 Years of Employee Ownership," Journal Communications internal pamphlet, 1987.

2. Joseph Blasi, "The Development and the Future of Employee Ownership in the Publicly Traded Corporation," in Karen M. Young, ed., *The Expanding Role of ESOPs in Public Companies* (Westport, Conn.: Quorum Books, 1990).

3. Quoted in "PepsiCo SharePower Stock Option Plan," PepsiCo pamphlet, 1990.

4. *1989 Profit Sharing Survey* (Chicago: Profit Sharing Council of America, 1989).

5. Robert Levering, Milton Moscowitz, and Michael Katz, *The 100 Best Companies to Work for in America* (Reading, Mass.: Addison-Wesley, 1989), p. 165.

Chapter 4

1. Richard J. Long, "Job Attitudes and Organizational Performance under Employee Ownership," *Academy of Management Journal* 23 (December 1980): 726–37.

2. Tove Hammer and Robert Stern, "Employee Ownership: Implications for the Organizational Distribution of Power," *Academy of Management Journal* 23 (March 1980): 78–100.

3. Katrina Berman, *Worker Owned Plywood Companies* (Pullman: Washington State University Press, 1967).

4. Michael Conte and Arnold Tannenbaum, *Employee Ownership* (Ann Arbor: University of Michigan Survey Research Center, 1980).

5. Thomas Marsh and Dale McAllister, "ESOP Tables: A Survey of Companies with Stock Ownership Plans," *Journal of Corporation Law* 6 (Spring 1981).

6. U.S. Senate, *Hearing before the Select Committee on Small Business*, 96th Cong., February 27, 1979.

7. Corey Rosen, Katherine J. Klein, and Karen M. Young, *Employee Ownership in America* (Lexington, Mass.: Lexington Books, 1986).

8. Ibid.

9. Richard Maturi, "Who's the Boss?" *CFO*, August 1989.

10. YSI, Inc., company pamphlet, 1988.

11. "YSI Focus," YSI culture statement.

12. The research is reported in Rosen, Klein, and Young, *Employee Ownership in America*.

13. John Butkus, "Employees Sing Praises of ESOP Despite Workload," *Stevens Point Journal*, April 6, 1989.

14. Cal Schacht, "Clay Equipment: A Study in Employee Ownership," in *Employee Ownership Report: 1987 Newsletters* (Oakland, Calif.: NCEO, 1988), p. 160.

Chapter 5

1. M. Carter McFarland, *Federal Government and Urban Problems* (Boulder, Colo.: Westview Press, 1978), p. 76.

2. Ibid., p. 79.

3. Paul R. Porter and David C. Sweet, *Rebuilding America's Cities: Roads to Recovery* (New Brunswick, N.J.: Center for Urban Policy Research, 1984), p. 163.

4. Stuart M. Butler, *Enterprise Zones* (New York: Universe Books, 1981), p. 80.

5. Roger Vaughn, *The Wealth of States: Policies for a Dynamic Economy* (Washington, D.C.: Council of State Planning Agencies, 1984), p. 42.

6. Michael C. D. MacDonald, *America's Cities* (New York: Simon and Schuster, 1984), p. 385.

7. Warner Woodworth, Christopher Meek, and William Foote Whyte, eds., *Industrial Democracy: Strategies for Community Revitalization* (Beverly Hills: Sage, 1985), p. 25.

8. Neal R. Pierce and Carol F. Steinbach, *Corrective Capitalism: The Rise of Community Economic Development Corporations* (New York: Ford Foundation, 1987), p. 303.

9. Linda M. Gardner, *Community Economic Development Strategies: Creating Successful Businesses*, Vol. 1: *Building the Base* (Berkeley: National Economic Development and Law Center, 1988), p. 88.

10. Personal interview, November 8, 1989.

11. Jan Gilbrecht, "End of the Rainbow," letter to the editor, *Image*, June 1, 1986.

12. John Logue, "The Role of States in Encouraging Employee Ownership," paper prepared for the National Center for Employee Ownership Conference on Employee Ownership Strategies for State and Local Governments, Washington, D.C., February 11, 1986.

Chapter 6

1. Domenico Mario Nuti, "On Traditional Cooperatives and James Meade's Labour-Capital Discriminating Partnerships" (Florence, Italy: European University Institute, February 22, 1988), unpublished paper.

2. David P. Ellerman, *The Socialization of Entrepreneurship: The Empresarial Division of the Caja Laboral Popular* (Somerville, Mass.: Industrial Cooperative Association, 1982).

3. Ibid.

4. Société Coopérative Ouvrière de Production, *L'état du movement* (Paris: SCOP, 1989).

5. U.S. General Accounting Office, *Federal Personnel: Status of the Federal Employee Direct Corporate Ownership Opportunity Plan* (Washington, D.C.: U.S. General Accounting Office, 1989), pp. 6–8.

6. "Asset-Stripping," *Economist*, July 2, 1983.

7. "People's Provincial: Workers' Drive Helps Company Turn the Corner," *Financial Times*, May 5, 1989.

8. Malcolm Hurlston, "Spring Breakthroughs for U.K. ESOPs," in *ESOP Report* (Washington, D.C.: ESOP Association, 1990), p. 5.

9. Gary H. Johncox, "MacMillan Bloedel's Experience with Employee Share Ownership," paper presented at the Employee Equity Investment Conference, Vancouver, September 26, 1989, p. 1.

10. Anthony Jensen, "Employee Ownership in Australia," in Robert Smiley and Ronald Gilbert, eds., *Employee Stock Ownership Plans* (New York: Prentice-Hall, 1989), pp. 21-4–21-10.

11. Shann Turnbull, "Louis Kelso's Impact on Employee Ownership in Australia," ibid., pp. 21-20–21-21.

12. Jensen, "Employee Ownership in Australia," p. 21-15.

13. Philip Revzin, "Selling Capitalism: France Urges Citizenry to Break with Habit, Become Stockholders," *Wall Street Journal*, November 5, 1986.

14. Thomas Koch, "Employee Ownership in West Germany" (Oakland, Calif.: NCEO, April 1990), unpublished paper, pp. 5, 13.

15. *Financial Times*, December 7, 1989.

16. Rania Fahmy, "ESOPs: A First in the Developing World," *Business Monthly: Journal of the American Chamber of Commerce in Egypt*, August 1989, pp. 24–27.

17. Michael Parks, "South Africa Firm to Give Stock to Workers," *Los Angeles Times*, November 27, 1987.

18. International Association for Financial Participation, *The Anglo American Corporation: Black and White Shareholders in South Africa* (Paris: International Association for Financial Participation, 1989), pp. 1, 6.

19. Edward Epstein, "Losing Faith in the Party," *San Francisco Chronicle*, April 10, 1990.

20. John Logue, "Employee Ownership with a Twist . . . of Vodka," *Owners at Work* 2 (Spring 1990): 1–2.

21. Ibid.

22. Krzysztof Stupnicki, "Polish Government Seeks to Build Political Support for Programme before Passing Law," *Privatization International* 2 (March 1990): 17.

23. Craig Forman, "East Bloc Legal Overhaul Lures Investors," *Wall Street Journal*, March 16, 1990.

24. Joseph Recinos, "The La Perla Model: Expanded Ownership without Land Distribution," paper presented at the U.S. AID Conference on Land Reform, Washington, D.C., March 1985.

25. Ibid.

26. Robert Rauth, "An ESOP Fable," *Reason* 18 (August–September 1986): 26–27.

27. Letter dated January 29, 1990, to Raul Rothblatt from V. Francisco Varua, vice-president, José Cojangco & Sons, Metro Manila, Philippines.

About the Authors

Gianna Durso has a B.A. from Princeton University. She was a staff member at the National Center for Employee Ownership from 1989 to 1990. While there she co-authored *International Developments in Employee Ownership* and edited the NCEO's *Journal of Employee Law and Finance*.

Darien A. McWhirter has a Ph.D. in political science from Yale University and a J.D. from the University of Texas. He is the author of *Your Rights at Work* and *Privacy in the Workplace*. He is the general counsel of the NCEO and the editor of the *Journal of Employee Law and Finance*.

Raul Rothblatt has a B.A. from the University of California. He was a staff member of the NCEO from 1989 to 1990, where he co-authored *International Developments in Employee Ownership*.

Corey Rosen has a Ph.D. in politics from Cornell University. He co-founded the NCEO in 1981 and is now its executive director. Before joining the center, he taught government at Ripon College and was a professional staff member of the U.S. Senate. He is the co-author of *Employee Ownership in America: The Equity Solution* and *Taking Stock: Employee Ownership at Work*.

Lauren Segarra has a B.A. from the University of Massachusetts. She is a staff member at the NCEO, where she specializes in community development and employee ownership outreach programs.

Sue Steiner has a B.A. from Brandeis University and an M.S.W. from San Francisco State University. From 1989 to 1990, she was projects director for the NCEO, where her principal responsibility was the development of alternative models to ESOPs for employee ownership.

Karen M. Young has an M.A. in organizational management from George Washington University. A co-founder of the NCEO, she now heads the center's employee involvement work and is its managing director. Before becoming associated with the center, she was a staff member of the U.S. Senate. She is the co-author of *Employee Ownership in America* and editor of *ESOPs in Public Companies*.

Index